PORTUGUESE

VOCABULARY

FOR ENGLISH SPEAKERS

ENGLISH-PORTUGUESE

The most useful words
To expand your lexicon and sharpen
your language skills

7000 words

Portuguese vocabulary for English speakers - 7000 words

By Andrey Taranov

T&P Books vocabularies are intended for helping you learn, memorize and review foreign words. The dictionary is divided into themes, covering all major spheres of everyday activities, business, science, culture, etc.

The process of learning words using T&P Books' theme-based dictionaries gives you the following advantages:

- Correctly grouped source information predetermines success at subsequent stages of word memorization
- Availability of words derived from the same root allowing memorization of word units (rather than separate words)
- Small units of words facilitate the process of establishing associative links needed for consolidation of vocabulary
- Level of language knowledge can be estimated by the number of learned words

T&P Books Publishing
www.tpbooks.com

ISBN: 978-1-78071-315-1

This book is also available in E-book formats.
Please visit www.tpbooks.com or the major online bookstores.

PORTUGUESE VOCABULARY
for English speakers

T&P Books vocabularies are intended to help you learn, memorize, and review foreign words. The vocabulary contains over 7000 commonly used words arranged thematically.

- Vocabulary contains the most commonly used words
- Recommended as an addition to any language course
- Meets the needs of beginners and advanced learners of foreign languages
- Convenient for daily use, revision sessions, and self-testing activities
- Allows you to assess your vocabulary

Special features of the vocabulary

- Words are organized according to their meaning, not alphabetically
- Words are presented in three columns to facilitate the reviewing and self-testing processes
- Words in groups are divided into small blocks to facilitate the learning process
- The vocabulary offers a convenient and simple transcription of each foreign word

The vocabulary has 198 topics including:

Basic Concepts, Numbers, Colors, Months, Seasons, Units of Measurement, Clothing & Accessories, Food & Nutrition, Restaurant, Family Members, Relatives, Character, Feelings, Emotions, Diseases, City, Town, Sightseeing, Shopping, Money, House, Home, Office, Working in the Office, Import & Export, Marketing, Job Search, Sports, Education, Computer, Internet, Tools, Nature, Countries, Nationalities and more ...

T&P BOOKS' THEME-BASED DICTIONARIES

The Correct System for Memorizing Foreign Words

Acquiring vocabulary is one of the most important elements of learning a foreign language, because words allow us to express our thoughts, ask questions, and provide answers. An inadequate vocabulary can impede communication with a foreigner and make it difficult to understand a book or movie well.

The pace of activity in all spheres of modern life, including the learning of modern languages, has increased. Today, we need to memorize large amounts of information (grammar rules, foreign words, etc.) within a short period. However, this does not need to be difficult. All you need to do is to choose the right training materials, learn a few special techniques, and develop your individual training system.

Having a system is critical to the process of language learning. Many people fail to succeed in this regard; they cannot master a foreign language because they fail to follow a system comprised of selecting materials, organizing lessons, arranging new words to be learned, and so on. The lack of a system causes confusion and eventually, lowers self-confidence.

T&P Books' theme-based dictionaries can be included in the list of elements needed for creating an effective system for learning foreign words. These dictionaries were specially developed for learning purposes and are meant to help students effectively memorize words and expand their vocabulary.

Generally speaking, the process of learning words consists of three main elements:

- Reception (creation or acquisition) of a training material, such as a word list
- Work aimed at memorizing new words
- Work aimed at reviewing the learned words, such as self-testing

All three elements are equally important since they determine the quality of work and the final result. All three processes require certain skills and a well-thought-out approach.

New words are often encountered quite randomly when learning a foreign language and it may be difficult to include them all in a unified list. As a result, these words remain written on scraps of paper, in book margins, textbooks, and so on. In order to systematize such words, we have to create and continually update a "book of new words." A paper notebook, a netbook, or a tablet PC can be used for these purposes.

This "book of new words" will be your personal, unique list of words. However, it will only contain the words that you came across during the learning process. For example, you might have written down the words "Sunday," "Tuesday," and "Friday." However, there are additional words for days of the week, for example, "Saturday," that are missing, and your list of words would be incomplete. Using a theme dictionary, in addition to the "book of new words," is a reasonable solution to this problem.

The theme-based dictionary may serve as the basis for expanding your vocabulary.

It will be your big "book of new words" containing the most frequently used words of a foreign language already included. There are quite a few theme-based dictionaries available, and you should ensure that you make the right choice in order to get the maximum benefit from your purchase.

Therefore, we suggest using theme-based dictionaries from T&P Books Publishing as an aid to learning foreign words. Our books are specially developed for effective use in the sphere of vocabulary systematization, expansion and review.

Theme-based dictionaries are not a magical solution to learning new words. However, they can serve as your main database to aid foreign-language acquisition. Apart from theme dictionaries, you can have copybooks for writing down new words, flash cards, glossaries for various texts, as well as other resources; however, a good theme dictionary will always remain your primary collection of words.

T&P Books' theme-based dictionaries are specialty books that contain the most frequently used words in a language.

The main characteristic of such dictionaries is the division of words into themes. For example, the *City* theme contains the words "street," "crossroads," "square," "fountain," and so on. The *Talking* theme might contain words like "to talk," "to ask," "question," and "answer".

All the words in a theme are divided into smaller units, each comprising 3–5 words. Such an arrangement improves the perception of words and makes the learning process less tiresome. Each unit contains a selection of words with similar meanings or identical roots. This allows you to learn words in small groups and establish other associative links that have a positive effect on memorization.

The words on each page are placed in three columns: a word in your native language, its translation, and its transcription. Such positioning allows for the use of techniques for effective memorization. After closing the translation column, you can flip through and review foreign words, and vice versa. "This is an easy and convenient method of review – one that we recommend you do often."

Our theme-based dictionaries contain transcriptions for all the foreign words. Unfortunately, none of the existing transcriptions are able to convey the exact nuances of foreign pronunciation. That is why we recommend using the transcriptions only as a supplementary learning aid. Correct pronunciation can only be acquired with the help of sound. Therefore our collection includes audio theme-based dictionaries.

The process of learning words using T&P Books' theme-based dictionaries gives you the following advantages:

- You have correctly grouped source information, which predetermines your success at subsequent stages of word memorization
- Availability of words derived from the same root (lazy, lazily, lazybones), allowing you to memorize word units instead of separate words
- Small units of words facilitate the process of establishing associative links needed for consolidation of vocabulary
- You can estimate the number of learned words and hence your level of language knowledge
- The dictionary allows for the creation of an effective and high-quality revision process
- You can revise certain themes several times, modifying the revision methods and techniques
- Audio versions of the dictionaries help you to work out the pronunciation of words and develop your skills of auditory word perception

The T&P Books' theme-based dictionaries are offered in several variants differing in the number of words: 1.500, 3.000, 5.000, 7.000, and 9.000 words. There are also dictionaries containing 15,000 words for some language combinations. Your choice of dictionary will depend on your knowledge level and goals.

We sincerely believe that our dictionaries will become your trusty assistant in learning foreign languages and will allow you to easily acquire the necessary vocabulary.

TABLE OF CONTENTS

PRONUNCIATION GUIDE

Letter	Portuguese example	T&P phonetic alphabet	English example
a	patinadora	[a]	shorter than in ask
ã	capitão	[ɑ̃]	nasal [a]
b	cabriolé	[b]	baby, book
b [1]	acabar	[β]	between b and v
c [2]	contador	[k]	clock, kiss
c [3]	injector	[s]	silent [s]
c [4]	ambulância	[s]	city, boss
ç	comemoração	[s]	city, boss
ch	champanha	[ʃ]	machine, shark
d	diário	[d]	day, doctor
e	expressão	[ɛ], [ɛ:]	habit, bad
e	grau científico	[e]	elm, medal
e	nove	[ə]	driver, teacher
f	fonética	[f]	face, food
g [5]	língua	[g]	game, gold
g [6]	estrangeiro	[ʒ]	forge, pleasure
gu [7]	fogueiro	[g]	game, gold
h [8]	hélice	[h]	silent [h]
i [9]	bandeira	[i]	shorter than in feet
i [10]	sino	[i]	shorter than in feet
j	juntos	[ʒ]	forge, pleasure
k [11]	empresa-broker	[k]	clock, kiss
l	bolsa	[l]	lace, people
lh	escolher	[ʎ]	daily, million
m [12]	menu	[m]	magic, milk
m [13]	passagem	[ŋ]	English, ring
n	piscina	[n]	name, normal
nh	desenho	[ɲ]	canyon, new
o [14]	escola de negócios	[o], [ɔ]	drop, baught
o [15]	ciclismo	[u]	book
p	prato	[p]	pencil, private
qu [16]	qualidade da imagem	[kv]	square, quality
qu [17]	querosene	[k]	clock, kiss
r	forno	[r]	rice, radio
r	resto	[ʁ]	fricative r
s [18]	sereia	[s]	city, boss
ss	passado	[s]	city, boss

Letter	Portuguese example	T&P phonetic alphabet	English example
s [19]	explosivo	[z]	zebra, please
s [20]	rede de lojas	[ʃ]	machine, shark
t	tordo	[t]	tourist, trip
u	truta	[u]	book
v	voar	[v]	very, river
v [21]	savana	[β]	between b and v
w [22]	cow-boy	[u]	book
x [23]	bruxa	[ʃ]	machine, shark
x [24]	exercício	[gz]	exam, exact
y	display	[j]	yes, New York
z [25]	amizade	[z]	zebra, please
z [26]	giz	[ʃ]	machine, shark

Combinations of letters

ia	embraiagem	[ja]	Kenya, piano
io [27]	estado-maior	[jɔ]	New York
io [28]	arroio	[ju]	youth, usually
io [29]	aniversário	[ju]	youth, usually
iu	ciumento	[ju]	youth, usually
un, um	fungo, algum	[ʊn]	soon
in, im	cinco, sim	[ĩ]	meeting, evening
en, em	cento, sempre	[ə̃]	nasal [e]

Comments

[1] usually between vowels
[2] before a, o, u and consonants
[3] before b, d, p, t
[4] in front of e, i
[5] before a, o, u and consonants
[6] before e, i
[7] before e, i
[8] at the beginning of words
[9] unstressed between vowel and consonant
[10] elsewhere
[11] in loanwords only
[12] before vowels and b, p
[13] before consonants and in em, im
[14] stressed
[15] unstressed, before a, e and in do, dos, o, os)
[16] before a, o and ü
[17] before e and i
[18] at the beginning of a word

[19] between vowels
[20] at the end of a word
[21] usually between vowels
[22] in loanwords only
[23] between vowels
[24] in ex- before a vowel
[25] between vowels
[26] at the end of a word
[27] stressed, after vowels
[28] unstressed, after vowels
[29] unstressed, after consonants

ABBREVIATIONS
used in the vocabulary

ab.	-	about
adj	-	adjective
adv	-	adverb
anim.	-	animate
as adj	-	attributive noun used as adjective
e.g.	-	for example
etc.	-	et cetera
fam.	-	familiar
fem.	-	feminine
form.	-	formal
inanim.	-	inanimate
masc.	-	masculine
math	-	mathematics
mil.	-	military
n	-	noun
pl	-	plural
pron.	-	pronoun
sb	-	somebody
sing.	-	singular
sth	-	something
v aux	-	auxiliary verb
vi	-	intransitive verb
vi, vt	-	intransitive, transitive verb
vt	-	transitive verb

m	-	masculine noun
f	-	feminine noun
m pl	-	masculine plural
f pl	-	feminine plural
m, f	-	masculine, feminine
vp	-	pronominal verb

BASIC CONCEPTS

Basic concepts. Part 1

1. Pronouns

I, me	**eu**	['eu]
you	**tu**	[tu]
he	**ele**	['ɛlə]
she	**ela**	['ɛlɐ]
we	**nós**	[nɔʃ]
you (to a group)	**vocês**	[vɔs'eʃ]
they (masc.)	**eles**	['ɛləʃ]
they (fem.)	**elas**	['ɛlɐʃ]

2. Greetings. Salutations. Farewells

Hello! (fam.)	**Olá!**	[ɔl'a]
Hello! (form.)	**Bom dia!**	[bõ d'iɐ]
Good morning!	**Bom dia!**	[bõ d'iɐ]
Good afternoon!	**Boa tarde!**	[b'oɐ t'ardə]
Good evening!	**Boa noite!**	[b'oɐ n'ojtə]
to say hello	**cumprimentar** (vt)	[kũprimẽt'aɾ]
Hi! (hello)	**Olá!**	[ɔl'a]
greeting (n)	**saudação** (f)	[sɐudɐs'ãu]
to greet (vt)	**saudar** (vt)	[sɐud'aɾ]
How are you? (form.)	**Como vai?**	[k'omu v'aj]
How are you? (fam.)	**Como vais?**	[k'omu v'ajʃ]
What's new?	**O que há de novo?**	[ukə a də n'ovu]
Bye-Bye! Goodbye!	**Até à vista!**	[ɐt'ɛ a v'iʃtɐ]
See you soon!	**Até breve!**	[ɐt'ɛ br'ɛvə]
Farewell!	**Adeus!**	[ɐd'euʃ]
to say goodbye	**despedir-se** (vp)	[dəʃpəd'irsə]
So long!	**Até logo!**	[ɐt'ɛ l'ɔgu]
Thank you!	**Obrigado! -a!**	[ɔbrig'adu -ɐ]
Thank you very much!	**Muito obrigado! -a!**	[m'ujtu ɔbrig'adu -ɐ]
You're welcome	**De nada**	[də n'adɐ]
Don't mention it!	**Não tem de quê**	[n'ãu tẽj də k'e]

It was nothing	**De nada**	[də n'adɐ]
Excuse me! (fam.)	**Desculpa!**	[dəʃk'ulpɐ]
Excuse me! (form.)	**Desculpe!**	[dəʃk'ulpə]
to excuse (forgive)	**desculpar** (vt)	[dəʃkulp'ar]
to apologize (vi)	**desculpar-se** (vp)	[dəʃkulp'arsə]
My apologies	**As minhas desculpas**	[ɐʃ m'iɲɐʃ dəʃk'ulpɐʃ]
I'm sorry!	**Desculpe!**	[dəʃk'ulpə]
to forgive (vt)	**desculpar** (vt)	[dəʃkulp'ar]
It's okay!	**Não faz mal**	[n'ãu faʃ m'al]
please (adv)	**por favor**	[pur fɐv'or]
Don't forget!	**Não se esqueça!**	[n'ãu sə əʃk'esɐ]
Certainly!	**Certamente!**	[sɛrtɐm'ẽtə]
Of course not!	**Claro que não!**	[kl'aru kə n'ãu]
Okay! (I agree)	**De acordo!**	[əʃt'a bẽj]
That's enough!	**Basta!**	[b'aʃtɐ]

3. Cardinal numbers. Part 1

0 zero	**zero**	[z'ɛru]
1 one	**um**	[ũ]
2 two	**dois**	[dojʃ]
3 three	**três**	[treʃ]
4 four	**quatro**	[ku'atru]
5 five	**cinco**	[s'ĩku]
6 six	**seis**	[s'ɐjʃ]
7 seven	**sete**	[s'ɛtə]
8 eight	**oito**	['ojtu]
9 nine	**nove**	[n'ɔvə]
10 ten	**dez**	[dɛʒ]
11 eleven	**onze**	['õzə]
12 twelve	**doze**	[d'ozə]
13 thirteen	**treze**	[tr'ezə]
14 fourteen	**catorze**	[kɐt'orzə]
15 fifteen	**quinze**	[k'ĩzə]
16 sixteen	**dezasseis**	[dəzɐs'ɐjʃ]
17 seventeen	**dezassete**	[dəzɐs'ɛtə]
18 eighteen	**dezoito**	[dəz'ɔjtu]
19 nineteen	**dezanove**	[dəzɐn'ɔvə]
20 twenty	**vinte**	[v'ĩtə]
21 twenty-one	**vinte e um**	[v'ĩtə i 'ũ]
22 twenty-two	**vinte e dois**	[v'ĩtə i d'ojʃ]
23 twenty-three	**vinte e três**	[v'ĩtə i tr'eʃ]
30 thirty	**trinta**	[tr'ĩtɐ]
31 thirty-one	**trinta e um**	[tr'ĩtɐ i 'ũ]

32 thirty-two	**trinta e dois**	[tr'ĩtɐ i d'ojʃ]
33 thirty-three	**trinta e três**	[tr'ĩtɐ i tr'eʃ]
40 forty	**quarenta**	[kuɐr'ẽtɐ]
41 forty-one	**quarenta e um**	[kuɐr'ẽtɐ i 'ũ]
42 forty-two	**quarenta e dois**	[kuɐr'ẽtɐ i d'ojʃ]
43 forty-three	**quarenta e três**	[kuɐr'ẽtɐ i tr'eʃ]
50 fifty	**cinquenta**	[sĩku'ẽtɐ]
51 fifty-one	**cinquenta e um**	[sĩku'ẽtɐ i 'ũ]
52 fifty-two	**cinquenta e dois**	[sĩku'ẽtɐ i d'ojʃ]
53 fifty-three	**cinquenta e três**	[sĩku'ẽtɐ i tr'eʃ]
60 sixty	**sessenta**	[səs'ẽtɐ]
61 sixty-one	**sessenta e um**	[səs'ẽtɐ i 'ũ]
62 sixty-two	**sessenta e dois**	[səs'ẽtɐ i d'ojʃ]
63 sixty-three	**sessenta e três**	[səs'ẽtɐ i tr'eʃ]
70 seventy	**setenta**	[sət'ẽtɐ]
71 seventy-one	**setenta e um**	[sət'ẽtɐ i 'ũ]
72 seventy-two	**setenta e dois**	[sət'ẽtɐ i d'ojʃ]
73 seventy-three	**setenta e três**	[sət'ẽtɐ i tr'eʃ]
80 eighty	**oitenta**	[ojt'ẽtɐ]
81 eighty-one	**oitenta e um**	[ojt'ẽtɐ i 'ũ]
82 eighty-two	**oitenta e dois**	[ojt'ẽtɐ i d'ojʃ]
83 eighty-three	**oitenta e três**	[ojt'ẽtɐ i tr'eʃ]
90 ninety	**noventa**	[nuv'ẽtɐ]
91 ninety-one	**noventa e um**	[nuv'ẽtɐ i 'ũ]
92 ninety-two	**noventa e dois**	[nuv'ẽtɐ i d'ojʃ]
93 ninety-three	**noventa e três**	[nuv'ẽtɐ i tr'eʃ]

4. Cardinal numbers. Part 2

100 one hundred	**cem**	[sẽj]
200 two hundred	**duzentos**	[duz'ẽtuʃ]
300 three hundred	**trezentos**	[trəz'ẽtuʃ]
400 four hundred	**quatrocentos**	[kuatrus'ẽtuʃ]
500 five hundred	**quinhentos**	[kiɲ'ẽtuʃ]
600 six hundred	**seiscentos**	[sɐjʃs'ẽtuʃ]
700 seven hundred	**setecentos**	[sɛtəs'ẽtuʃ]
800 eight hundred	**oitocentos**	[ojtus'ẽtuʃ]
900 nine hundred	**novecentos**	[nɔvəs'ẽtuʃ]
1000 one thousand	**mil**	[mil]
2000 two thousand	**dois mil**	[d'ojʃ mil]
3000 three thousand	**três mil**	[tr'eʃ mil]
10000 ten thousand	**dez mil**	[d'ɛʒ mil]

one hundred thousand	**cem mil**	[sẽj mil]
million	**um milhão**	[ũ miʎ'ãu]
billion	**mil milhões**	[mil miʎ'ojʃ]

5. Numbers. Fractions

fraction	**fração** (f)	[fras'ãu]
one half	**um meio**	[ũ m'ɐju]
one third	**um terço**	[ũ t'ersu]
one quarter	**um quarto**	[ũ ku'artu]
one eighth	**um oitavo**	[ũ ojt'avu]
one tenth	**um décimo**	[ũ d'ɛsimu]
two thirds	**dois terços**	[d'ojʃ t'ersuʃ]
three quarters	**três quartos**	[treʃ ku'artuʃ]

6. Numbers. Basic operations

subtraction	**subtração** (f)	[subtras'ãu]
to subtract (vi, vt)	**subtrair** (vi, vt)	[subtrɐ'iɾ]
division	**divisão** (f)	[diviz'ãu]
to divide (vt)	**dividir** (vt)	[divid'iɾ]
addition	**adição** (f)	[ɐdis'ãu]
to add up (vt)	**somar** (vt)	[sum'aɾ]
to add (vi, vt)	**adicionar** (vt)	[ɐdisjun'aɾ]
multiplication	**multiplicação** (f)	[multiplikɐs'ãu]
to multiply (vt)	**multiplicar** (vt)	[multiplik'aɾ]

7. Numbers. Miscellaneous

digit, figure	**algarismo, dígito** (m)	[algɐɾ'iʒmu], [d'iʒitu]
number	**número** (m)	[n'uməɾu]
numeral	**numeral** (m)	[numəɾ'al]
minus sign	**menos** (m)	[m'enuʃ]
plus sign	**mais** (m)	[m'ajʃ]
formula	**fórmula** (f)	[f'ɔrmulɐ]
calculation	**cálculo** (m)	[k'alkulu]
to count (vt)	**contar, calcular** (vt)	[kõt'aɾ], [kalkul'aɾ]
to count up	**fazer a contagem**	[fɐz'er ɐ kõt'aʒẽj]
to compare (vt)	**comparar** (vt)	[kõpɐɾ'aɾ]
How much?	**Quanto?**	[ku'ãtu]
How many?	**Quantos? -as?**	[ku'ãtuʃ -ɐʃ]
sum, total	**soma** (f)	[s'omɐ]

result	**resultado** (m)	[Rəzult'adu]
remainder	**resto** (m)	[R'ɛʃtu]
a few ...	**alguns ...**	[alg'ũʃ]
few (not many)	**poucos, poucas**	[p'okuʃ], [p'okɐʃ]
a little (~ tired)	**um pouco ...**	[ũ p'oku]
the rest	**resto** (m)	[R'ɛʃtu]
one and a half	**um e meio**	[ũ i m'ɐju]
dozen	**dúzia** (f)	[d'uziɐ]
in half (adv)	**ao meio**	[au m'ɐju]
equally (evenly)	**em partes iguais**	[ẽ p'artəʃ igu'ajʃ]
half	**metade** (f)	[mət'adə]
time (three ~s)	**vez** (f)	[veʒ]

8. The most important verbs. Part 1

to advise (vt)	**aconselhar** (vt)	[ɐkõsəʎ'ar]
to agree (say yes)	**concordar** (vt)	[kõkurd'ar]
to answer (vi, vt)	**responder** (vt)	[Rəʃpõd'er]
to apologize (vi)	**desculpar-se** (vp)	[dəʃkulp'arsə]
to arrive (vi)	**chegar** (vi)	[ʃəg'ar]
to ask (~ oneself)	**perguntar** (vt)	[pərgũt'ar]
to ask (~ sb to do sth)	**pedir** (vt)	[pəd'ir]
to be (~ a teacher)	**ser** (vi)	[ser]
to be (~ on a diet)	**estar** (vi)	[əʃt'ar]
to be afraid	**ter medo**	[ter m'edu]
to be hungry	**ter fome**	[ter f'ɔmə]
to be interested in ...	**interessar-se** (vp)	[ĩtərəs'arsə]
to be needed	**ser necessário**	[ser nəsəs'ariu]
to be surprised	**surpreender-se** (vp)	[surpriẽd'ersə]
to be thirsty	**ter sede**	[ter s'edə]
to begin (vt)	**começar** (vt)	[kuməs'ar]
to belong to ...	**pertencer** (vt)	[pərtẽs'er]
to boast (vi)	**gabar-se** (vp)	[gɐb'arsə]
to break (split into pieces)	**quebrar** (vt)	[kəbr'ar]
to call (for help)	**chamar** (vt)	[ʃɐm'ar]
can (v aux)	**poder** (v aux)	[pud'er]
to catch (vt)	**pegar** (vt)	[pəg'ar]
to change (vt)	**mudar** (vt)	[mud'ar]
to choose (select)	**escolher** (vt)	[əʃkuʎ'er]
to come down	**descer** (vi)	[dəʃs'er]
to come in (enter)	**entrar** (vi)	[ẽtr'ar]
to compare (vt)	**comparar** (vt)	[kõpɐr'ar]
to complain (vi, vt)	**reclamar** (vi)	[Rəklɐm'ar]

to confuse (mix up)	**confundir** (vt)	[kõfũd'iɾ]
to continue (vt)	**continuar** (vt)	[kõtinu'aɾ]
to control (vt)	**controlar** (vt)	[kõtrul'aɾ]
to cook (dinner)	**preparar** (vt)	[prəpeɾ'aɾ]
to cost (vt)	**custar** (vt)	[kuʃt'aɾ]
to count (add up)	**contar** (vt)	[kõt'aɾ]
to count on ...	**contar com ...**	[kõt'aɾ kõ]
to create (vt)	**criar** (vt)	[kri'aɾ]
to cry (weep)	**chorar** (vi)	[ʃur'aɾ]

9. The most important verbs. Part 2

to deceive (vi, vt)	**enganar** (vt)	[ẽgɐn'aɾ]
to decorate (tree, street)	**decorar** (vt)	[dəkur'aɾ]
to defend (a country, etc.)	**defender** (vt)	[dəfẽd'eɾ]
to demand (request firmly)	**exigir** (vt)	[eziʒ'iɾ]
to dig (vt)	**cavar** (vt)	[kɐv'aɾ]
to discuss (vt)	**discutir** (vt)	[diʃkut'iɾ]
to do (vt)	**fazer** (vt)	[fɐz'eɾ]
to doubt (have doubts)	**duvidar** (vt)	[duvid'aɾ]
to drop (let fall)	**deixar cair** (vt)	[dɐjʃ'aɾ kɐ'iɾ]
to excuse (forgive)	**desculpar** (vt)	[dəʃkulp'aɾ]
to exist (vi)	**existir** (vi)	[eziʃt'iɾ]
to expect (foresee)	**prever** (vt)	[prəv'eɾ]
to explain (vt)	**explicar** (vt)	[əʃplik'aɾ]
to fall (vi)	**cair** (vi)	[kɐ'iɾ]
to find (vt)	**encontrar** (vt)	[ẽkõtr'aɾ]
to finish (vt)	**terminar** (vt)	[təɾmin'aɾ]
to fly (vi)	**voar** (vi)	[vu'aɾ]
to follow ... (come after)	**seguir ...**	[səg'iɾ]
to forget (vi, vt)	**esquecer** (vi, vt)	[əʃkɛs'eɾ]
to forgive (vt)	**perdoar** (vt)	[pərdu'aɾ]
to give (vt)	**dar** (vt)	[daɾ]
to give a hint	**dar uma dica**	[daɾ 'umɐ d'ikɐ]
to go (on foot)	**ir** (vi)	[iɾ]
to go for a swim	**ir nadar**	[iɾ nɐd'aɾ]
to go out (from ...)	**sair** (vi)	[sɐ'iɾ]
to guess right	**adivinhar** (vt)	[ɐdiviɲ'aɾ]
to have (vt)	**ter** (vt)	[teɾ]
to have breakfast	**tomar o pequeno-almoço**	[tum'aɾ u pək'enu alm'osu]
to have dinner	**jantar** (vi)	[ʒɐ̃t'aɾ]
to have lunch	**almoçar** (vi)	[almus'aɾ]
to hear (vt)	**ouvir** (vt)	[ov'iɾ]

to help (vt)	**ajudar** (vt)	[ɐʒud'aɾ]
to hide (vt)	**esconder** (vt)	[əʃkõd'eɾ]
to hope (vi, vt)	**esperar** (vt)	[əʃpəɾ'aɾ]
to hunt (vi, vt)	**caçar** (vi)	[kɐs'aɾ]
to hurry (vi)	**estar com pressa**	[əʃt'aɾ kõ pɾ'ɛsɐ]

10. The most important verbs. Part 3

to inform (vt)	**informar** (vt)	[ĩfurm'aɾ]
to insist (vi, vt)	**insistir** (vi)	[ĩsiʃt'iɾ]
to insult (vt)	**insultar** (vt)	[ĩsult'aɾ]
to invite (vt)	**convidar** (vt)	[kõvid'aɾ]
to joke (vi)	**fazer piadas**	[fɐz'eɾ pj'adɐʃ]
to keep (vt)	**guardar** (vt)	[guɐɾd'aɾ]
to keep silent	**ficar em silêncio**	[fik'aɾ ẽ sil'ẽsiu]
to kill (vt)	**matar** (vt)	[mɐt'aɾ]
to know (sb)	**conhecer** (vt)	[kuɲəs'eɾ]
to know (sth)	**saber** (vt)	[sɐb'eɾ]
to laugh (vi)	**rir** (vi)	[ʀiɾ]
to liberate (city, etc.)	**libertar** (vt)	[libəɾt'aɾ]
to like (I like ...)	**gostar** (vt)	[guʃt'aɾ]
to look for ... (search)	**buscar** (vt)	[buʃk'aɾ]
to love (sb)	**amar** (vt)	[ɐm'aɾ]
to make a mistake	**errar** (vi)	[ɛʀ'aɾ]
to manage, to run	**dirigir** (vt)	[diɾiʒ'iɾ]
to mean (signify)	**significar** (vt)	[signifik'aɾ]
to mention (talk about)	**mencionar** (vt)	[mẽsiun'aɾ]
to miss (school, etc.)	**faltar a ...**	[falt'aɾ ɐ]
to notice (see)	**perceber** (vt)	[pəɾsəb'eɾ]
to object (vi, vt)	**objetar** (vt)	[ɔbʒɛt'aɾ]
to observe (see)	**observar** (vt)	[ɔbsəɾv'aɾ]
to open (vt)	**abrir** (vt)	[ɐbɾ'iɾ]
to order (meal, etc.)	**pedir** (vt)	[pəd'iɾ]
to order (mil.)	**ordenar** (vt)	[ɔɾdən'aɾ]
to own (possess)	**possuir** (vt)	[pusu'iɾ]
to participate (vi)	**participar** (vi)	[pɐɾtisip'aɾ]
to pay (vi, vt)	**pagar** (vt)	[pɐg'aɾ]
to permit (vt)	**permitir** (vt)	[pəɾmit'iɾ]
to plan (vt)	**planear** (vt)	[plɐnj'aɾ]
to play (children)	**brincar, jogar** (vi, vt)	[bɾĩk'aɾ], [ʒug'aɾ]
to pray (vi, vt)	**rezar, orar** (vi)	[ʀəz'aɾ], [ɔɾ'aɾ]
to prefer (vt)	**preferir** (vt)	[pɾəfəɾ'iɾ]
to promise (vt)	**prometer** (vt)	[pɾumət'eɾ]
to pronounce (vt)	**pronunciar** (vt)	[pɾunũsj'aɾ]

to propose (vt)	**propor** (vt)	[prup'oɾ]
to punish (vt)	**punir** (vt)	[pun'iɾ]
to read (vi, vt)	**ler** (vt)	[leɾ]
to recommend (vt)	**recomendar** (vt)	[ʀəkumẽd'aɾ]
to refuse (vi, vt)	**negar-se** (vt)	[nəg'arsə]
to regret (be sorry)	**lamentar** (vt)	[lɐmẽt'aɾ]
to rent (sth from sb)	**alugar** (vt)	[ɐlug'aɾ]
to repeat (say again)	**repetir** (vt)	[ʀəpət'iɾ]
to reserve, to book	**reservar** (vt)	[ʀəzərv'aɾ]
to run (vi)	**correr** (vi)	[kuʀ'eɾ]

11. The most important verbs. Part 4

to save (rescue)	**salvar** (vt)	[salv'aɾ]
to say (~ thank you)	**dizer** (vt)	[diz'eɾ]
to scold (vt)	**repreender** (vt)	[ʀəpriẽd'eɾ]
to see (vt)	**ver** (vt)	[veɾ]
to sell (vt)	**vender** (vt)	[vẽd'eɾ]
to send (vt)	**enviar** (vt)	[ẽvj'aɾ]
to shoot (vi)	**atirar** (vi)	[ɐtiɾ'aɾ]
to shout (vi)	**gritar** (vi)	[grit'aɾ]
to show (vt)	**mostrar** (vt)	[muʃtr'aɾ]
to sign (document)	**assinar** (vt)	[ɐsin'aɾ]
to sit down (vi)	**sentar-se** (vp)	[sẽt'arsə]
to smile (vi)	**sorrir** (vi)	[suʀ'iɾ]
to speak (vi, vt)	**falar** (vi)	[fɐl'aɾ]
to steal (money, etc.)	**roubar** (vt)	[ʀob'aɾ]
to stop (please ~ calling me)	**cessar** (vt)	[səs'aɾ]
to stop (for pause, etc.)	**parar** (vi)	[pɐɾ'aɾ]
to study (vt)	**estudar** (vt)	[əʃtud'aɾ]
to swim (vi)	**nadar** (vi)	[nɐd'aɾ]
to take (vt)	**pegar** (vt)	[pəg'aɾ]
to think (vi, vt)	**pensar** (vt)	[pẽs'aɾ]
to threaten (vt)	**ameaçar** (vt)	[ɐmiɐs'aɾ]
to touch (with hands)	**tocar** (vt)	[tuk'aɾ]
to translate (vt)	**traduzir** (vt)	[trɐduz'iɾ]
to trust (vt)	**confiar** (vt)	[kõfj'aɾ]
to try (attempt)	**tentar** (vt)	[tẽt'aɾ]
to turn (~ to the left)	**virar** (vi)	[viɾ'aɾ]
to underestimate (vt)	**subestimar** (vt)	[subəʃtim'aɾ]
to understand (vt)	**compreender** (vt)	[kõpriẽd'eɾ]
to unite (vt)	**unir** (vt)	[un'iɾ]
to wait (vt)	**esperar** (vi, vt)	[əʃpəɾ'aɾ]

to want (wish, desire)	**querer** (vt)	[kər'er]
to warn (vt)	**advertir** (vt)	[ɐdvərt'ir]
to work (vi)	**trabalhar** (vi)	[trɐbɐʎ'ar]
to write (vt)	**escrever** (vt)	[əʃkrəv'er]
to write down	**anotar** (vt)	[ɐnut'ar]

12. Colors

color	**cor** (f)	[kor]
shade (tint)	**matiz** (m)	[mɐt'iʒ]
hue	**tom** (m)	[tõ]
rainbow	**arco-íris** (m)	['arku 'iriʃ]
white (adj)	**branco**	[br'ãku]
black (adj)	**preto**	[pr'etu]
gray (adj)	**cinzento**	[sĩz'ẽtu]
green (adj)	**verde**	[v'erdə]
yellow (adj)	**amarelo**	[ɐmɐr'ɛlu]
red (adj)	**vermelho**	[vərm'ɐʎu]
blue (adj)	**azul**	[ɐz'ul]
light blue (adj)	**azul claro**	[ɐz'ul kl'aru]
pink (adj)	**cor-de-rosa**	[kor də ʀ'ɔzɐ]
orange (adj)	**cor de laranja**	[kor də lɐr'ãʒɐ]
violet (adj)	**violeta**	[viul'etɐ]
brown (adj)	**castanho**	[kɐʃt'ɐɲu]
golden (adj)	**dourado**	[dor'adu]
silvery (adj)	**prateado**	[pretj'adu]
beige (adj)	**bege**	[b'ɛʒə]
cream (adj)	**creme**	[kr'ɛmə]
turquoise (adj)	**turquesa**	[turk'ezɐ]
cherry red (adj)	**vermelho cereja**	[vərm'ɐʎu sər'ɐʒɐ]
lilac (adj)	**lilás**	[lil'aʃ]
crimson (adj)	**carmesim**	[kɐrməz'ĩ]
light (adj)	**claro**	[kl'aru]
dark (adj)	**escuro**	[əʃk'uru]
bright, vivid (adj)	**vivo**	[v'ivu]
colored (pencils)	**de cor**	[də kor]
color (e.g., ~ film)	**a cores**	[ɐ k'orəʃ]
black-and-white (adj)	**preto e branco**	[pr'etu i br'ãku]
plain (one-colored)	**de uma só cor**	[də 'umɐ sɔ kor]
multicolored (adj)	**multicor, multicolor**	[multik'or], [multikul'or]

13. Questions

Who?	**Quem?**	[kẽj]
What?	**Que?**	[ke]
Where? (at, in)	**Onde?**	['õdə]
Where (to)?	**Para onde?**	[p'ɐrɐ 'õdə]
From where?	**De onde?**	[də 'õdə]
When?	**Quando?**	[ku'ãdu]
Why? (What for?)	**Para quê?**	[p'ɐrɐ ke]
Why? (reason)	**Porquê?**	[purk'e]
What for?	**Para quê?**	[p'ɐrɐ ke]
How? (in what way)	**Como?**	[k'omu]
What? (What kind of ...?)	**Qual?**	[ku'al]
Which?	**Qual?**	[ku'al]
To whom?	**A quem?**	[ɐ kẽj]
About whom?	**De quem?**	[də kẽj]
About what?	**Do quê?**	[du ke]
With whom?	**Com quem?**	[kõ kẽj]
How many?	**Quantos? -as?**	[ku'ãtuʃ -ɐʃ]
How much?	**Quanto?**	[ku'ãtu]
Whose?	**De quem?**	[də kẽj]

14. Function words. Adverbs. Part 1

Where? (at, in)	**Onde?**	['õdə]
here (adv)	**aqui**	[ɐk'i]
there (adv)	**lá, ali**	[la], [ɐl'i]
somewhere (to be)	**em algum lugar**	[ɛn alg'ũ lug'aɾ]
nowhere (not anywhere)	**em lugar nenhum**	[ẽ lug'ar nəɲ'ũ]
by (near, beside)	**ao pé de ...**	['au pɛ də]
by the window	**ao pé da janela**	['au pɛ dɐ ʒɐn'ɛlɐ]
Where (to)?	**Para onde?**	[p'ɐrɐ 'õdə]
here (e.g., come ~!)	**para cá**	[p'ɐrɐ ka]
there (e.g., to go ~)	**para lá**	[p'ɐrɐ la]
from here (adv)	**daqui**	[dɐk'i]
from there (adv)	**de lá, dali**	[də la], [dɐl'i]
close (adv)	**perto**	[p'ɛrtu]
far (adv)	**longe**	[l'õʒə]
near (e.g., ~ Paris)	**perto de ...**	[p'ɛrtu də]
nearby (adv)	**ao lado de**	[au l'adu də]
not far (adv)	**perto, não fica longe**	[p'ɛrtu], [n'ãu f'ikɐ l'õʒə]

left (adj)	**esquerdo**	[əʃk'erdu]
on the left	**à esquerda**	[a əʃk'erdɐ]
to the left	**para esquerda**	[p'ɐrɐ əʃk'erdɐ]
right (adj)	**direito**	[dir'ɐjtu]
on the right	**à direita**	[a dir'ɐjtɐ]
to the right	**para direita**	[p'ɐrɐ dir'ɐjtɐ]
in front (adv)	**à frente**	[a fr'ẽtə]
front (as adj)	**da frente**	[dɐ fr'ẽtə]
ahead (look ~)	**para a frente**	[p'ɐrɐ a fr'ẽtə]
behind (adv)	**atrás de ...**	[ɐtr'aʃ də]
from behind	**por detrás**	[pur dətr'aʃ]
back (towards the rear)	**para trás**	[p'ɐrɐ tr'aʃ]
middle	**meio** (m), **metade** (f)	[m'ɐju], [mət'adə]
in the middle	**no meio**	[nu m'ɐju]
at the side	**de lado**	[də l'adu]
everywhere (adv)	**em todo lugar**	[ãn t'odu lug'ar]
around (in all directions)	**ao redor**	['au ʀəd'ɔr]
from inside	**de dentro**	[də d'ẽtru]
somewhere (to go)	**para algum lugar**	[p'ɐrɐ alg'ũ lug'ar]
straight (directly)	**diretamente**	[dirɛtɐm'ẽtə]
back (e.g., come ~)	**de volta**	[də v'ɔltɐ]
from anywhere	**de algum lugar**	[də alg'ũ lug'ar]
from somewhere	**de um lugar**	[də ũ lug'ar]
firstly (adv)	**em primeiro lugar**	[ẽ prim'ɐjru lug'ar]
secondly (adv)	**em segundo lugar**	[ẽ səg'ũdu lug'ar]
thirdly (adv)	**em terceiro lugar**	[ẽ tərs'ɐjru lug'ar]
suddenly (adv)	**de repente**	[də ʀəp'ẽtə]
at first (adv)	**inicialmente**	[inisialm'ẽtə]
for the first time	**pela primeira vez**	[p'elɐ prim'ɐjrɐ v'eʒ]
long before ...	**muito antes de ...**	[m'ujtu 'ãtəʃ də]
anew (over again)	**novamente**	[nɔvɐm'ẽtə]
for good (adv)	**para sempre**	[p'ɐrɐ s'ẽprə]
never (adv)	**nunca**	[n'ũkɐ]
again (adv)	**de novo**	[də n'ovu]
now (adv)	**agora**	[ɐg'ɔrɐ]
often (adv)	**frequentemente**	[frəkuẽtəm'ẽtə]
then (adv)	**então**	[ẽt'ãu]
urgently (quickly)	**urgentemente**	[urʒẽtəm'ẽtə]
usually (adv)	**usualmente**	[uzualm'ẽtə]
by the way, ...	**a propósito**	[ɐ prup'ɔzitu]
possible (that is ~)	**é possível**	[ɛ pus'ivɛl]

probably (adv)	**provavelmente**	[pruvavɛlm'ẽtə]
maybe (adv)	**talvez**	[talv'eʒ]
besides ...	**além disso, ...**	[al'ẽj d'isu]
that's why ...	**por isso ...**	[pur 'isu]
in spite of ...	**apesar de ...**	[ɐpəz'ar də]
thanks to ...	**graças a ...**	[gr'asɐʃ ɐ]
what (pron.)	**que**	[kə]
that (conj.)	**que**	[kə]
something	**algo**	[algu]
anything (something)	**alguma coisa**	[alg'umɐ k'ojzɐ]
nothing	**nada**	[n'adɐ]
who (pron.)	**quem**	[kẽj]
someone	**alguém**	[alg'ẽj]
somebody	**alguém**	[alg'ẽj]
nobody	**ninguém**	[nĩg'ẽj]
nowhere (a voyage to ~)	**para lugar nenhum**	[p'ɐrɐ lug'ar nəɲ'ũ]
nobody's	**de ninguém**	[də nĩg'ẽj]
somebody's	**de alguém**	[də alg'ẽj]
so (I'm ~ glad)	**tão**	[t'ãu]
also (as well)	**também**	[tãb'ẽj]
too (as well)	**também**	[tãb'ẽj]

15. Function words. Adverbs. Part 2

Why?	**Porquê?**	[purk'e]
for some reason	**por alguma razão**	[pur alg'umɐ ʀɐz'ãu]
because ...	**porque ...**	[p'urkə]
for some purpose	**não se sabe para que**	[n'ãu sə s'abə p'ɐrɐ kə]
and	**e**	[i]
or	**ou**	['ou]
but	**mas**	[meʃ]
for (e.g., ~ me)	**para**	[p'ɐrɐ]
too (~ many people)	**demasiado, muito**	[dəmɐzi'adu], [m'ujtu]
only (exclusively)	**só, somente**	[sɔ], [sɔm'ẽtə]
exactly (adv)	**exatamente**	[ezatɐm'ẽtə]
about (more or less)	**cerca de**	[s'erkɐ də]
approximately (adv)	**aproximadamente**	[ɐprɔsimadɐm'ẽtə]
approximate (adj)	**aproximado**	[ɐprɔsim'adu]
almost (adv)	**quase**	[ku'azə]
the rest	**resto** (m)	[ʀ'ɛʃtu]
the other (second)	**o outro**	[u 'otru]
other (different)	**outro**	['otru]

each (adj)	**cada**	[k'ɐdɐ]
any (no matter which)	**qualquer**	[kualk'ɛɾ]
many (adv)	**muitos, muitas**	[m'ujtuʃ -ɐʃ]
much (adv)	**muito**	[m'ujtu]
many people	**muitas pessoas**	[m'ujtɐʃ pəs'oɐʃ]
all (everyone)	**todos**	[t'oduʃ]
in return for ...	**em troca de ...**	[ẽ tr'ɔkɐ də]
in exchange (adv)	**em troca**	[ẽ tr'ɔkɐ]
by hand (made)	**à mão**	[a m'ãu]
hardly (negative opinion)	**é pouco provável**	[ɛ p'oku pruv'avɛl]
probably (adv)	**provavelmente**	[pruvavɛlm'ẽtə]
on purpose (adv)	**de propósito**	[də prup'ɔzitu]
by accident (adv)	**por acidente**	[puɾ ɐsid'ẽtə]
very (adv)	**muito**	[m'ujtu]
for example (adv)	**por exemplo**	[puɾ ez'ẽplu]
between	**entre**	['ẽtrə]
among	**entre, no meio de ...**	['ẽtrə], [nu m'ɐju də]
so much (such a lot)	**tanto**	[t'ãtu]
especially (adv)	**especialmente**	[əʃpəsjalm'ẽtə]

Basic concepts. Part 2

16. Weekdays

Monday	**segunda-feira** (f)	[səg'ũdɐ f'ɐjɾɐ]
Tuesday	**terça-feira** (f)	[t'ersɐ f'ɐjɾɐ]
Wednesday	**quarta-feira** (f)	[ku'art f'ɐjɾɐ]
Thursday	**quinta-feira** (f)	[k'ĩtɐ f'ɐjɾɐ]
Friday	**sexta-feira** (f)	[s'ɐʃtɐ f'ɐjɾɐ]
Saturday	**sábado** (m)	[s'abɐdu]
Sunday	**domingo** (m)	[dum'ĩgu]
today (adv)	**hoje**	['oʒə]
tomorrow (adv)	**amanhã**	[amɐɲ'ã]
the day after tomorrow	**depois de amanhã**	[dəp'ojʃ də amɐɲ'ã]
yesterday (adv)	**ontem**	['õtẽj]
the day before yesterday	**anteontem**	[ãtj'õtẽj]
day	**dia** (m)	[d'iɐ]
working day	**dia** (m) **de trabalho**	[d'iɐ də tɾɐb'aʎu]
public holiday	**feriado** (m)	[fərj'adu]
day off	**dia** (m) **de folga**	[d'iɐ də f'ɔlgɐ]
weekend	**fim** (m) **de semana**	[fĩ də səm'ɐnɐ]
all day long	**o dia todo**	[u d'iɐ t'odu]
next day (adv)	**no dia seguinte**	[nu d'iɐ səg'ĩtə]
two days ago	**há dois dias**	[a d'ojʃ d'iɐʃ]
the day before	**na véspera**	[nɐ v'ɛʃpəɾɐ]
daily (adj)	**diário**	[dj'ariu]
every day (adv)	**todos os dias**	[t'oduʃ uʃ d'iɐʃ]
week	**semana** (f)	[səm'ɐnɐ]
last week (adv)	**na semana passada**	[nɐ səm'ɐnɐ pɐs'adɐ]
next week (adv)	**na próxima semana**	[nɐ pr'ɔsimɐ səm'ɐnɐ]
weekly (adj)	**semanal**	[səmɐn'al]
every week (adv)	**semanalmente**	[səmɐnalm'ẽtə]
twice a week	**duas vezes por semana**	[d'uɐʃ v'ezəʃ p'ur səm'ɐnɐ]
every Tuesday	**cada terça-feira**	[k'ɐdɐ tersɐ f'ɐjɾɐ]

17. Hours. Day and night

morning	**manhã** (f)	[mɐɲ'ã]
in the morning	**de manhã**	[də mɐɲ'ã]
noon, midday	**meio-dia** (m)	[m'ɐju d'iɐ]

in the afternoon **à tarde** [a t'ardə]
evening **noite** (f) [n'ojtə]
in the evening **à noite** [a n'ojtə]
night **noite** (f) [n'ojtə]
at night **à noite** [a n'ojtə]
midnight **meia-noite** (f) [m'ɐjɐ n'ojtə]

second **segundo** (m) [səg'ũdu]
minute **minuto** (m) [min'utu]
hour **hora** (f) ['ɔrɐ]
half an hour **meia hora** (f) [m'ɐjɐ 'ɔrɐ]
quarter of an hour **quarto** (m) **de hora** [ku'artu də 'ɔrɐ]
fifteen minutes **quinze minutos** [k'ĩzə min'utuʃ]
24 hours **vinte e quatro horas** [v'ĩtə i ku'atru 'ɔrɐʃ]

sunrise **nascer** (m) **do sol** [nɐʃs'er du sɔl]
dawn **amanhecer** (m) [ɐmɐɲəs'er]
early morning **madrugada** (f) [mɐdrug'adɐ]
sunset **pôr do sol** (m) [por du s'ɔl]

early in the morning **de madrugada** [də mɐdrug'adɐ]
this morning **hoje de manhã** ['oʒə də mɐɲ'ã]
tomorrow morning **amanhã de manhã** [amɐɲ'ã də mɐɲ'ã]

this afternoon **hoje à tarde** ['oʒə a t'ardə]
in the afternoon **à tarde** [a t'ardə]
tomorrow afternoon **amanhã à tarde** [amɐɲ'ã a t'ardə]

tonight (this evening) **hoje à noite** ['oʒə a n'ojtə]
tomorrow night **amanhã à noite** [amɐɲ'ã a n'ojtə]

at 3 o'clock sharp **às três horas em ponto** [aʃ treʃ 'ɔrɐʃ ẽ p'õtu]
about 4 o'clock **por volta das quatro** [pur v'ɔltɐ dɐʃ ku'atru]
by 12 o'clock **às doze** [aʃ d'ozə]

in 20 minutes **dentro de vinte minutos** [d'ẽtru də v'ĩtə min'utuʃ]
in an hour **dentro duma hora** [d'ẽtru d'umɐ 'ɔrɐ]
on time (adv) **a tempo** [ɐ t'ẽpu]

a quarter of ... **menos um quarto** [m'enuʃ 'ũ ku'artu]
within an hour **durante uma hora** [dur'ãtə 'umɐ 'ɔrɐ]
every 15 minutes **a cada quinze minutos** [ɐ k'ɐdɐ k'ĩzə min'utuʃ]
round the clock **as vinte e quatro horas** [ɐʃ v'ĩtə i ku'atru 'ɔrɐʃ]

18. Months. Seasons

January **janeiro** (m) [ʒɐn'ɐjru]
February **fevereiro** (m) [fəvər'ɐjru]
March **março** (m) [m'arsu]
April **abril** (m) [ɐbr'il]

May	**maio** (m)	[m'aju]
June	**junho** (m)	[ʒ'uɲu]
July	**julho** (m)	[ʒ'uʎu]
August	**agosto** (m)	[ɐg'oʃtu]
September	**setembro** (m)	[sət'ẽbru]
October	**outubro** (m)	[ot'ubru]
November	**novembro** (m)	[nuv'ẽbru]
December	**dezembro** (m)	[dəz'ẽbru]
spring	**primavera** (f)	[primɐv'ɛrɐ]
in spring	**na primavera**	[nɐ primɐv'ɛrɐ]
spring (as adj)	**primaveril**	[primɐvər'il]
summer	**verão** (m)	[vər'ãu]
in summer	**no verão**	[nu vər'ãu]
summer (as adj)	**de verão**	[də vər'ãu]
fall	**outono** (m)	[ot'onu]
in fall	**no outono**	[nu ot'onu]
fall (as adj)	**outonal**	[otun'al]
winter	**inverno** (m)	[ĩv'ɛrnu]
in winter	**no inverno**	[nu ĩv'ɛrnu]
winter (as adj)	**de inverno**	[də ĩv'ɛrnu]
month	**mês** (m)	[meʃ]
this month	**este mês**	['eʃtə meʃ]
next month	**no próximo mês**	[nu pr'ɔsimu meʃ]
last month	**no mês passado**	[nu meʃ pɐs'adu]
a month ago	**há um mês**	[a ũ meʃ]
in a month	**dentro de um mês**	[d'ẽtru də ũ meʃ]
in two months	**dentro de dois meses**	[d'ẽtru də d'ojʃ m'ezəʃ]
the whole month	**durante todo o mês**	[dur'ãtə t'odu u meʃ]
all month long	**um mês inteiro**	[ũ meʃ ĩt'ɐjru]
monthly (~ magazine)	**mensal**	[mẽs'al]
monthly (adv)	**mensalmente**	[mẽsalm'ẽtə]
every month	**cada mês**	[k'ɐdɐ meʃ]
twice a month	**duas vezes por mês**	[d'uɐʃ v'ezəʃ pur meʃ]
year	**ano** (m)	['ɐnu]
this year	**este ano**	['eʃtə 'ɐnu]
next year	**no próximo ano**	[nu pr'ɔsimu 'ɐnu]
last year	**no ano passado**	[nu 'ɐnu pɐs'adu]
a year ago	**há um ano**	[a ũ 'ɐnu]
in a year	**dentro dum ano**	[d'ẽtru dũ 'ɐnu]
in two years	**dentro de 2 anos**	[d'ẽtru də d'ojʃ 'ɐnuʃ]
the whole year	**durante todo o ano**	[dur'ãtə t'odu u 'ɐnu]
all year long	**um ano inteiro**	[ũ 'ɐnu ĩt'ɐjru]

every year	**cada ano**	[k'ɐdɐ 'ɐnu]
annual (adj)	**anual**	[ɐnu'al]
annually (adv)	**anualmente**	[ɐnualm'ẽtə]
4 times a year	**quatro vezes por ano**	[ku'atru v'ezəʃ pur 'ɐnu]
date (e.g., today's ~)	**data** (f)	[d'atɐ]
date (e.g., ~ of birth)	**data** (f)	[d'atɐ]
calendar	**calendário** (m)	[kɐlẽd'ariu]
half a year	**meio ano**	[m'ɐju 'ɐnu]
six months	**seis meses**	[s'ɐjʃ m'ezəʃ]
season (summer, etc.)	**estação** (f)	[əʃtɐs'ãu]
century	**século** (m)	[s'ɛkulu]

19. Time. Miscellaneous

time	**tempo** (m)	[t'ẽpu]
instant (n)	**momento** (m)	[mum'ẽtu]
moment	**instante** (m)	[ĩʃt'ãtə]
instant (adj)	**instantâneo**	[ĩʃtãt'ɐniu]
lapse (of time)	**período** (m) **de tempo**	[pər'iudu də t'ẽpu]
life	**vida** (f)	[v'idɐ]
eternity	**eternidade** (f)	[etərnid'adə]
epoch	**época** (f)	['ɛpukɐ]
era	**era** (f)	['ɛrɐ]
cycle	**ciclo** (m)	[s'iklu]
period	**período** (m)	[pər'iudu]
term (short-~)	**prazo** (m)	[pr'azu]
the future	**futuro** (m)	[fut'uru]
future (as adj)	**futuro**	[fut'uru]
next time	**da próxima vez**	[dɐ pr'ɔsimɐ veʒ]
the past	**passado** (m)	[pɐs'adu]
past (recent)	**passado**	[pɐs'adu]
last time	**na vez passada**	[nɐ veʒ pɐs'adɐ]
later (adv)	**mais tarde**	[m'ajʃ t'ardə]
after (prep.)	**depois**	[dəp'ojʃ]
nowadays (adv)	**atualmente**	[ɐtualm'ẽtə]
now (adv)	**agora**	[ɐg'ɔrɐ]
immediately (adv)	**imediatamente**	[imədjatɐm'ẽtə]
soon (adv)	**logo, brevemente**	[l'ɔgu], [brɛvəm'ẽtə]
in advance (beforehand)	**de antemão**	[də ãtəm'ãu]
a long time ago	**há muito tempo**	[a m'ujtu t'ẽpu]
recently (adv)	**há pouco tempo**	[a p'oku t'ẽpu]
destiny	**destino** (m)	[dəʃt'inu]
memories (childhood ~)	**recordações** (f pl)	[ʀəkurdɐs'ojʃ]
archives	**arquivo** (m)	[ɐrk'ivu]

during ...	**durante ...**	[dur'ãtə]
long, a long time (adv)	**durante muito tempo**	[dur'ãtə m'ujtu t'ẽpu]
not long (adv)	**pouco tempo**	[p'oku t'ẽpu]
early (in the morning)	**cedo**	[s'edu]
late (not early)	**tarde**	[t'ardə]
forever (for good)	**para sempre**	[p'ɐrɐ s'ẽprə]
to start (begin)	**começar** (vt)	[kuməs'ar]
to postpone (vt)	**adiar** (vt)	[ɐdj'ar]
at the same time	**simultaneamente**	[simultɐniɐm'ẽtə]
permanently (adv)	**permanentemente**	[pərmɐnẽtəm'ẽtə]
constant (noise, pain)	**constante**	[kõʃt'ãtə]
temporary (adj)	**temporário**	[tẽpur'ariu]
sometimes (adv)	**às vezes**	[aʃ v'ezəʃ]
rarely (adv)	**raramente**	[ʀarɐm'ẽtə]
often (adv)	**frequentemente**	[frəkuẽtəm'ẽtə]

20. Opposites

rich (adj)	**rico**	[ʀ'iku]
poor (adj)	**pobre**	[p'ɔbrə]
ill, sick (adj)	**doente**	[du'ẽtə]
healthy (adj)	**são**	[s'ãu]
big (adj)	**grande**	[gr'ãdə]
small (adj)	**pequeno**	[pək'enu]
quickly (adv)	**rapidamente**	[ʀapidɐm'ẽtə]
slowly (adv)	**lentamente**	[lẽtɐm'ẽtə]
fast (adj)	**rápido**	[ʀ'apidu]
slow (adj)	**lento**	[l'ẽtu]
cheerful (adj)	**alegre**	[ɐl'ɛgrə]
sad (adj)	**triste**	[tr'iʃtə]
together (adv)	**juntos**	[ʒ'ũtuʃ]
separately (adv)	**separadamente**	[səpɐradɐm'ẽtə]
aloud (to read)	**em voz alta**	[ẽ vɔʒ 'altɐ]
silently (to oneself)	**para si**	[p'ɐrɐ si]
tall (adj)	**alto**	['altu]
low (adj)	**baixo**	[b'ajʃu]
deep (adj)	**profundo**	[pruf'ũdu]
shallow (adj)	**pouco fundo**	[p'oku f'ũdu]

yes	**sim**	[sĩ]
no	**não**	[nãu]
distant (in space)	**distante**	[diʃt'ãtə]
nearby (adj)	**próximo**	[pr'ɔsimu]
far (adv)	**longe**	[l'õʒə]
nearby (adv)	**perto**	[p'ɛrtu]
long (adj)	**longo**	[l'õgu]
short (adj)	**curto**	[k'urtu]
good (kindhearted)	**bondoso**	[bõd'ozu]
evil (adj)	**mau**	[m'au]
married (adj)	**casado**	[kɐz'adu]
single (adj)	**solteiro**	[sɔlt'ɐjru]
to forbid (vt)	**proibir** (vt)	[pruib'ir]
to permit (vt)	**permitir** (vt)	[pərmit'ir]
end	**fim** (m)	[fĩ]
beginning	**começo** (m)	[kum'esu]
left (adj)	**esquerdo**	[əʃk'erdu]
right (adj)	**direito**	[dir'ɐjtu]
first (adj)	**primeiro**	[prim'ɐjru]
last (adj)	**último**	['ultimu]
crime	**crime** (m)	[kr'imə]
punishment	**castigo** (m)	[kɐʃt'igu]
to order (vt)	**ordenar** (vt)	[ɔrdən'ar]
to obey (vi, vt)	**obedecer** (vt)	[ɔbədəs'er]
straight (adj)	**reto**	[ʀ'ɛtu]
curved (adj)	**curvo**	[k'urvu]
paradise	**paraíso** (m)	[pɐrɐ'izu]
hell	**inferno** (m)	[ĩf'ɛrnu]
to be born	**nascer** (vi)	[nɐʃs'er]
to die (vi)	**morrer** (vi)	[muʀ'er]
strong (adj)	**forte**	[f'ɔrtə]
weak (adj)	**fraco**	[fr'aku]
old (adj)	**idoso**	[id'ozu]
young (adj)	**jovem**	[ʒ'ɔvẽj]
old (adj)	**velho**	[v'ɛʎu]
new (adj)	**novo**	[n'ovu]

hard (adj)	**duro**	[d'uru]
soft (adj)	**mole**	[m'ɔlə]
warm (adj)	**morno**	[m'ornu]
cold (adj)	**frio**	[fr'iu]
fat (adj)	**gordo**	[g'ordu]
thin (adj)	**magro**	[m'agru]
narrow (adj)	**estreito**	[əʃtr'ɐjtu]
wide (adj)	**largo**	[l'argu]
good (adj)	**bom**	[bõ]
bad (adj)	**mau**	[m'au]
brave (adj)	**valente**	[vɐl'ẽtə]
cowardly (adj)	**cobarde**	[kub'ardə]

21. Lines and shapes

square	**quadrado** (m)	[kuɐdr'adu]
square (as adj)	**quadrado**	[kuɐdr'adu]
circle	**círculo** (m)	[s'irkulu]
round (adj)	**redondo**	[ʀəd'õdu]
triangle	**triângulo** (m)	[trj'ãgulu]
triangular (adj)	**triangular**	[triãgul'ar]
oval	**oval** (f)	[ɔv'al]
oval (as adj)	**oval**	[ɔv'al]
rectangle	**retângulo** (m)	[ʀɛt'ãgulu]
rectangular (adj)	**retangular**	[ʀɛtãgul'ar]
pyramid	**pirâmide** (f)	[pir'ɐmidə]
rhombus	**rombo** (m)	[ʀ'õbu]
trapezoid	**trapézio** (m)	[trɐp'ɛziu]
cube	**cubo** (m)	[k'ubu]
prism	**prisma** (m)	[pr'iʒmɐ]
circumference	**circunferência** (f)	[sirkũfər'ẽsiɐ]
sphere	**esfera** (f)	[əʃf'ɛrɐ]
ball (solid sphere)	**globo** (m)	[gl'obu]
diameter	**diâmetro** (m)	[dj'ɐmətru]
radius	**raio** (m)	[ʀ'aju]
perimeter (circle's ~)	**perímetro** (m)	[pər'imətru]
center	**centro** (m)	[s'ẽtru]
horizontal (adj)	**horizontal**	[ɔrizõt'al]
vertical (adj)	**vertical**	[vərtik'al]
parallel (n)	**paralela** (f)	[pɐrɐl'ɛlɐ]
parallel (as adj)	**paralelo**	[pɐrɐl'ɛlu]

line	**linha** (f)	[l'iɲɐ]
stroke	**traço** (m)	[tr'asu]
straight line	**reta** (f)	[ʀ'ɛtɐ]
curve (curved line)	**curva** (f)	[k'urvɐ]
thin (line, etc.)	**fino**	[f'inu]
contour (outline)	**contorno** (m)	[kõt'ornu]
intersection	**interseção** (f)	[ĩtərsɛs'ãu]
right angle	**ângulo** (m) **reto**	[ãgulu ʀ'ɛtu]
segment	**segmento** (m)	[sɛgm'ẽtu]
sector	**setor** (m)	[sɛt'or]
side (of triangle)	**lado** (m)	[l'adu]
angle	**ângulo** (m)	[ãgulu]

22. Units of measurement

weight	**peso** (m)	[p'ezu]
length	**comprimento** (m)	[kõprim'ẽtu]
width	**largura** (f)	[lɐrg'urɐ]
height	**altura** (f)	[alt'urɐ]
depth	**profundidade** (f)	[prufũdid'adə]
volume	**volume** (m)	[vul'umə]
area	**área** (f)	['ariɐ]
gram	**grama** (m)	[gr'ɐmɐ]
milligram	**miligrama** (m)	[miligr'ɐmɐ]
kilogram	**quilograma** (m)	[kilugr'ɐmɐ]
ton	**tonelada** (f)	[tunəl'adɐ]
pound	**libra** (f)	[l'ibrɐ]
ounce	**onça** (f)	['õsɐ]
meter	**metro** (m)	[m'ɛtru]
millimeter	**milímetro** (m)	[mil'imətru]
centimeter	**centímetro** (m)	[sẽt'imətru]
kilometer	**quilómetro** (m)	[kil'ɔmətru]
mile	**milha** (f)	[m'iʎɐ]
inch	**polegada** (f)	[puləg'adɐ]
foot	**pé** (m)	[pɛ]
yard	**jarda** (f)	[ʒ'ardɐ]
square meter	**metro** (m) **quadrado**	[m'ɛtru kuɐdr'adu]
hectare	**hectare** (m)	[ɛkt'arə]
liter	**litro** (m)	[l'itru]
degree	**grau** (m)	[gr'au]
volt	**volt** (m)	[v'ɔltə]
ampere	**ampere** (m)	[ãp'ɛrə]
horsepower	**cavalo-vapor** (m)	[kɐv'alu vɐp'or]
quantity	**quantidade** (f)	[kuãtid'adə]

a little bit of ...	**um pouco de ...**	[ũ p'oku də]
half	**metade** (f)	[mət'adə]
dozen	**dúzia** (f)	[d'uziɐ]
piece (item)	**peça** (f)	[p'ɛsɐ]
size	**dimensão** (f)	[dimẽs'ãu]
scale (map ~)	**escala** (f)	[əʃk'alɐ]
minimal (adj)	**mínimo**	[m'inimu]
the smallest (adj)	**menor, mais pequeno**	[mən'ɔɾ], [m'ajʃ pək'enu]
medium (adj)	**médio**	[m'ɛdiu]
maximal (adj)	**máximo**	[m'asimu]
the largest (adj)	**maior, mais grande**	[mɐj'ɔɾ], [m'ajʃ gɾ'ãdə]

23. Containers

jar (glass)	**boião** (m) **de vidro**	[boj'ãu də v'idɾu]
can	**lata** (f)	[l'atɐ]
bucket	**balde** (m)	[b'aldə]
barrel	**barril** (m)	[bɐʀ'il]
basin (for washing)	**bacia** (f)	[bɐs'iɐ]
tank (for liquid, gas)	**tanque** (m)	[t'ãkə]
hip flask	**cantil** (m) **de bolso**	[kãt'il də b'olsu]
jerrycan	**bidão** (m) **de gasolina**	[bid'ãu də gɐzul'inɐ]
cistern (tank)	**cisterna** (f)	[siʃt'ɛrnɐ]
mug	**caneca** (f)	[kɐn'ɛkɐ]
cup (of coffee, etc.)	**chávena** (f)	[ʃ'avənɐ]
saucer	**pires** (m)	[p'irəʃ]
glass (tumbler)	**copo** (m)	[k'ɔpu]
wineglass	**taça** (m) **de vinho**	[t'asɐ də v'iɲu]
saucepan	**panela** (f)	[pɐn'ɛlɐ]
bottle (~ of wine)	**garrafa** (f)	[gɐʀ'afɐ]
neck (of the bottle)	**gargalo** (m)	[gɐrg'alu]
carafe	**jarro, garrafa** (f)	[ʒ'aʀu], [gɐʀ'afɐ]
pitcher (earthenware)	**jarro** (m) **de barro**	[ʒ'aʀu də b'aʀu]
vessel (container)	**vasilhame** (m)	[vɐziʎ'ɐmə]
pot (crock)	**pote** (m)	[p'ɔtə]
vase	**vaso** (m)	[v'azu]
bottle (~ of perfume)	**frasco, frasquinho** (m)	[fɾ'aʃku], [fɾɐʃk'iɲu]
vial, small bottle	**frasco** (m)	[fɾ'aʃku]
tube (of toothpaste)	**tubo** (m)	[t'ubu]
sack (bag)	**saca** (f)	[s'akɐ]
bag (paper ~, plastic ~)	**saco** (m)	[s'aku]
pack (of cigarettes, etc.)	**maço** (m)	[m'asu]

box (e.g., shoebox)	**caixa** (f)	[k'ajʃɐ]
crate	**engradado** (m)	[ẽgrɐd'adu]
basket	**cesto** (m), **cesta** (f)	[s'eʃtu], [s'eʃtɐ]

24. Materials

material	**material** (m)	[mɐtərj'al]
wood	**madeira** (f)	[mɐd'ɐjrɐ]
wooden (adj)	**de madeira**	[də mɐd'ɐjrɐ]
glass (n)	**vidro** (m)	[v'idru]
glass (as adj)	**de vidro**	[də v'idru]
stone (n)	**pedra** (f)	[p'ɛdrɐ]
stone (as adj)	**de pedra**	[də p'ɛdrɐ]
plastic (n)	**plástico** (m)	[pl'aʃtiku]
plastic (as adj)	**de plástico**	[də pl'aʃtiku]
rubber (n)	**borracha** (f)	[buʀ'aʃɐ]
rubber (as adj)	**de borracha**	[də buʀ'aʃɐ]
cloth, fabric (n)	**tecido, pano** (m)	[təs'idu], [p'ɐnu]
fabric (as adj)	**de tecido**	[də təs'idu]
paper (n)	**papel** (m)	[pɐp'ɛl]
paper (as adj)	**de papel**	[də pɐp'ɛl]
cardboard (n)	**cartão** (m)	[kɐrt'ãu]
cardboard (as adj)	**de cartão**	[də kɐrt'ãu]
polyethylene	**polietileno** (m)	[pɔliɛtil'enu]
cellophane	**celofane** (m)	[səluf'ɐnə]
linoleum	**linóleo** (m)	[lin'ɔliu]
plywood	**contraplacado** (m)	[kõtrɐplɐk'adu]
porcelain (n)	**porcelana** (f)	[pursəl'ɐnɐ]
porcelain (as adj)	**de porcelana**	[də pursəl'ɐnɐ]
clay (n)	**barro** (f)	[b'aʀu]
clay (as adj)	**de barro**	[də b'aʀu]
ceramics (n)	**cerâmica** (f)	[sər'ɐmikɐ]
ceramic (as adj)	**de cerâmica**	[də sər'ɐmikɐ]

25. Metals

metal (n)	**metal** (m)	[mət'al]
metal (as adj)	**metálico**	[mət'aliku]
alloy (n)	**liga** (f)	[l'igɐ]

gold (n)	**ouro** (m)	['oru]
gold, golden (adj)	**de ouro**	[də 'oru]
silver (n)	**prata** (f)	[pr'atɐ]
silver (as adj)	**de prata**	[də pr'atɐ]
iron (n)	**ferro** (m)	[f'ɛʀu]
iron (adj), made of iron	**de ferro**	[də f'ɛʀu]
steel (n)	**aço** (m)	['asu]
steel (as adj)	**de aço**	[də 'asu]
copper (n)	**cobre** (m)	[k'ɔbrə]
copper (as adj)	**de cobre**	[də k'ɔbrə]
aluminum (n)	**alumínio** (m)	[ɐlum'iniu]
aluminum (as adj)	**de alumínio**	[də ɐlum'iniu]
bronze (n)	**bronze** (m)	[br'õzə]
bronze (as adj)	**de bronze**	[də br'õzə]
brass	**latão** (m)	[lɐt'ãu]
nickel	**níquel** (m)	[n'ikɛl]
platinum	**platina** (f)	[plɐt'inɐ]
mercury	**mercúrio** (m)	[mərk'uriu]
tin	**estanho** (m)	[əʃt'ɐɲu]
lead	**chumbo** (m)	[ʃ'ũbu]
zinc	**zinco** (m)	[z'ĩku]

HUMAN BEING

Human being. The body

26. Humans. Basic concepts

human being	**ser** (m) **humano**	[ser um'ɐnu]
man (adult male)	**homem** (m)	['ɔmẽj]
woman	**mulher** (f)	[muʎ'ɛr]
child	**criança** (f)	[krj'ãsɐ]
girl	**menina** (f)	[mən'inɐ]
boy	**menino** (m)	[mən'inu]
teenager	**adolescente** (m)	[ɐduləʃs'ẽtə]
old man	**velhote, idoso** (m)	[vɛʎ'ɔtə], [id'ozu]
old woman	**velhota** (f)	[vɛʎ'ɔtɐ]

27. Human anatomy

organism	**organismo** (m)	[ɔrgɐn'iʒmu]
heart	**coração** (m)	[kurɐs'ãu]
blood	**sangue** (m)	[s'ãgə]
artery	**artéria** (f)	[ɐrt'ɛriɐ]
vein	**veia** (f)	[v'ɐjɐ]
brain	**cérebro** (m)	[s'ɛrəbru]
nerve	**nervo** (m)	[n'ervu]
nerves	**nervos** (m pl)	[n'ervuʃ]
vertebra	**vértebra** (f)	[v'ɛrtəbrɐ]
spine	**coluna** (f) **vertebral**	[kul'unɐ vərtəbr'al]
stomach (organ)	**estômago** (m)	[əʃt'omɐgu]
intestines, bowel	**intestinos** (m pl)	[ĩtəʃt'inuʃ]
intestine (e.g., large ~)	**intestino** (m)	[ĩtəʃt'inu]
liver	**fígado** (m)	[f'igɐdu]
kidney	**rim** (m)	[ʀĩ]
bone	**osso** (m)	['osu]
skeleton	**esqueleto** (m)	[əʃkəl'etu]
rib	**costela** (f)	[kuʃt'ɛlɐ]
skull	**crânio** (m)	[kr'ɐniu]
muscle	**músculo** (m)	[m'uʃkulu]
biceps	**bíceps** (m)	[b'isɛps]

triceps **triceps** (m) [tris'ɛʃ]
tendon **tendão** (m) [tẽd'ãu]
joint **articulação** (f) [ɐrtikulɐs'ãu]
lungs **pulmões** (m pl) [pulm'ojʃ]
genitals **órgãos** (m pl) **genitais** ['ɔrg'ãuʃ ʒənit'ajʃ]
skin **pele** (f) [p'ɛlə]

28. Head

head **cabeça** (f) [kɐb'esɐ]
face **cara** (f) [k'arɐ]
nose **nariz** (m) [nɐr'iʒ]
mouth **boca** (f) [b'okɐ]

eye **olho** (m) ['oʎu]
eyes **olhos** (m pl) ['ɔʎuʃ]
pupil **pupila** (f) [pup'ilɐ]
eyebrow **sobrancelha** (f) [subrãs'ɐʎɐ]
eyelash **pestana** (f) [pəʃt'ɐnɐ]
eyelid **pálpebra** (f) [p'alpəbrɐ]

tongue **língua** (f) [l'ĩguɐ]
tooth **dente** (m) [d'ẽtə]
lips **lábios** (m pl) [l'abiuʃ]
cheekbones **maçãs** (f pl) **do rosto** [mɐs'ãʃ du ʀ'oʃtu]
gum **gengiva** (f) [ʒẽʒ'ivɐ]
palate **céu** (f) **da boca** [s'ɛu dɐ b'okɐ]

nostrils **narinas** (f pl) [nɐr'inɐʃ]
chin **queixo** (m) [k'ɐjʃu]
jaw **mandíbula** (f) [mãd'ibulɐ]
cheek **bochecha** (f) [buʃ'ɐʃɐ]

forehead **testa** (f) [t'ɛʃtɐ]
temple **têmpora** (f) [t'ẽpurɐ]
ear **orelha** (f) [ɔr'ɐʎɐ]
back of the head **nuca** (f) [n'ukɐ]
neck **pescoço** (m) [pəʃk'osu]
throat **garganta** (f) [gɐrg'ãtɐ]

hair **cabelos** (m pl) [kɐb'eluʃ]
hairstyle **penteado** (m) [pẽtj'adu]
haircut **corte** (m) **de cabelo** [k'ɔrtə də kɐb'elu]
wig **peruca** (f) [pər'ukɐ]

mustache **bigode** (m) [big'ɔdə]
beard **barba** (f) [b'arbɐ]
to have (a beard, etc.) **usar, ter** (vt) [uz'ar], [ter]
braid **trança** (f) [tr'ãsɐ]
sideburns **suíças** (f pl) [su'isɐʃ]

red-haired (adj)	**ruivo**	[ʀ'ujvu]
gray (hair)	**grisalho**	[griz'aʎu]
bald (adj)	**calvo**	[k'alvu]
bald patch	**calva** (f)	[k'alvɐ]
ponytail	**rabo-de-cavalo** (m)	[ʀabu də kɐv'alu]
bangs	**franja** (f)	[fr'ãʒɐ]

29. Human body

hand	**mão** (f)	[m'ãu]
arm	**braço** (m)	[br'asu]
finger	**dedo** (m)	[d'edu]
toe	**dedo** (m)	[d'edu]
thumb	**polegar** (m)	[puləg'aɾ]
little finger	**dedo** (m) **mindinho**	[d'edu mĩd'iɲu]
nail	**unha** (f)	['uɲɐ]
fist	**punho** (m)	[p'uɲu]
palm	**palma** (f) **da mão**	[p'almɐ dɐ m'ãu]
wrist	**pulso** (m)	[p'ulsu]
forearm	**antebraço** (m)	[ãtəbr'asu]
elbow	**cotovelo** (m)	[kutuv'elu]
shoulder	**ombro** (m)	['õbru]
leg	**perna** (f)	[p'ɛrnɐ]
foot	**pé** (m)	[pɛ]
knee	**joelho** (m)	[ʒu'ɐʎu]
calf (part of leg)	**barriga** (f) **da perna**	[bɐʀ'igɐ dɐ p'ɛrnɐ]
hip	**coxa** (f)	[k'oʃɐ]
heel	**calcanhar** (m)	[kalkɐɲ'aɾ]
body	**corpo** (m)	[k'orpu]
stomach	**barriga** (f)	[bɐʀ'igɐ]
chest	**peito** (m)	[p'ɐjtu]
breast	**seio** (m)	[s'ɐju]
flank	**lado** (m)	[l'adu]
back	**costas** (f pl)	[k'ɔʃtɐʃ]
lower back	**região** (f) **lombar**	[ʀəʒj'ãu lõb'aɾ]
waist	**cintura** (f)	[sĩt'urɐ]
navel	**umbigo** (m)	[ũb'igu]
buttocks	**nádegas** (f pl)	[n'adəgɐʃ]
bottom	**traseiro** (m)	[trɐz'ɐjru]
beauty mark	**sinal** (m)	[sin'al]
birthmark	**sinal** (m) **de nascença**	[sin'al də nɐʃs'ẽsɐ]
tattoo	**tatuagem** (f)	[tɐtu'aʒẽj]
scar	**cicatriz** (f)	[sikɐtr'iʒ]

Clothing & Accessories

30. Outerwear. Coats

clothes	**roupa** (f)	[R'opɐ]
outer clothes	**roupa** (f) **exterior**	[R'opɐ əʃtərj'or]
winter clothes	**roupa** (f) **de inverno**	[R'opɐ də ĩv'ɛrnu]
overcoat	**sobretudo** (m)	[sobrət'udu]
fur coat	**casaco** (m) **de peles**	[kɐz'aku də p'ɛləʃ]
fur jacket	**casaco curto** (m) **de peles**	[kɐz'aku k'urtu də p'ɛləʃ]
down coat	**colchão** (m) **de penas**	[kɔlʃ'ãu də p'enɐʃ]
jacket (e.g., leather ~)	**casaco, blusão** (m)	[kɐz'aku], [bluz'ãu]
raincoat	**capa** (f)	[k'apɐ]
waterproof (adj)	**impermeável**	[ĩpərmj'avɛl]

31. Men's & women's clothing

shirt	**camisa** (f)	[kɐm'izɐ]
pants	**calças** (f pl)	[k'alsɐʃ]
jeans	**calças** (f pl) **de ganga**	[k'alsɐʃ də g'ãgɐ]
jacket (of man's suit)	**casaco** (m)	[kɐz'aku]
suit	**fato** (m)	[f'atu]
dress (frock)	**vestido** (m)	[vəʃt'idu]
skirt	**saia** (f)	[s'ajɐ]
blouse	**blusa** (f)	[bl'uzɐ]
knitted jacket	**casaco** (m) **de malha**	[kɐz'aku də m'aʎɐ]
jacket (of woman's suit)	**casaquinho** (m)	[kɐzɐk'iɲu]
T-shirt	**t-shirt, camiseta** (f)	[t'iʃərt], [kɐmiz'etɐ]
shorts (short trousers)	**calções** (m pl)	[kals'ojʃ]
tracksuit	**fato** (m) **de treino**	[f'atu də tr'ɐjnu]
bathrobe	**roupão** (m) **de banho**	[Rop'ãu də b'ɐɲu]
pajamas	**pijama** (m)	[piʒ'ɐmɐ]
sweater	**suéter** (m)	[su'ɛtɛr]
pullover	**pulôver** (m)	[pul'ovɛr]
vest	**colete** (m)	[kul'etə]
tailcoat	**casaca** (f)	[kɐz'akɐ]
tuxedo	**smoking** (m)	[sm'okĩg]
uniform	**uniforme** (m)	[unif'ɔrmə]

workwear	**roupa** (f) **de trabalho**	[ʀ'ope də treb'aʎu]
overalls	**fato-macaco** (m)	[f'atu mek'aku]
coat (e.g., doctor's smock)	**bata** (f)	[b'ate]

32. Clothing. Underwear

underwear	**roupa** (f) **interior**	[ʀ'ope ĩtərj'or]
boxers	**cuecas boxer** (f pl)	[ku'ɛkeʃ b'ɔkser]
panties	**cuecas** (f pl)	[ku'ɛkeʃ]
undershirt (A-shirt)	**camisola** (f) **interior**	[kemiz'ɔle ĩtərj'or]
socks	**peúgas** (f pl)	[pj'ugeʃ]
nightgown	**camisa** (f) **de noite**	[kem'ize də n'ojtə]
bra	**sutiã** (m)	[sutj'ã]
knee highs	**meias 3/4** (f pl)	[m'ejeʃ tr'eʃ ku'atru]
tights	**meias-calças** (f pl)	[m'ejeʃ k'alseʃ]
stockings (thigh highs)	**meias** (f pl)	[m'ejeʃ]
bathing suit	**fato** (m) **de banho**	[f'atu də b'eɲu]

33. Headwear

hat	**chapéu** (m)	[ʃep'ɛu]
fedora	**chapéu** (m) **de feltro**	[ʃep'ɛu də f'eltru]
baseball cap	**boné** (m) **de beisebol**	[bɔn'ɛ də b'ɛjzbɔl]
flatcap	**boné** (m)	[bɔn'ɛ]
beret	**boina** (f)	[b'ɔjne]
hood	**capuz** (m)	[kep'uʃ]
panama hat	**panamá** (m)	[penem'a]
knitted hat	**gorro** (m) **de malha**	[g'oʀu də m'aʎe]
headscarf	**lenço** (m)	[l'ẽsu]
women's hat	**chapéu** (m) **de mulher**	[ʃep'ɛu də muʎ'ɛr]
hard hat	**capacete** (m) **de proteção**	[kepes'etə də prutɛs'ãu]
garrison cap	**bivaque** (m)	[biv'akə]
helmet	**capacete** (m)	[kepes'etə]
derby	**chapéu** (m) **de coco**	[ʃep'ɛu də k'oku]
top hat	**chapéu** (m) **alto**	[ʃep'ɛu 'altu]

34. Footwear

footwear	**calçado** (m)	[kals'adu]
ankle boots	**botinas** (f pl)	[but'ineʃ]
shoes (low-heeled ~)	**sapatos** (m pl)	[sep'atuʃ]

boots (cowboy ~)	**botas** (f pl)	[b'ɔteʃ]
slippers	**pantufas** (f pl)	[pãt'ufeʃ]
tennis shoes	**ténis** (m pl)	[t'ɛniʃ]
sneakers	**sapatilhas** (f pl)	[sepet'iʎeʃ]
sandals	**sandálias** (f pl)	[sãd'alieʃ]
cobbler	**sapateiro** (m)	[sepet'ejru]
heel	**salto** (m)	[s'altu]
pair (of shoes)	**par** (m)	[par]
shoestring	**atacador** (m)	[eteked'or]
to lace (vt)	**amarrar** (vt)	[emeʀ'ar]
shoehorn	**calçadeira** (f)	[kalsed'ejre]
shoe polish	**graxa** (f) **para calçado**	[gr'aʃe p'ere kals'adu]

35. Textile. Fabrics

cotton (n)	**algodão** (m)	[algud'ãu]
cotton (as adj)	**de algodão**	[də algud'ãu]
flax (n)	**linho** (m)	[l'iɲu]
flax (as adj)	**de linho**	[də l'iɲu]
silk (n)	**seda** (f)	[s'ede]
silk (as adj)	**de seda**	[də s'ede]
wool (n)	**lã** (f)	[lã]
woolen (adj)	**de lã**	[də lã]
velvet	**veludo** (m)	[vəl'udu]
suede	**camurça** (f)	[kem'urse]
corduroy	**bombazina** (f)	[bõbez'ine]
nylon (n)	**nylon** (m)	[n'ajlɔn]
nylon (as adj)	**de nylon**	[də n'ajlɔn]
polyester (n)	**poliéster** (m)	[pɔli'ɛstɛr]
polyester (as adj)	**de poliéster**	[də pɔli'ɛstɛr]
leather (n)	**couro** (m)	[k'oru]
leather (as adj)	**de couro**	[də k'oru]
fur (n)	**pele** (f)	[p'ɛlə]
fur (e.g., ~ coat)	**de peles, de pele**	[də p'ɛləʃ], [də p'ɛlə]

36. Personal accessories

gloves	**luvas** (f pl)	[l'uveʃ]
mittens	**mitenes** (f pl)	[mit'ɛnəʃ]
scarf (muffler)	**cachecol** (m)	[kaʃək'ɔl]
glasses	**óculos** (m pl)	['ɔkuluʃ]

frame (eyeglass ~)	**armação** (f) **de óculos**	[ɐrmɐs'ãu də 'ɔkuluʃ]
umbrella	**guarda-chuva** (m)	[guardɐ ʃ'uvɐ]
walking stick	**bengala** (f)	[bẽg'alɐ]
hairbrush	**escova** (f) **para o cabelo**	[əʃk'ovɐ p'ɐrɐ u kɐb'elu]
fan	**leque** (m)	[l'ɛkə]
necktie	**gravata** (f)	[grɐv'atɐ]
bow tie	**gravata-borboleta** (f)	[grɐv'atɐ burbul'etɐ]
suspenders	**suspensórios** (m pl)	[suʃpẽs'ɔriuʃ]
handkerchief	**lenço** (m)	[l'ẽsu]
comb	**pente** (m)	[p'ẽtə]
barrette	**travessão** (m)	[trɐvəs'ãu]
hairpin	**gancho** (m) **de cabelo**	[g'ãʃu də kɐb'elu]
buckle	**fivela** (f)	[fiv'ɛlɐ]
belt	**cinto** (m)	[s'ĩtu]
shoulder strap	**correia** (f)	[kuʀ'ɐjɐ]
bag (handbag)	**bolsa** (f)	[b'olsɐ]
purse	**bolsa** (f) **de senhora**	[b'olsɐ də səɲ'orɐ]
backpack	**mochila** (f)	[muʃ'ilɐ]

37. Clothing. Miscellaneous

fashion	**moda** (f)	[m'ɔdɐ]
in vogue (adj)	**na moda**	[nɐ m'ɔdɐ]
fashion designer	**estilista** (m)	[əʃtil'iʃtɐ]
collar	**colarinho** (m), **gola** (f)	[kulɐr'iɲu], [g'ɔlɐ]
pocket	**bolso** (m)	[b'olsu]
pocket (as adj)	**de bolso**	[də b'olsu]
sleeve	**manga** (f)	[m'ãgɐ]
hanging loop	**cabide** (m)	[kɐb'idə]
fly (on trousers)	**braguilha** (f)	[brɐg'iʎɐ]
zipper (fastener)	**fecho de correr** (m)	[f'ɐʃu də kuʀ'er]
fastener	**fecho** (m), **colchete** (m)	[f'ɐʃu], [kolʃ'etə]
button	**botão** (m)	[but'ãu]
buttonhole	**casa** (f) **de botão**	[k'azɐ də but'ãu]
to come off (ab. button)	**cair** (vi)	[kɐ'ir]
to sew (vi, vt)	**coser, costurar** (vi)	[kuz'er], [kuʃtur'ar]
to embroider (vi, vt)	**bordar** (vt)	[burd'ar]
embroidery	**bordado** (m)	[burd'adu]
sewing needle	**agulha** (f)	[ɐg'uʎɐ]
thread	**fio** (m)	[f'iu]
seam	**costura** (f)	[kuʃt'urɐ]
to get dirty (vi)	**sujar-se** (vp)	[suʒ'arsə]
stain (mark, spot)	**mancha** (f)	[m'ãʃɐ]

to crease, crumple (vi)	**amarrotar-se** (vp)	[ɐmɐʀut'arsə]
to tear (vt)	**rasgar** (vt)	[ʀɐʒg'aɾ]
clothes moth	**traça** (f)	[tɾ'asɐ]

38. Personal care. Cosmetics

toothpaste	**pasta** (f) **de dentes**	[p'aʃtɐ də d'ẽtəʃ]
toothbrush	**escova** (f) **de dentes**	[əʃk'ovɐ də d'ẽtəʃ]
to brush one's teeth	**escovar os dentes**	[əʃkuv'aɾ uʃ d'ẽtəʃ]
razor	**máquina** (f) **de barbear**	[m'akinɐ də bɐɾbi'aɾ]
shaving cream	**creme** (m) **de barbear**	[kɾ'ɛmə də bɐɾbj'aɾ]
to shave (vi)	**barbear-se** (vp)	[bɐɾbj'arsə]
soap	**sabonete** (m)	[sɐbun'etə]
shampoo	**champô** (m)	[ʃãp'o]
scissors	**tesoura** (f)	[təz'oɾɐ]
nail file	**lima** (f) **de unhas**	[l'imɐ də 'uɲɐʃ]
nail clippers	**corta-unhas** (m)	[k'ɔɾtɐ 'uɲɐʃ]
tweezers	**pinça** (f)	[p'ĩsɐ]
cosmetics	**cosméticos** (m pl)	[kuʒm'ɛtikuʃ]
face mask	**máscara** (f)	[m'aʃkɐɾɐ]
manicure	**manicura** (f)	[mɐnik'uɾɐ]
to have a manicure	**fazer a manicura**	[fɐz'eɾ ɐ mɐnik'uɾɐ]
pedicure	**pedicure** (f)	[pədik'uɾə]
make-up bag	**bolsa** (f) **de maquilhagem**	[b'olsɐ də mɐkiʎ'aʒẽj]
face powder	**pó** (m)	[pɔ]
powder compact	**caixa** (f) **de pó**	[k'ajʃɐ də pɔ]
blusher	**blush** (m)	[blɐʃ]
perfume (bottled)	**perfume** (m)	[pərf'umə]
toilet water (perfume)	**água** (f) **de toilette**	['aguɐ də tual'ɛtə]
lotion	**loção** (m)	[lus'ãu]
cologne	**água-de-colónia** (f)	['aguɐ də kul'ɔniɐ]
eyeshadow	**sombra** (f) **para os olhos**	[s'õbɾɐ p'eɾɐ uʃ 'ɔʎuʃ]
eyeliner	**lápis** (m) **delineador**	[l'apiʃ dəliniɐd'oɾ]
mascara	**máscara** (f), **rímel** (m)	[m'aʃkɐɾɐ], [ʀ'imɛl]
lipstick	**batom** (m)	[b'atõ]
nail polish, enamel	**verniz** (m) **de unhas**	[vərn'iʒ də 'uɲɐʃ]
hair spray	**laca** (f) **para cabelos**	[l'akɐ p'eɾɐ kɐb'eluʃ]
deodorant	**desodorizante** (m)	[dəzɔdɔɾiz'ãtə]
cream	**creme** (m)	[kɾ'ɛmə]
face cream	**creme** (m) **de rosto**	[kɾ'ɛmə də ʀ'oʃtu]
hand cream	**creme** (m) **de mãos**	[kɾ'ɛmə də m'ãuʃ]

anti-wrinkle cream	**creme** (m) **antirrugas**	[kr'ɛmə ãtiʀ'ugɐʃ]
day cream	**creme** (m) **de dia**	[kr'ɛmə də d'iɐ]
night cream	**creme** (m) **de noite**	[kr'ɛmə də n'ojtə]
day (as adj)	**de dia**	[də d'iɐ]
night (as adj)	**da noite**	[dɐ n'ojtə]
tampon	**tampão** (m)	[tãp'ãu]
toilet paper	**papel** (m) **higiénico**	[pɐp'ɛl iʒj'ɛniku]
hair dryer	**secador** (m) **elétrico**	[səkɐd'or el'ɛtriku]

39. Jewelry

jewelry	**joias** (f pl)	[ʒ'ɔjɐʃ]
precious (e.g., ~ stone)	**precioso**	[prəsj'ozu]
hallmark	**marca** (f) **de contraste**	[m'arkɐ də kõtr'aʃtə]
ring	**anel** (m)	[ɐn'ɛl]
wedding ring	**aliança** (f)	[ɐlj'ãsɐ]
bracelet	**pulseira** (f)	[puls'ɐjrɐ]
earrings	**brincos** (m pl)	[br'ĩkuʃ]
necklace (~ of pearls)	**colar** (m)	[kul'ar]
crown	**coroa** (f)	[kur'oɐ]
bead necklace	**colar** (m) **de contas**	[kul'ar də k'õtɐʃ]
diamond	**diamante** (m)	[diɐm'ãtə]
emerald	**esmeralda** (f)	[əʒmər'aldɐ]
ruby	**rubi** (m)	[ʀub'i]
sapphire	**safira** (f)	[sɐf'irɐ]
pearl	**pérola** (f)	[p'ɛrulɐ]
amber	**âmbar** (m)	[ãbar]

40. Watches. Clocks

watch (wristwatch)	**relógio** (m) **de pulso**	[ʀəl'ɔʒiu də p'ulsu]
dial	**mostrador** (m)	[muʃtrɐd'or]
hand (of clock, watch)	**ponteiro** (m)	[põt'ɐjru]
metal watch band	**bracelete** (f) **em aço**	[brɐsəl'ɛtə ɛn 'asu]
watch strap	**bracelete** (f) **em pele**	[brɐsəl'ɛtə ẽ p'ɛlə]
battery	**pilha** (f)	[p'iʎɐ]
to be dead (battery)	**acabar** (vi)	[ɐkɐb'ar]
to change a battery	**trocar a pilha**	[truk'ar ɐ p'iʎɐ]
to run fast	**estar adiantado**	[əʃt'ar ɐdiãt'adu]
to run slow	**estar atrasado**	[əʃt'ar ɐtrɐz'adu]
wall clock	**relógio** (m) **de parede**	[ʀəl'ɔʒiu də pɐr'edə]
hourglass	**ampulheta** (f)	[ãpuʎ'etɐ]

sundial	**relógio** (m) **de sol**	[ʀəl'ɔʒiu də sɔl]
alarm clock	**despertador** (m)	[dəʃpərtɐd'or]
watchmaker	**relojoeiro** (m)	[ʀəluʒu'ɐjru]
to repair (vt)	**reparar** (vt)	[ʀəpɐr'ar]

Food. Nutricion

41. Food

meat **carne** (f) [k'arnə]
chicken **galinha** (f) [gɐl'iɲɐ]
young chicken **frango** (m) [fr'ãgu]
duck **pato** (m) [p'atu]
goose **ganso** (m) [g'ãsu]
game **caça** (f) [k'asɐ]
turkey **peru** (m) [pər'u]

pork **carne** (f) **de porco** [k'arnə də p'orku]
veal **carne** (f) **de vitela** [k'arnə də vit'ɛlɐ]
lamb **carne** (f) **de carneiro** [k'arnə də kɐrn'ɐjru]
beef **carne** (f) **de vaca** [k'arnə də v'akɐ]
rabbit **carne** (f) **de coelho** [k'arnə də ku'ɐʎu]

sausage (salami, etc.) **chouriço** (m) [ʃor'isu]
vienna sausage **salsicha** (f) [sals'iʃɐ]
bacon **bacon** (m) [b'ɐjkɐn]
ham **fiambre** (f) [fj'ãbrə]
gammon (ham) **presunto** (m) [prəz'ũtu]

pâté **patê** (m) [pɐt'e]
liver **iscas** (f pl) ['iʃkɐʃ]

lard **toucinho** (m) [tos'iɲu]
ground beef **carne** (f) **moída** [k'arnə mu'idɐ]
tongue **língua** (f) [l'ĩguɐ]

egg **ovo** (m) ['ovu]
eggs **ovos** (m pl) ['ɔvuʃ]
egg white **clara** (f) **do ovo** [kl'arɐ du 'ovu]
egg yolk **gema** (f) **do ovo** [ʒ'emɐ du 'ovu]

fish **peixe** (m) [p'ɐjʃə]
seafood **marisco** (m) [mɐr'iʃku]
crustaceans **crustáceos** (m pl) [kruʃt'asiuʃ]
caviar **caviar** (m) [kavj'ar]

crab **caranguejo** (m) [kɐrãg'ɐʒu]
shrimp **camarão** (m) [kɐmɐr'ãu]
oyster **ostra** (f) ['ɔʃtrɐ]
spiny lobster **lagosta** (f) [lɐg'oʃtɐ]
octopus **polvo** (m) [p'olvu]

squid	**lula** (f)	[l'ulɐ]
sturgeon	**esturjão** (m)	[əʃturʒ'ãu]
salmon	**salmão** (m)	[salm'ãu]
halibut	**halibute** (m)	[alib'utə]
cod	**bacalhau** (m)	[bɐkɐʎ'au]
mackerel	**cavala** (m), **sarda** (f)	[kɐv'alɐ], [s'ardɐ]
tuna	**atum** (m)	[ɐt'ũ]
eel	**enguia** (f)	[ẽg'iɐ]
trout	**truta** (f)	[tr'utɐ]
sardine	**sardinha** (f)	[sɐrd'iɲɐ]
pike	**lúcio** (m)	[l'usiu]
herring	**arenque** (m)	[ɐr'ẽkə]
bread	**pão** (m)	[p'ãu]
cheese	**queijo** (m)	[k'ɐjʒu]
sugar	**açúcar** (m)	[ɐs'ukar]
salt	**sal** (m)	[sal]
rice	**arroz** (m)	[ɐʀ'ɔʒ]
pasta	**massas** (f pl)	[m'asɐʃ]
noodles	**talharim** (m)	[tɐʎɐr'ĩ]
butter	**manteiga** (f)	[mãt'ɐjgɐ]
vegetable oil	**óleo** (m)	['ɔliu]
sunflower oil	**óleo** (m) **de girassol**	['ɔliu də ʒirɐs'ɔl]
margarine	**margarina** (f)	[mɐrgɐr'inɐ]
olives	**azeitonas** (f pl)	[ɐzɐjt'onɐʒ]
olive oil	**azeite** (m)	[ɐz'ɐjtə]
milk	**leite** (m)	[l'ɐjtə]
condensed milk	**leite** (m) **condensado**	[l'ɐjtə kõdẽs'adu]
yogurt	**iogurte** (m)	[iɔg'urtə]
sour cream	**creme** (m) **azedo**	[kr'ɛmə ɐz'edu]
cream (of milk)	**nata** (f) **do leite**	[n'atɐ du l'ɐjtə]
mayonnaise	**maionese** (f)	[majun'ezə]
buttercream	**creme** (m)	[kr'ɛmə]
cereal grain (wheat, etc.)	**grãos** (m pl) **de cereais**	[gr'ãuʃ də sərj'ajʃ]
flour	**farinha** (f)	[fɐr'iɲɐ]
canned food	**conservas** (f pl)	[kõs'ɛrvɐʃ]
cornflakes	**flocos** (m pl) **de milho**	[fl'ɔkuʃ də m'iʎu]
honey	**mel** (m)	[mɛl]
jam	**doce** (m)	[d'osə]
chewing gum	**pastilha** (f) **elástica**	[pɐʃt'iʎɐ el'aʃtikɐ]

42. Drinks

water	**água** (f)	['agʊɐ]
drinking water	**água** (f) **potável**	['agʊɐ put'avɛl]
mineral water	**água** (f) **mineral**	['agʊɐ minər'al]
still (adj)	**sem gás**	[sẽj gaʃ]
carbonated (adj)	**gaseificada**	[gɐziifik'adɐ]
sparkling (adj)	**com gás**	[kõ gaʃ]
ice	**gelo** (m)	[ʒ'elu]
with ice	**com gelo**	[kõ ʒ'elu]
non-alcoholic (adj)	**sem álcool**	[sɛm 'alkuɔl]
soft drink	**bebida** (f) **sem álcool**	[bəb'idɐ sɛn 'alkuɔl]
cool soft drink	**refresco** (m)	[ʀəfr'eʃku]
lemonade	**limonada** (f)	[limun'adɐ]
liquor	**bebidas** (f pl) **alcoólicas**	[bəb'idɐʃ alku'ɔlikɐʃ]
wine	**vinho** (m)	[v'iɲu]
white wine	**vinho** (m) **branco**	[v'iɲu br'ãku]
red wine	**vinho** (m) **tinto**	[v'iɲu t'ĩtu]
liqueur	**licor** (m)	[lik'or]
champagne	**champanhe** (m)	[ʃãp'ɐɲə]
vermouth	**vermute** (m)	[vərm'utə]
whisky	**uísque** (m)	[u'iʃkə]
vodka	**vodca, vodka** (f)	[v'ɔdkɐ]
gin	**gim** (m)	[ʒĩ]
cognac	**conhaque** (m)	[kuɲ'akə]
rum	**rum** (m)	[ʀũ]
coffee	**café** (m)	[kɐf'ɛ]
black coffee	**café** (m) **puro**	[kɐf'ɛ p'uru]
coffee with milk	**café** (m) **com leite**	[kɐf'ɛ kõ l'ɐjtə]
cappuccino	**cappuccino** (m)	[kaputʃ'inu]
instant coffee	**café** (m) **solúvel**	[kɐf'ɛ sul'uvɛl]
milk	**leite** (m)	[l'ɐjtə]
cocktail	**coquetel** (m)	[kɔkət'ɛl]
milk shake	**batido** (m) **de leite**	[bɐt'idu də l'ɐjtə]
juice	**sumo** (m)	[s'umu]
tomato juice	**sumo** (m) **de tomate**	[s'umu də tum'atə]
orange juice	**sumo** (m) **de laranja**	[s'umu də lɐr'ãʒɐ]
freshly squeezed juice	**sumo** (m) **fresco**	[s'umu fr'eʃku]
beer	**cerveja** (f)	[sərv'ɐʒɐ]
light beer	**cerveja** (f) **clara**	[sərv'ɐʒɐ kl'arɐ]
dark beer	**cerveja** (m) **preta**	[sərv'ɐʒɐ pr'etɐ]
tea	**chá** (m)	[ʃa]

black tea	**chá** (m) **preto**	[ʃa pr'etu]
green tea	**chá** (m) **verde**	[ʃa v'erdə]

43. Vegetables

vegetables	**legumes** (m pl)	[ləg'uməʃ]
greens	**verduras** (f pl)	[vərd'urɐʃ]
tomato	**tomate** (m)	[tum'atə]
cucumber	**pepino** (m)	[pəp'inu]
carrot	**cenoura** (f)	[sən'orɐ]
potato	**batata** (f)	[bɐt'atɐ]
onion	**cebola** (f)	[səb'olɐ]
garlic	**alho** (m)	['aʎu]
cabbage	**couve** (f)	[k'ovə]
cauliflower	**couve-flor** (f)	[k'ovə fl'or]
Brussels sprouts	**couve-de-bruxelas** (f)	[k'ovə də bruʃ'ɛlɐʃ]
broccoli	**brócolos** (m pl)	[br'ɔkuluʃ]
beetroot	**beterraba** (f)	[bətəʀ'abɐ]
eggplant	**beringela** (f)	[bərĩʒ'ɛlɐ]
zucchini	**curgete** (f)	[kurʒ'ɛtə]
pumpkin	**abóbora** (f)	[ɐb'ɔburɐ]
turnip	**nabo** (m)	[n'abu]
parsley	**salsa** (f)	[s'alsɐ]
dill	**funcho, endro** (m)	[f'ũʃu], ['ẽdru]
lettuce	**alface** (f)	[alf'asə]
celery	**aipo** (m)	['ajpu]
asparagus	**espargo** (m)	[əʃp'argu]
spinach	**espinafre** (m)	[əʃpin'afrə]
pea	**ervilha** (f)	[erv'iʎɐ]
beans	**fava** (f)	[f'avɐ]
corn (maize)	**milho** (m)	[m'iʎu]
kidney bean	**feijão** (m)	[fɐjʒ'ãu]
pepper	**pimentão** (m)	[pimẽt'ãu]
radish	**rabanete** (m)	[ʀɐbɐn'etə]
artichoke	**alcachofra** (f)	[alkɐʃ'ofrɐ]

44. Fruits. Nuts

fruit	**fruta** (f)	[fr'utɐ]
apple	**maçã** (f)	[mɐs'ã]
pear	**pera** (f)	[p'erɐ]
lemon	**limão** (m)	[lim'ãu]

orange	**laranja** (f)	[lɐr'ãʒɐ]
strawberry	**morango** (m)	[mur'ãgu]
mandarin	**tangerina** (f)	[tãʒər'inɐ]
plum	**ameixa** (f)	[ɐm'ɐjʃɐ]
peach	**pêssego** (m)	[p'esəgu]
apricot	**damasco** (m)	[dɐm'aʃku]
raspberry	**framboesa** (f)	[frãbu'ezɐ]
pineapple	**ananás** (m)	[ɐnɐn'aʃ]
banana	**banana** (f)	[bɐn'ɐnɐ]
watermelon	**melancia** (f)	[məlãs'iɐ]
grape	**uva** (f)	['uvɐ]
sour cherry	**ginja** (f)	[ʒ'ĩʒɐ]
sweet cherry	**cereja** (f)	[sər'ɐʒɐ]
melon	**meloa** (f), **melão** (m)	[məl'oɐ], [məl'ãu]
grapefruit	**toranja** (f)	[tur'ãʒɐ]
avocado	**abacate** (m)	[ɐbɐk'atə]
papaya	**papaia** (f), **mamão** (m)	[pɐp'ajɐ], [mɐm'ãu]
mango	**manga** (f)	[m'ãgɐ]
pomegranate	**romã** (f)	[ʀum'ã]
redcurrant	**groselha** (f) **vermelha**	[gruz'ɐʎɐ vərm'ɐʎɐ]
blackcurrant	**groselha** (f) **preta**	[gruz'ɐʎɐ pr'etɐ]
gooseberry	**groselha** (f) **espinhosa**	[gruz'ɐʎɐ əʃpiɲ'ɔzɐ]
bilberry	**mirtilo** (m)	[mirt'ilu]
blackberry	**amora silvestre** (f)	[ɐm'ɔrɐ silv'ɛʃtrə]
raisin	**uvas** (f pl) **passas**	['uvɐʃ p'asɐʃ]
fig	**figo** (m)	[f'igu]
date	**tâmara** (f)	[t'ɐmɐrɐ]
peanut	**amendoim** (m)	[ɐmẽdu'ĩ]
almond	**amêndoa** (f)	[ɐm'ẽduɐ]
walnut	**noz** (f)	[nɔʒ]
hazelnut	**avelã** (f)	[ɐvəl'ã]
coconut	**coco** (m)	[k'oku]
pistachios	**pistáchios** (m pl)	[piʃt'aʃiuʃ]

45. Bread. Candy

confectionery (pastry)	**pastelaria** (f)	[pɐʃtəlɐr'iɐ]
bread	**pão** (m)	[p'ãu]
cookies	**bolacha** (f)	[bul'aʃɐ]
chocolate (n)	**chocolate** (m)	[ʃukul'atə]
chocolate (as adj)	**de chocolate**	[də ʃukul'atə]
candy	**rebuçado** (m)	[ʀəbus'adu]
cake (e.g., cupcake)	**bolo** (m)	[b'olu]

cake (e.g., birthday ~)	**bolo** (m) **de aniversário**	[b'olu də ɐnivərs'ariu]
pie (e.g., apple ~)	**tarte** (f)	[t'artə]
filling (for cake, pie)	**recheio** (m)	[ʀəʃ'ɐju]
whole fruit jam	**doce** (m)	[d'osə]
marmalade	**geleia** (f) **de frutas**	[ʒəl'ɐjɐ də fr'utɐʃ]
waffle	**waffle** (m)	[w'ɐjfəl]
ice-cream	**gelado** (m)	[ʒəl'adu]
pudding	**pudim** (m)	[pud'ĩ]

46. Cooked dishes

course, dish	**prato** (m)	[pr'atu]
cuisine	**cozinha** (f)	[kuz'iɲɐ]
recipe	**receita** (f)	[ʀəs'ɐjtɐ]
portion	**porção** (f)	[purs'ãu]
salad	**salada** (f)	[sɐl'adɐ]
soup	**sopa** (f)	[s'opɐ]
clear soup (broth)	**caldo** (m)	[k'aldu]
sandwich (bread)	**sandes** (f)	[s'ãdəʃ]
fried eggs	**ovos** (m pl) **estrelados**	['ɔvuʃ əʃtrəl'aduʃ]
cutlet (croquette)	**croquete** (m)	[kruk'etə]
hamburger (beefburger)	**hambúrguer** (m)	[ãb'urgɛr]
beefsteak	**bife** (m)	[b'ifə]
stew	**guisado** (m)	[giz'adu]
side dish	**conduto** (m)	[kõd'utu]
spaghetti	**espaguete** (m)	[əʃpɐg'etə]
mashed potatoes	**puré** (m) **de batata**	[pur'ɛ də bɐt'atɐ]
pizza	**pizza** (f)	[p'itzɐ]
porridge (oatmeal, etc.)	**papa** (f)	[p'apɐ]
omelet	**omelete** (f)	[ɔməl'ɛtə]
boiled (e.g., ~ beef)	**cozido**	[kuz'idu]
smoked (adj)	**fumado**	[fum'adu]
fried (adj)	**frito**	[fr'itu]
dried (adj)	**seco**	[s'eku]
frozen (adj)	**congelado**	[kõʒəl'adu]
pickled (adj)	**em vinagre**	[ẽ vin'agrə]
sweet (sugary)	**doce, açucarado**	[d'osə], [ɐsukɐr'adu]
salty (adj)	**salgado**	[salg'adu]
cold (adj)	**frio**	[fr'iu]
hot (adj)	**quente**	[k'ẽtə]
bitter (adj)	**amargo**	[ɐm'argu]
tasty (adj)	**gostoso**	[guʃt'ozu]
to cook in boiling water	**cozinhar em água a ferver**	[kuziɲ'ar ɛn 'aguɐ ɐ fərv'er]

to cook (dinner)	**fazer, preparar** (vt)	[fɐz'er], [prəpɐr'ar]
to fry (vt)	**fritar** (vt)	[frit'ar]
to heat up (food)	**aquecer** (vt)	[ɐkɛs'er]
to salt (vt)	**salgar** (vt)	[salg'ar]
to pepper (vt)	**apimentar** (vt)	[ɐpimẽt'ar]
to grate (vt)	**ralar** (vt)	[ʀɐl'ar]
peel (n)	**casca** (f)	[k'aʃkɐ]
to peel (vt)	**descascar** (vt)	[dəʃkɐʃk'ar]

47. Spices

salt	**sal** (m)	[sal]
salty (adj)	**salgado**	[salg'adu]
to salt (vt)	**salgar** (vt)	[salg'ar]
black pepper	**pimenta** (f) **preta**	[pim'ẽtɐ pr'etɐ]
red pepper	**pimenta** (f) **vermelha**	[pim'ẽtɐ vərm'ɐʎɐ]
mustard	**mostarda** (f)	[muʃt'ardɐ]
horseradish	**raiz-forte** (f)	[ʀɐ'iʃ f'ɔrtə]
condiment	**condimento** (m)	[kõdim'ẽtu]
spice	**especiaria** (f)	[əʃpəsiɐr'iɐ]
sauce	**molho** (m)	[m'oʎu]
vinegar	**vinagre** (m)	[vin'agrə]
anise	**anis** (m)	[ɐn'iʃ]
basil	**manjericão** (m)	[mãʒərik'ãu]
cloves	**cravo** (m)	[kr'avu]
ginger	**gengibre** (m)	[ʒẽʒ'ibrə]
coriander	**coentro** (m)	[ku'ẽtru]
cinnamon	**canela** (f)	[kɐn'ɛlɐ]
sesame	**sésamo** (m)	[s'ɛzɐmu]
bay leaf	**folhas** (f pl) **de louro**	[f'oʎɐʃ də l'oru]
paprika	**páprica** (f)	[p'aprikɐ]
caraway	**cominho** (m)	[kum'iɲu]
saffron	**açafrão** (m)	[ɐsɐfr'ãu]

48. Meals

food	**comida** (f)	[kum'idɐ]
to eat (vi, vt)	**comer** (vt)	[kum'er]
breakfast	**pequeno-almoço** (m)	[pək'enu alm'osu]
to have breakfast	**tomar o pequeno-almoço**	[tum'ar u pək'enu alm'osu]
lunch	**almoço** (m)	[alm'osu]
to have lunch	**almoçar** (vi)	[almus'ar]

dinner	**jantar** (m)	[ʒãt'ar]
to have dinner	**jantar** (vi)	[ʒãt'ar]
appetite	**apetite** (m)	[ɐpət'itə]
Enjoy your meal!	**Bom apetite!**	[bõ ɐpət'itə]
to open (~ a bottle)	**abrir** (vt)	[ɐbr'ir]
to spill (liquid)	**derramar** (vt)	[dəʀɐm'ar]
to spill out (vi)	**derramar-se** (vp)	[dəʀɐm'arsə]
to boil (vi)	**estar a ferver**	[əʃt'ar ɐ fərv'er]
to boil (vt)	**ferver** (vt)	[fərv'er]
boiled (~ water)	**fervido**	[fərv'idu]
to chill, cool down (vt)	**arrefecer** (vt)	[ɐʀəfəs'er]
to chill (vi)	**arrefecer-se** (vp)	[ɐʀəfəs'ersə]
taste, flavor	**sabor, gosto** (m)	[sɐb'or], [g'oʃtu]
aftertaste	**gostinho** (m)	[guʃt'iɲu]
to be on a diet	**fazer dieta**	[fɐz'er dj'ɛtɐ]
diet	**dieta** (f)	[dj'ɛtɐ]
vitamin	**vitamina** (f)	[vitɐm'inɐ]
calorie	**caloria** (f)	[kɐlur'iɐ]
vegetarian (n)	**vegetariano** (m)	[vəʒətɐrj'ɐnu]
vegetarian (adj)	**vegetariano**	[vəʒətɐrj'ɐnu]
fats (nutrient)	**gorduras** (f pl)	[gurd'urɐʃ]
proteins	**proteínas** (f pl)	[prɔtɐ'inɐʃ]
carbohydrates	**hidratos** (m pl) **de carbono**	[idr'atuʃ də kɐrb'ɔnu]
slice (of lemon, ham)	**fatia** (f)	[fɐt'iɐ]
piece (of cake, pie)	**bocado, pedaço** (m)	[buk'adu], [pəd'asu]
crumb (of bread)	**migalha** (f)	[mig'aʎɐ]

49. Table setting

spoon	**colher** (f)	[kuʎ'ɛr]
knife	**faca** (f)	[f'akɐ]
fork	**garfo** (m)	[g'arfu]
cup (of coffee)	**chávena** (f)	[ʃ'avənɐ]
plate (dinner ~)	**prato** (m)	[pr'atu]
saucer	**pires** (m)	[p'irəʃ]
napkin (on table)	**guardanapo** (m)	[guɐrdɐn'apu]
toothpick	**palito** (m)	[pɐl'itu]

50. Restaurant

restaurant	**restaurante** (m)	[ʀəʃtaur'ãtə]
coffee house	**café** (m)	[kɐf'ɛ]

pub, bar	**bar** (m)	[bar]
tearoom	**salão** (m) **de chá**	[sɐl'ãu də ʃa]
waiter	**empregado** (m) **de mesa**	[ẽprəg'adu də m'ezɐ]
waitress	**empregada** (f) **de mesa**	[ẽprəg'adɐ də m'ezɐ]
bartender	**barman** (m)	[b'armɐn]
menu	**ementa** (f)	[em'ẽtɐ]
wine list	**lista** (f) **de vinhos**	[l'iʃtɐ də v'iɲuʃ]
to book a table	**reservar uma mesa**	[ʀəzərv'ar 'umɐ m'ezɐ]
course, dish	**prato** (m)	[pr'atu]
to order (meal)	**pedir** (vt)	[pəd'ir]
to make an order	**pedir** (vi)	[pəd'ir]
aperitif	**aperitivo** (m)	[ɐpərit'ivu]
appetizer	**entrada** (f)	[ẽtr'adɐ]
dessert	**sobremesa** (f)	[sobrəm'ezɐ]
check	**conta** (f)	[k'õtɐ]
to pay the check	**pagar a conta**	[pɐg'ar ɐ k'õtɐ]
to give change	**dar o troco**	[dar u tr'oku]
tip	**gorjeta** (f)	[gurʒ'etɐ]

Family, relatives and friends

51. Personal information. Forms

name, first name	**nome** (m)	[n'omə]
family name	**apelido** (m)	[ɐpəl'idu]
date of birth	**data** (f) **de nascimento**	[d'atɐ də nɐʃsim'ẽtu]
place of birth	**local** (m) **de nascimento**	[luk'al də nɐʃsim'ẽtu]
nationality	**nacionalidade** (f)	[nɐsiunɐlid'adə]
place of residence	**lugar** (m) **de residência**	[lug'ar də ʀəzid'ẽsiɐ]
country	**país** (m)	[pɐ'iʃ]
profession (occupation)	**profissão** (f)	[prufis'ãu]
gender, sex	**sexo** (m)	[s'ɛksu]
height	**estatura** (f)	[əʃtɐt'urɐ]
weight	**peso** (m)	[p'ezu]

52. Family members. Relatives

mother	**mãe** (f)	[mẽj]
father	**pai** (m)	[paj]
son	**filho** (m)	[f'iʎu]
daughter	**filha** (f)	[f'iʎɐ]
younger daughter	**filha** (f) **mais nova**	[f'iʎɐ m'ajʃ n'ɔvɐ]
younger son	**filho** (m) **mais novo**	[f'iʎu m'ajʃ n'ovu]
eldest daughter	**filha** (f) **mais velha**	[f'iʎɐ m'ajʃ v'ɛʎɐ]
eldest son	**filho** (m) **mais velho**	[f'iʎu m'ajʃ v'ɛʎu]
brother	**irmão** (m)	[irm'ãu]
elder brother	**irmão mais velho**	[irm'ãu m'ajʃ v'ɛʎu]
younger brother	**irmão mais novo**	[irm'ãu m'ajʃ n'ovu]
sister	**irmã** (f)	[irm'ã]
elder sister	**irmã mais velha**	[irm'ã m'ajʃ v'ɛʎɐ]
younger sister	**irmã mais nova**	[irm'ã m'ajʃ n'ɔvɐ]
cousin (masc.)	**primo** (m)	[pr'imu]
cousin (fem.)	**prima** (f)	[pr'imɐ]
mom	**mamã** (f)	[mɐm'ã]
dad, daddy	**papá** (m)	[pɐp'a]
parents	**pais** (pl)	[p'ajʃ]
child	**criança** (f)	[krj'ãsɐ]
children	**crianças** (f pl)	[krj'ãsɐʃ]

grandmother	**avó** (f)	[ɐv'ɔ]
grandfather	**avô** (m)	[ɐv'o]
grandson	**neto** (m)	[n'ɛtu]
granddaughter	**neta** (f)	[n'ɛtɐ]
grandchildren	**netos** (pl)	[n'ɛtuʃ]
uncle	**tio** (m)	[t'iu]
aunt	**tia** (f)	[t'iɐ]
nephew	**sobrinho** (m)	[subr'iɲu]
niece	**sobrinha** (f)	[subr'iɲɐ]
mother-in-law (wife's mother)	**sogra** (f)	[s'ɔgrɐ]
father-in-law (husband's father)	**sogro** (m)	[s'ogru]
son-in-law (daughter's husband)	**genro** (m)	[ʒ'ẽʀu]
stepmother	**madrasta** (f)	[mɐdr'aʃtɐ]
stepfather	**padrasto** (m)	[pɐdr'aʃtu]
infant	**criança** (f) **de colo**	[krj'ãsɐ də k'ɔlu]
baby (infant)	**bebé** (m)	[bəb'ɛ]
little boy, kid	**menino** (m)	[mən'inu]
wife	**mulher** (f)	[muʎ'ɛr]
husband	**marido** (m)	[mɐr'idu]
spouse (husband)	**esposo** (m)	[əʃp'ozu]
spouse (wife)	**esposa** (f)	[əʃp'ozɐ]
married (masc.)	**casado**	[kɐz'adu]
married (fem.)	**casada**	[kɐz'adɐ]
single (unmarried)	**solteiro**	[sɔlt'ɐjru]
bachelor	**solteirão** (m)	[sɔltɐjr'ãu]
divorced (masc.)	**divorciado**	[divursj'adu]
widow	**viúva** (f)	[vj'uvɐ]
widower	**viúvo** (m)	[vj'uvu]
relative	**parente** (m)	[pɐr'ẽtə]
close relative	**parente** (m) **próximo**	[pɐr'ẽtə pr'ɔsimu]
distant relative	**parente** (m) **distante**	[pɐr'ẽtə diʃt'ãtə]
relatives	**parentes** (m pl)	[pɐr'ẽtəʃ]
orphan (boy)	**órfão** (m)	['ɔrfãu]
orphan (girl)	**órfã** (f)	['ɔrfã]
guardian (of minor)	**tutor** (m)	[tut'or]
to adopt (a boy)	**adotar** (vt)	[ɐdɔt'ar]
to adopt (a girl)	**adotar** (vt)	[ɐdɔt'ar]

53. Friends. Coworkers

friend (masc.)	**amigo** (m)	[ɐm'igu]
friend (fem.)	**amiga** (f)	[ɐm'igɐ]

friendship	**amizade** (f)	[ɐmiz'adə]
to be friends	**ser amigos**	[ser ɐm'iguʃ]
buddy (masc.)	**amigo** (m)	[ɐm'igu]
buddy (fem.)	**amiga** (f)	[ɐm'igɐ]
partner	**parceiro** (m)	[pɐrs'ɐjru]
chief (boss)	**chefe** (m)	[ʃ'ɛfə]
superior	**superior** (m)	[supərj'or]
owner, proprietor	**proprietário** (m)	[pruprіɛt'ariu]
subordinate	**subordinado** (m)	[suburdin'adu]
colleague	**colega** (m)	[kul'ɛgɐ]
acquaintance (person)	**conhecido** (m)	[kuɲəs'idu]
fellow traveler	**companheiro** (m) **de viagem**	[kõpɐɲ'ɐjru də vj'aʒẽj]
classmate	**colega** (m) **de classe**	[kul'ɛgɐ də kl'asə]
neighbor (masc.)	**vizinho** (m)	[viz'iɲu]
neighbor (fem.)	**vizinha** (f)	[viz'iɲɐ]
neighbors	**vizinhos** (pl)	[viz'iɲuʃ]

54. Man. Woman

woman	**mulher** (f)	[muʎ'ɛr]
girl (young woman)	**rapariga** (f)	[ʀɐpɐr'igɐ]
bride	**noiva** (f)	[n'ojvɐ]
beautiful (adj)	**bonita**	[bun'itɐ]
tall (adj)	**alta**	['altɐ]
slender (adj)	**esbelta**	[əʒb'ɛltɐ]
short (adj)	**de estatura média**	[də əʃtɐt'urɐ m'ɛdiɐ]
blonde (n)	**loura** (f)	[l'orɐ]
brunette (n)	**morena** (f)	[mur'enɐ]
ladies' (adj)	**de senhora**	[də səɲ'orɐ]
virgin (girl)	**virgem** (f)	[v'irʒẽj]
pregnant (adj)	**grávida**	[gr'avidɐ]
man (adult male)	**homem** (m)	['ɔmẽj]
blond (n)	**louro** (m)	[l'oru]
brunet (n)	**moreno** (m)	[mur'enu]
tall (adj)	**alto**	['altu]
short (adj)	**de estatura média**	[də əʃtɐt'urɐ m'ɛdiɐ]
rude (rough)	**rude**	[ʀ'udə]
stocky (adj)	**atarracado**	[ɐtɐʀɐk'adu]
robust (adj)	**robusto**	[ʀub'uʃtu]
strong (adj)	**forte**	[f'ɔrtə]

strength	**força** (f)	[f'orsɐ]
stout, fat (adj)	**gordo**	[g'ordu]
swarthy (adj)	**moreno**	[mur'enu]
well-built (adj)	**esbelto**	[əʒb'ɛltu]
elegant (adj)	**elegante**	[eləg'ãtə]

55. Age

age	**idade** (f)	[id'adə]
youth (young age)	**juventude** (f)	[ʒuvẽt'udə]
young (adj)	**jovem**	[ʒ'ɔvẽj]
younger (adj)	**mais novo**	[m'ajʃ n'ovu]
older (adj)	**mais velho**	[m'ajʃ v'ɛʎu]
young man	**jovem** (m)	[ʒ'ɔvẽj]
teenager	**adolescente** (m)	[ɐduləʃs'ẽtə]
guy, fellow	**rapaz** (m)	[ʀɐp'aʒ]
old man	**velhote** (m)	[vɛʎ'ɔtə]
old woman	**velhota** (f)	[vɛʎ'ɔtɐ]
adult	**adulto**	[ɐd'ultu]
middle-aged (adj)	**de meia-idade**	[də mɐjɐ id'adə]
elderly (adj)	**de certa idade**	[də s'ɛrtɐ id'adə]
old (adj)	**idoso**	[id'ozu]
retirement	**reforma** (f)	[ʀəf'ɔrmɐ]
to retire (from job)	**reformar-se** (vp)	[ʀəfurm'arsə]
retiree	**reformado** (m)	[ʀəfurm'adu]

56. Children

child	**criança** (f)	[krj'ãsɐ]
children	**crianças** (f pl)	[krj'ãsɐʃ]
twins	**gémeos** (m pl)	[ʒ'ɛmiuʃ]
cradle	**berço** (m)	[b'ersu]
rattle	**guizo** (m)	[g'izu]
diaper	**fralda** (f)	[fr'aldɐ]
pacifier	**chucha** (f)	[ʃ'uʃɐ]
baby carriage	**carrinho** (m) **de bebé**	[kɐʀ'iɲu də bəb'ɛ]
kindergarten	**jardim** (m) **de infância**	[ʒɐrd'ĩ də ĩf'ãsiɐ]
babysitter	**babysitter** (f)	[bɐbisit'er]
childhood	**infância** (f)	[ĩf'ãsiɐ]
doll	**boneca** (f)	[bun'ɛkɐ]

toy	**brinquedo** (m)	[brĩk'edu]
construction set	**jogo** (m) **de armar**	[ʒ'ogu də ɐrm'ar]
well-bred (adj)	**bem-educado**	[bẽj eduk'adu]
ill-bred (adj)	**mal-educado**	[mal eduk'adu]
spoiled (adj)	**mimado**	[mim'adu]
to be naughty	**ser travesso**	[ser trɐv'ɛsu]
mischievous (adj)	**travesso, traquinas**	[trɐv'ɛsu], [trɐk'inɐʃ]
mischievousness	**travessura** (f)	[trɐvəs'urɐ]
mischievous child	**criança** (f) **travessa**	[krj'ãsɐ trɐv'ɛsɐ]
obedient (adj)	**obediente**	[ɔbədj'ẽtə]
disobedient (adj)	**desobediente**	[dəzɔbədj'ẽtə]
docile (adj)	**dócil**	[d'ɔsil]
clever (smart)	**inteligente**	[ĩtəliʒ'ẽtə]
child prodigy	**menino** (m) **prodígio**	[mən'inu prud'iʒiu]

57. Married couples. Family life

to kiss (vt)	**beijar** (vt)	[bɐjʒ'ar]
to kiss (vi)	**beijar-se** (vp)	[bɐjʒ'arsə]
family (n)	**família** (f)	[fɐm'iliɐ]
family (as adj)	**familiar**	[fɐmilj'ar]
couple	**casal** (m)	[kɐz'al]
marriage (state)	**matrimónio** (m)	[mɐtrim'ɔniu]
hearth (home)	**lar** (m)	[lar]
dynasty	**dinastia** (f)	[dinɐʃt'iɐ]
date	**encontro** (m)	[ẽk'õtru]
kiss	**beijo** (m)	[b'ɐjʒu]
love (for sb)	**amor** (m)	[ɐm'or]
to love (sb)	**amar** (vt)	[ɐm'ar]
beloved	**amado, querido**	[ɐm'adu], [kər'idu]
tenderness	**ternura** (f)	[tərn'urɐ]
tender (affectionate)	**terno, afetuoso**	[t'ɛrnu], [ɐfɛtu'ozu]
faithfulness	**fidelidade** (f)	[fidəlid'adə]
faithful (adj)	**fiel**	[fj'ɛl]
care (attention)	**cuidado** (m)	[kuid'adu]
caring (~ father)	**carinhoso**	[kɐriɲ'ozu]
newlyweds	**recém-casados** (m pl)	[ʀəs'ẽj kɐz'aduʃ]
honeymoon	**lua de mel** (f)	[l'uɐ də mɛl]
to get married (ab. woman)	**casar-se** (vp)	[kɐz'arsə]
to get married (ab. man)	**casar-se** (vp)	[kɐz'arsə]
wedding	**boda** (f)	[b'odɐ]

golden wedding	**bodas** (f pl) **de ouro**	[b'odɐʃ də 'oɾu]
anniversary	**aniversário** (m)	[ɐnivərs'ariu]
lover (masc.)	**amante** (m)	[ɐm'ãtə]
mistress	**amante** (f)	[ɐm'ãtə]
adultery	**adultério** (m)	[ɐdult'ɛɾiu]
to cheat on ... (commit adultery)	**cometer adultério**	[kumət'er ɐdult'ɛɾiu]
jealous (adj)	**ciumento**	[sium'ẽtu]
to be jealous	**ser ciumento**	[ser sium'ẽtu]
divorce	**divórcio** (m)	[div'ɔɾsiu]
to divorce (vi)	**divorciar-se** (vp)	[divuɾsj'arsə]
to quarrel (vi)	**discutir, brigar** (vi)	[diʃkut'iɾ], [brig'aɾ]
to be reconciled	**fazer as pazes**	[fɐz'er ɐʃ p'azəʃ]
together (adv)	**juntos**	[ʒ'ũtuʃ]
sex	**sexo** (m)	[s'ɛksu]
happiness	**felicidade** (f)	[fəlisid'adə]
happy (adj)	**feliz**	[fəl'iʃ]
misfortune (accident)	**infelicidade** (f)	[ĩfəlisid'adə]
unhappy (adj)	**infeliz**	[ĩfəl'iʃ]

Character. Feelings. Emotions

58. Feelings. Emotions

feeling (emotion)	**sentimento** (m)	[sẽtim'ẽtu]
feelings	**sentimentos** (m pl)	[sẽtim'ẽtuʃ]
to feel (vt)	**sentir** (vt)	[sẽt'ir]
hunger	**fome** (f)	[f'ɔmə]
to be hungry	**ter fome**	[ter f'ɔmə]
thirst	**sede** (f)	[s'edə]
to be thirsty	**ter sede**	[ter s'edə]
sleepiness	**sonolência** (f)	[sunul'ẽsiɐ]
to feel sleepy	**ter sono**	[ter s'onu]
tiredness	**cansaço** (m)	[kãs'asu]
tired (adj)	**cansado**	[kãs'adu]
to get tired	**estar cansado**	[əʃt'ar kãs'adu]
mood (humor)	**humor** (m)	[um'or]
boredom	**tédio** (m)	[t'ɛdiu]
to be bored	**aborrecer-se** (vp)	[ɐbuʀəs'ersə]
seclusion	**isolamento** (m)	[izulɐm'ẽtu]
to seclude oneself	**isolar-se**	[izul'arsə]
to worry (make anxious)	**preocupar** (vt)	[priɔkup'ar]
to be worried	**preocupar-se** (vp)	[priɔkup'arsə]
worrying (n)	**preocupação** (f)	[priɔkupɐs'ãu]
anxiety	**ansiedade** (f)	[ãsiɛd'adə]
preoccupied (adj)	**preocupado**	[priɔkup'adu]
to be nervous	**estar nervoso**	[əʃt'ar nərv'ozu]
to panic (vi)	**entrar em pânico**	[ẽtr'ar ẽ p'ɐniku]
hope	**esperança** (f)	[əʃpər'ãsɐ]
to hope (vi, vt)	**esperar** (vt)	[əʃpər'ar]
certainty	**certeza** (f)	[sərt'ezɐ]
certain, sure (adj)	**certo**	[s'ɛrtu]
uncertainty	**indecisão** (f)	[ĩdəsiz'ãu]
uncertain (adj)	**indeciso**	[ĩdəs'izu]
drunk (adj)	**ébrio, bêbado**	['ɛbriu], [b'ebɐdu]
sober (adj)	**sóbrio**	[s'ɔbriu]
weak (adj)	**fraco**	[fr'aku]
happy (adj)	**feliz**	[fəl'iʃ]
to scare (vt)	**assustar** (vt)	[ɐsuʃt'ar]

fury (madness)	**fúria** (f)	[f'uriɐ]
rage (fury)	**ira, raiva** (f)	[irɐ], [ʀ'ajvɐ]
depression	**depressão** (f)	[dəprəs'ãu]
discomfort	**desconforto** (m)	[dəʃkõf'ortu]
comfort	**conforto** (m)	[kõf'ortu]
to regret (be sorry)	**lamentar** (vt)	[lɐmẽt'ar]
regret	**lamento** (m)	[lɐm'ẽtu]
bad luck	**azar** (m), **má sorte** (f)	[ɐz'ar], [ma s'ɔrtə]
sadness	**tristeza** (f)	[triʃt'ezɐ]
shame (remorse)	**vergonha** (f)	[vərg'oɲɐ]
gladness	**alegria** (f)	[ɐləgr'iɐ]
enthusiasm, zeal	**entusiasmo** (m)	[ẽtuzj'aʒmu]
enthusiast	**entusiasta** (m)	[ẽtuzj'aʃtɐ]
to show enthusiasm	**mostrar entusiasmo**	[muʃtr'ar ẽtuzj'aʒmu]

59. Character. Personality

character	**caráter** (m)	[kɐr'atɛr]
character flaw	**falha** (f) **de caráter**	[f'aʎɐ də kɐr'atɛr]
mind	**mente** (f)	[m'ẽtə]
reason	**razão** (f)	[ʀɐz'ãu]
conscience	**consciência** (f)	[kõʃsj'ẽsiɐ]
habit (custom)	**hábito** (m)	['abitu]
ability	**habilidade** (f)	[ɐbilid'adə]
can (e.g., ~ swim)	**saber**	[sɐb'er]
patient (adj)	**paciente**	[pɐsj'ẽtə]
impatient (adj)	**impaciente**	[ĩpɐsj'ẽtə]
curious (inquisitive)	**curioso**	[kurj'ozu]
curiosity	**curiosidade** (f)	[kuriuzid'adə]
modesty	**modéstia** (f)	[mud'ɛʃtiɐ]
modest (adj)	**modesto**	[mud'ɛʃtu]
immodest (adj)	**imodesto**	[imud'ɛʃtu]
laziness	**preguiça** (f)	[prəg'isɐ]
lazy (adj)	**preguiçoso**	[prəgis'ozu]
lazy person (masc.)	**preguiçoso** (m)	[prəgis'ozu]
cunning (n)	**astúcia** (f)	[ɐʃt'usiɐ]
cunning (as adj)	**astuto**	[ɐʃt'utu]
distrust	**desconfiança** (f)	[dəʃkõfj'ãsɐ]
distrustful (adj)	**desconfiado**	[dəʃkõfj'adu]
generosity	**generosidade** (f)	[ʒənəruzid'adə]
generous (adj)	**generoso**	[ʒənər'ozu]
talented (adj)	**talentoso**	[tɐlẽt'ozu]

talent	**talento** (m)	[tel'ẽtu]
courageous (adj)	**corajoso**	[kurɐʒ'ozu]
courage	**coragem** (f)	[kur'aʒẽj]
honest (adj)	**honesto**	[on'ɛʃtu]
honesty	**honestidade** (f)	[onɛʃtid'adə]
careful (cautious)	**prudente**	[prud'ẽtə]
brave (courageous)	**valente**	[vel'ẽtə]
serious (adj)	**sério**	[s'ɛriu]
strict (severe, stern)	**severo**	[səv'ɛru]
decisive (adj)	**decidido**	[dəsid'idu]
indecisive (adj)	**indeciso**	[ĩdəs'izu]
shy, timid (adj)	**tímido**	[t'imidu]
shyness, timidity	**timidez** (f)	[timid'eʃ]
confidence (trust)	**confiança** (f)	[kõfj'ãsɐ]
to believe (trust)	**confiar** (vt)	[kõfj'ar]
trusting (naïve)	**crédulo**	[kr'ɛdulu]
sincerely (adv)	**sinceramente**	[sĩsɛrɐm'ẽtə]
sincere (adj)	**sincero**	[sĩs'ɛru]
sincerity	**sinceridade** (f)	[sĩsərid'adə]
open (person)	**aberto**	[ɐb'ɛrtu]
calm (adj)	**calmo**	[k'almu]
frank (sincere)	**franco**	[fr'ãku]
naïve (adj)	**ingénuo**	[ĩʒ'ɛnuu]
absent-minded (adj)	**distraído**	[diʃtrɐ'idu]
funny (odd)	**engraçado**	[ẽgrɐs'adu]
greed	**ganância** (f)	[gɐn'ãsiɐ]
greedy (adj)	**ganacioso**	[gɐnɐsj'ozu]
stingy (adj)	**avarento**	[ɐvɐr'ẽtu]
evil (adj)	**mau**	[m'au]
stubborn (adj)	**teimoso**	[tɐjm'ozu]
unpleasant (adj)	**desagradável**	[dəzɐgrɐd'avɛl]
selfish person (masc.)	**egoísta** (m)	[egu'iʃtɐ]
selfish (adj)	**egoísta**	[egu'iʃtɐ]
coward	**cobarde** (m)	[kub'ardə]
cowardly (adj)	**cobarde**	[kub'ardə]

60. Sleep. Dreams

to sleep (vi)	**dormir** (vi)	[durm'ir]
sleep, sleeping	**sono** (m)	[s'onu]
dream	**sonho** (m)	[s'oɲu]
to dream (in sleep)	**sonhar** (vi)	[suɲ'ar]
sleepy (adj)	**sonolento**	[sunul'ẽtu]

bed	**cama** (f)	[k'emɐ]
mattress	**colchão** (m)	[kɔlʃ'ãu]
blanket (comforter)	**cobertor** (m)	[kubərt'or]
pillow	**almofada** (f)	[almuf'adɐ]
sheet	**lençol** (m)	[lẽs'ɔl]
insomnia	**insónia** (f)	[ĩs'ɔniɐ]
sleepless (adj)	**insone**	[ĩs'ɔnə]
sleeping pill	**sonífero** (m)	[sun'ifəru]
to take a sleeping pill	**tomar um sonífero**	[tum'ar ũ sun'ifəru]
to feel sleepy	**estar sonolento**	[əʃt'ar sunul'ẽtu]
to yawn (vi)	**bocejar** (vi)	[busəʒ'ar]
to go to bed	**ir para a cama**	[ir p'erɐ ɐ k'emɐ]
to make up the bed	**fazer a cama**	[fɐz'er ɐ k'emɐ]
to fall asleep	**adormecer** (vi)	[ɐdurməs'er]
nightmare	**pesadelo** (m)	[pəzɐd'elu]
snoring	**ronco** (m)	[ʀ'õku]
to snore (vi)	**ressonar** (vi)	[ʀəsun'ar]
alarm clock	**despertador** (m)	[dəʃpərtɐd'or]
to wake (vt)	**acordar, despertar** (vt)	[ɐkurd'ar], [dəʃpərt'ar]
to wake up	**acordar** (vi)	[ɐkurd'ar]
to get up (vi)	**levantar-se** (vp)	[ləvãt'arsə]
to wash up (vi)	**lavar-se** (vp)	[lɐv'arsə]

61. Humour. Laughter. Gladness

humor (wit, fun)	**humor** (m)	[um'or]
sense of humor	**sentido** (m) **de humor**	[sẽt'idu də um'or]
to have fun	**divertir-se** (vp)	[divərt'irsə]
cheerful (adj)	**alegre**	[ɐl'ɛgrə]
merriment, fun	**alegria** (f)	[ɐləgr'iɐ]
smile	**sorriso** (m)	[suʀ'izu]
to smile (vi)	**sorrir** (vi)	[suʀ'ir]
to start laughing	**começar a rir**	[kuməs'ar ɐ ʀir]
to laugh (vi)	**rir** (vi)	[ʀir]
laugh, laughter	**riso** (m)	[ʀ'izu]
anecdote	**anedota** (f)	[ɐnəd'ɔtɐ]
funny (anecdote, etc.)	**engraçado**	[ẽgrɐs'adu]
funny (odd)	**ridículo**	[ʀid'ikulu]
to joke (vi)	**fazer piadas**	[fɐz'er pj'adɐʃ]
joke (verbal)	**piada** (f)	[pj'adɐ]
joy (emotion)	**alegria** (f)	[ɐləgr'iɐ]
to rejoice (vi)	**regozijar-se** (vp)	[ʀəguziʒ'arsə]
glad, cheerful (adj)	**alegre**	[ɐl'ɛgrə]

62. Discussion, conversation. Part 1

communication	**comunicação** (f)	[kumunikɐs'ãu]
to communicate	**comunicar-se** (vp)	[kumunik'arsə]
conversation	**conversa** (f)	[kõv'ɛrsɐ]
dialog	**diálogo** (m)	[dj'alugu]
discussion (discourse)	**discussão** (f)	[diʃkus'ãu]
debate	**debate** (m)	[dəb'atə]
to debate (vi)	**debater** (vt)	[dəbɐt'er]
interlocutor	**interlocutor** (m)	[ĩtɛrlukut'or]
topic (theme)	**tema** (m)	[t'emɐ]
point of view	**ponto** (m) **de vista**	[p'õtu də v'iʃtɐ]
opinion (viewpoint)	**opinião** (f)	[ɔpinj'ãu]
speech (talk)	**discurso** (m)	[diʃk'ursu]
discussion (of report, etc.)	**discussão** (f)	[diʃkus'ãu]
to discuss (vt)	**discutir** (vt)	[diʃkut'ir]
talk (conversation)	**conversa** (f)	[kõv'ɛrsɐ]
to talk (vi)	**conversar** (vi)	[kõvərs'ar]
meeting	**encontro** (m)	[ẽk'õtru]
to meet (vi, vt)	**encontrar-se** (vp)	[ẽkõtr'arsə]
proverb	**provérbio** (m)	[pruv'ɛrbiu]
saying	**ditado** (m)	[dit'adu]
riddle (poser)	**adivinha** (f)	[ɐdiv'iɲɐ]
to ask a riddle	**dizer uma adivinha**	[diz'er 'umɐ ɐdiv'iɲɐ]
password	**senha** (f)	[s'ɐɲɐ]
secret	**segredo** (m)	[səgr'edu]
oath (vow)	**juramento** (m)	[ʒurɐm'ẽtu]
to swear (an oath)	**jurar** (vi)	[ʒur'ar]
promise	**promessa** (f)	[prum'ɛsɐ]
to promise (vt)	**prometer** (vt)	[prumət'er]
advice (counsel)	**conselho** (m)	[kõs'ɐʎu]
to advise (vt)	**aconselhar** (vt)	[ɐkõsəʎ'ar]
to follow one's advice	**seguir o conselho**	[səg'ir u kõs'ɐʎu]
to listen to ... (obey)	**escutar** (vt)	[əʃkut'ar]
news	**novidade** (f)	[nuvid'adə]
sensation (news)	**sensação** (f)	[sẽsɐs'ãu]
information (data)	**informação** (f)	[ĩfurmɐs'ãu]
conclusion (decision)	**conclusão** (f)	[kõkluz'ãu]
voice	**voz** (f)	[vɔʒ]
compliment	**elogio** (m)	[eluʒ'iu]
kind (nice)	**amável**	[ɐm'avɛl]
word	**palavra** (f)	[pɐl'avrɐ]
phrase	**frase** (f)	[fr'azə]

answer — **resposta** (f) — [ʀəʃp'ɔʃtɐ]
truth — **verdade** (f) — [vərd'adə]
lie — **mentira** (f) — [mẽt'irɐ]

thought — **pensamento** (m) — [pẽsɐm'ẽtu]
idea (inspiration) — **ideia** (f) — [id'ɛjɐ]
fantasy — **fantasia** (f) — [fãtɐz'iɐ]

63. Discussion, conversation. Part 2

respected (adj) — **estimado** — [əʃtim'adu]
to respect (vt) — **respeitar** (vt) — [ʀəʃpɐjt'aɾ]
respect — **respeito** (m) — [ʀəʃp'ɐjtu]
Dear ... (letter) — **Estimado ... , Caro ...** — [əʃtim'adu], [k'aru]

to introduce (present) — **apresentar** (vt) — [ɐprəzẽt'aɾ]
to make acquaintance — **conhecer** (vt) — [kuɲəs'eɾ]
intention — **intenção** (f) — [ĩtẽs'ãu]
to intend (have in mind) — **tencionar** (vt) — [tẽsiun'aɾ]
wish — **desejo** (m) — [dəz'ɐʒu]
to wish (~ good luck) — **desejar** (vt) — [dəzəʒ'aɾ]

surprise (astonishment) — **surpresa** (f) — [surpr'ezɐ]
to surprise (amaze) — **surpreender** (vt) — [surpriẽd'eɾ]
to be surprised — **surpreender-se** (vp) — [surpriẽd'ersə]

to give (vt) — **dar** (vt) — [daɾ]
to take (get hold of) — **pegar** (vt) — [pəg'aɾ]
to give back — **devolver** (vt) — [dəvɔlv'eɾ]
to return (give back) — **devolver** (vt) — [dəvɔlv'eɾ]

to apologize (vi) — **desculpar-se** (vp) — [dəʃkulp'arsə]
apology — **desculpa** (f) — [dəʃk'ulpɐ]
to forgive (vt) — **perdoar** (vt) — [pərdu'aɾ]

to talk (speak) — **falar** (vi) — [fɐl'aɾ]
to listen (vi) — **escutar** (vt) — [əʃkut'aɾ]
to hear out — **ouvir até o fim** — [ov'ir ɐt'ɛ u fĩ]
to understand (vt) — **compreender** (vt) — [kõpriẽd'eɾ]

to show (display) — **mostrar** (vt) — [muʃtr'aɾ]
to look at ... — **olhar para ...** — [ɔʎ'ar p'ɐrɐ]
to call (with one's voice) — **chamar** (vt) — [ʃɐm'aɾ]
to distract (disturb) — **distrair** (vt) — [diʃtrɐ'iɾ]
to disturb (vt) — **perturbar** (vt) — [pərturb'aɾ]
to pass (to hand sth) — **entregar** (vt) — [ẽtrəg'aɾ]

demand (request) — **pedido** (m) — [pəd'idu]
to request (ask) — **pedir** (vt) — [pəd'iɾ]
demand (firm request) — **exigência** (f) — [eziʒ'ẽsiɐ]

to demand (request firmly)	**exigir** (vt)	[eziʒ'iɾ]
to tease (nickname)	**chamar nomes** (vt)	[ʃem'aɾ n'oməʃ]
to mock (make fun of)	**zombar** (vt)	[zõb'aɾ]
mockery, derision	**zombaria** (f)	[zõbeɾ'iɐ]
nickname	**apelido** (m)	[ɐpəl'idu]
allusion	**alusão** (f)	[ɐluz'ãu]
to allude (vi)	**aludir** (vt)	[ɐlud'iɾ]
to imply (vt)	**subentender** (vt)	[subẽtẽd'eɾ]
description	**descrição** (f)	[dəʃkris'ãu]
to describe (vt)	**descrever** (vt)	[dəʃkrəv'eɾ]
praise (compliments)	**elogio** (m)	[eluʒ'iu]
to praise (vt)	**elogiar** (vt)	[eluʒj'aɾ]
disappointment	**desapontamento** (m)	[dəzɐpõtɐm'ẽtu]
to disappoint (vt)	**desapontar** (vt)	[dəzɐpõt'aɾ]
to be disappointed	**desapontar-se** (vp)	[dəzɐpõt'aɾsə]
supposition	**suposição** (f)	[supuzis'ãu]
to suppose (assume)	**supor** (vt)	[sup'oɾ]
warning (caution)	**advertência** (f)	[ɐdvəɾt'ẽsiɐ]
to warn (vt)	**advertir** (vt)	[ɐdvəɾt'iɾ]

64. Discussion, conversation. Part 3

to talk into (convince)	**convencer** (vt)	[kõvẽs'eɾ]
to calm down (vt)	**acalmar** (vt)	[ɐkalm'aɾ]
silence (~ is golden)	**silêncio** (m)	[sil'ẽsiu]
to keep silent	**ficar em silêncio**	[fik'aɾ ẽ sil'ẽsiu]
to whisper (vi, vt)	**sussurrar** (vt)	[susuʀ'aɾ]
whisper	**sussurro** (m)	[sus'uʀu]
frankly, sincerely (adv)	**francamente**	[frãkɐm'ẽtə]
in my opinion ...	**a meu ver ...**	[ɐ m'eu veɾ]
detail (of the story)	**detalhe** (m)	[dət'aʎə]
detailed (adj)	**detalhado**	[dətɐʎ'adu]
in detail (adv)	**detalhadamente**	[dətɐʎadɐm'ẽtə]
hint, clue	**dica** (f)	[d'ikɐ]
to give a hint	**dar uma dica**	[daɾ 'umɐ d'ikɐ]
look (glance)	**olhar** (m)	[ɔʎ'aɾ]
to have a look	**dar uma vista de olhos**	[daɾ 'umɐ v'iʃtɐ də 'ɔʎuʃ]
fixed (look)	**fixo**	[f'iksu]
to blink (vi)	**piscar** (vi)	[piʃk'aɾ]
to wink (vi)	**pestanejar** (vt)	[pəʃtənəʒ'aɾ]
to nod (in assent)	**acenar** (vt)	[ɐsən'aɾ]

sigh	**suspiro** (m)	[suʃp'iru]
to sigh (vi)	**suspirar** (vi)	[suʃpir'ar]
to shudder (vi)	**estremecer** (vi)	[əʃtrəməs'er]
gesture	**gesto** (m)	[ʒ'ɛʃtu]
to touch (one's arm, etc.)	**tocar** (vt)	[tuk'ar]
to seize (by the arm)	**agarrar** (vt)	[ɐgɐʀ'ar]
to tap (on the shoulder)	**bater de leve**	[bɐt'er də l'ɛvə]
Look out!	**Cuidado!**	[kuid'adu]
Really?	**A sério?**	[ɐ s'ɛriu]
Are you sure?	**Tens a certeza?**	[tẽjʃ ɐ sərt'ezɐ]
Good luck!	**Boa sorte!**	[b'oɐ s'ɔrtə]
I see!	**Compreendi!**	[kõpriẽd'i]
It's a pity!	**Que pena!**	[kə p'enɐ]

65. Agreement. Refusal

consent (agreement)	**consentimento** (m)	[kõsẽtim'ẽtu]
to agree (say yes)	**consentir** (vi)	[kõsẽt'ir]
approval	**aprovação** (f)	[ɐpruvɐs'ãu]
to approve (vt)	**aprovar** (vt)	[ɐpruv'ar]
refusal	**recusa** (f)	[ʀək'uzɐ]
to refuse (vi, vt)	**negar-se** (vt)	[nəg'arsə]
Great!	**Está ótimo!**	[əʃt'a 'ɔtimu]
All right!	**Muito bem!**	[m'ũjtu bẽj]
Okay! (I agree)	**Está bem!**	[əʃt'a bẽj]
forbidden (adj)	**proibido**	[pruib'idu]
it's forbidden	**é proibido**	[ɛ pruib'idu]
it's impossible	**é impossível**	[ɛ ĩpus'ivɛl]
incorrect (adj)	**incorreto**	[ĩkuʀ'ɛtu]
to reject (~ a demand)	**rejeitar** (vt)	[ʀəʒɐjt'ar]
to support (cause, idea)	**apoiar** (vt)	[ɐpoj'ar]
to accept (~ an apology)	**aceitar** (vt)	[ɐsɐjt'ar]
to confirm (vt)	**confirmar** (vt)	[kõfirm'ar]
confirmation	**confirmação** (f)	[kõfirmɐs'ãu]
permission	**permissão** (f)	[pərmis'ãu]
to permit (vt)	**permitir** (vt)	[pərmit'ir]
decision	**decisão** (f)	[dəsiz'ãu]
to say nothing	**não dizer nada**	[n'ãu diz'er n'adɐ]
condition (term)	**condição** (f)	[kõdis'ãu]
excuse (pretext)	**pretexto** (m)	[prət'ɛʃtu]
praise (compliments)	**elogio** (m)	[eluʒ'iu]
to praise (vt)	**elogiar** (vt)	[eluʒj'ar]

66. Success. Good luck. Failure

success	**êxito, sucesso** (m)	['ɛzitu], [sus'ɛsu]
successfully (adv)	**com êxito**	[kõ 'ɛzitu]
successful (adj)	**bem sucedido**	[bẽj susəd'idu]
good luck	**sorte** (f)	[s'ɔrtə]
Good luck!	**Boa sorte!**	[b'oɐ s'ɔrtə]
lucky (e.g., ~ day)	**feliz**	[fəl'iʃ]
lucky (fortunate)	**sortudo, felizardo**	[surt'udu], [fəliz'ardu]
failure	**fracasso** (m)	[frɐk'asu]
misfortune	**pouca sorte** (f)	[p'okɐ s'ɔrtə]
bad luck	**azar** (m), **má sorte** (f)	[ɐz'ar], [ma s'ɔrtə]
unsuccessful (adj)	**mal sucedido**	[mal susəd'idu]
catastrophe	**catástrofe** (f)	[kɐt'aʃtrufə]
pride	**orgulho** (m)	[ɔrg'uʎu]
proud (adj)	**orgulhoso**	[ɔrguʎ'ozu]
to be proud	**estar orgulhoso**	[əʃt'ar ɔrguʎ'ozu]
winner	**vencedor** (m)	[vẽsəd'or]
to win (vi)	**vencer** (vi)	[vẽs'er]
to lose (not win)	**perder** (vt)	[pərd'er]
try	**tentativa** (f)	[tẽtɐt'ivɐ]
to try (vi)	**tentar** (vt)	[tẽt'ar]
chance (opportunity)	**chance** (m)	[ʃ'ãsə]

67. Quarrels. Negative emotions

shout (scream)	**grito** (m)	[gr'itu]
to shout (vi)	**gritar** (vi)	[grit'ar]
to start to cry out	**começar a gritar**	[kuməs'ar ɐ grit'ar]
quarrel	**discussão** (f)	[diʃkus'ãu]
to quarrel (vi)	**discutir** (vt)	[diʃkut'ir]
fight (scandal)	**escândalo** (m)	[əʃk'ãdɐlu]
to have a fight	**criar escândalo**	[kri'ar əʃk'ãdɐlu]
conflict	**conflito** (m)	[kõfl'itu]
misunderstanding	**mal-entendido** (m)	[malẽtẽd'idu]
insult	**insulto** (m)	[ĩs'ultu]
to insult (vt)	**insultar** (vt)	[ĩsult'ar]
insulted (adj)	**insultado**	[ĩsult'adu]
resentment	**ofensa** (f)	[ɔf'ẽsɐ]
to offend (vt)	**ofender** (vt)	[ɔfẽd'er]
to take offense	**ofender-se** (vp)	[ɔfẽd'ersə]
indignation	**indignação** (f)	[ĩdignɐs'ãu]
to be indignant	**indignar-se** (vp)	[ĩdign'arsə]

complaint	**queixa** (f)	[k'ɐjʃɐ]
to complain (vi, vt)	**queixar-se** (vp)	[kɐjʃ'arsə]
apology	**desculpa** (f)	[dəʃk'ulpɐ]
to apologize (vi)	**desculpar-se** (vp)	[dəʃkulp'arsə]
to beg pardon	**pedir perdão**	[pəd'ir pərd'ãu]
criticism	**crítica** (f)	[kr'itikɐ]
to criticize (vt)	**criticar** (vt)	[kritik'ar]
accusation	**acusação** (f)	[ɐkuzɐs'ãu]
to accuse (vt)	**acusar** (vt)	[ɐkuz'ar]
revenge	**vingança** (f)	[vĩg'ãsɐ]
to revenge (vt)	**vingar** (vt)	[vĩg'ar]
to pay back	**pagar de volta**	[pɐg'ar də v'ɔltɐ]
disdain	**desprezo** (m)	[dəʃpr'ezu]
to despise (vt)	**desprezar** (vt)	[dəʃprəz'ar]
hatred, hate	**ódio** (m)	['ɔdiu]
to hate (vt)	**odiar** (vt)	[odj'ar]
nervous (adj)	**nervoso**	[nərv'ozu]
to be nervous	**estar nervoso**	[əʃt'ar nərv'ozu]
angry (mad)	**zangado**	[zãg'adu]
to make angry	**zangar** (vt)	[zãg'ar]
humiliation	**humilhação** (f)	[umiʎɐs'ãu]
to humiliate (vt)	**humilhar** (vt)	[umiʎ'ar]
to humiliate oneself	**humilhar-se** (vp)	[umiʎ'arsə]
shock	**choque** (m)	[ʃ'ɔkə]
to shock (vt)	**chocar** (vt)	[ʃuk'ar]
trouble (annoyance)	**aborrecimento** (m)	[ɐbuʀəsim'ẽtu]
unpleasant (adj)	**desagradável**	[dəzɐgrɐd'avɛl]
fear (dread)	**medo** (m)	[m'edu]
terrible (storm, heat)	**terrível**	[təʀ'ivɛl]
scary (e.g., ~ story)	**assustador**	[ɐsuʃtɐd'or]
horror	**horror** (m)	[ɔʀ'or]
awful (crime, news)	**horrível**	[ɔʀ'ivɛl]
to begin to tremble	**começar a tremer**	[kuməs'ar ɐ trəm'er]
to cry (weep)	**chorar** (vi)	[ʃur'ar]
to start crying	**começar a chorar**	[kuməs'ar ɐ ʃur'ar]
tear	**lágrima** (f)	[l'agrimɐ]
fault	**falta** (f)	[f'altɐ]
guilt (feeling)	**culpa** (f)	[k'ulpɐ]
dishonor (disgrace)	**desonra** (f)	[dəz'õʀɐ]
protest	**protesto** (m)	[prut'ɛʃtu]
stress	**stress** (m)	[str'ɛs]

to disturb (vt)	**perturbar** (vt)	[pərturb'ar]
to be furious	**zangar-se com ...**	[zãg'arsə kõ]
mad, angry (adj)	**zangado**	[zãg'adu]
to end (~ a relationship)	**terminar** (vt)	[tərmin'ar]
to swear (at sb)	**praguejar**	[prɐgəʒ'ar]
to be scared	**assustar-se**	[ɐsuʃt'arsə]
to hit (strike with hand)	**golpear** (vt)	[gɔlpj'ar]
to fight (vi)	**bater-se** (vp)	[bɐt'ersə]
to settle (a conflict)	**resolver** (vt)	[ʀəzɔlv'er]
discontented (adj)	**descontente**	[dəʃkõt'ẽtə]
furious (adj)	**furioso**	[furj'ozu]
It's not good!	**Não está bem!**	[n'ãu əʃt'a bẽj]
It's bad!	**É mau!**	[ɛ m'au]

Medicine

68. Diseases

sickness	**doença** (f)	[du'ẽsɐ]
to be sick	**estar doente**	[əʃt'ar du'ẽtə]
health	**saúde** (f)	[sɐ'udə]
runny nose (coryza)	**nariz** (m) **a escorrer**	[nɐr'iʃ ɐ əʃkuʀ'er]
angina	**amigdalite** (f)	[ɐmigdɐl'itə]
cold (illness)	**constipação** (f)	[kõʃtipɐs'ãu]
to catch a cold	**constipar-se** (vp)	[kõʃtip'arsə]
bronchitis	**bronquite** (f)	[brõk'itə]
pneumonia	**pneumonia** (f)	[pneumun'iɐ]
flu, influenza	**gripe** (f)	[gr'ipə]
near-sighted (adj)	**míope**	[m'iupə]
far-sighted (adj)	**presbita**	[prəʒb'itɐ]
strabismus (crossed eyes)	**estrabismo** (m)	[əʃtrɐb'iʒmu]
cross-eyed (adj)	**estrábico**	[əʃtr'abiku]
cataract	**catarata** (f)	[kɐtɐr'atɐ]
glaucoma	**glaucoma** (m)	[glauk'omɐ]
stroke	**AVC** (m), **apoplexia** (f)	[avɛs'ɛ], [ɐpɔplɛks'iɐ]
heart attack	**ataque** (m) **cardíaco**	[ɐt'akə kɐrd'iɐku]
myocardial infarction	**enfarte** (m) **do miocárdio**	[ẽf'artə du miɔk'ardiu]
paralysis	**paralisia** (f)	[pɐrɐliz'iɐ]
to paralyze (vt)	**paralisar** (vt)	[pɐrɐliz'ar]
allergy	**alergia** (f)	[ɐlərʒ'iɐ]
asthma	**asma** (f)	['aʒmɐ]
diabetes	**diabetes** (f)	[diɐb'ɛtəʃ]
toothache	**dor** (f) **de dentes**	[dor də d'ẽtəʃ]
caries	**cárie** (f)	[k'ariə]
diarrhea	**diarreia** (f)	[diɐʀ'ɐjɐ]
constipation	**prisão** (f) **de ventre**	[priz'ãu də v'ẽtrə]
stomach upset	**desarranjo** (m) **intestinal**	[dəzɐʀ'ãʒu ĩtəʃtin'al]
food poisoning	**intoxicação** (f) **alimentar**	[ĩtɔksikɐs'ãu ɐlimẽt'ar]
to have a food poisoning	**intoxicar-se**	[ĩtɔksik'arsə]
arthritis	**artrite** (f)	[ɐrtr'itə]
rickets	**raquitismo** (m)	[ʀɐkit'iʒmu]
rheumatism	**reumatismo** (m)	[ʀiumɐt'iʒmu]

atherosclerosis	**arteriosclerose** (f)	[ɐrtəriɔʃklər'ɔzə]
gastritis	**gastrite** (f)	[gɐʃtr'itə]
appendicitis	**apendicite** (f)	[ɐpẽdis'itə]
cholecystitis	**colecistite** (f)	[kulɛsiʃt'itə]
ulcer	**úlcera** (f)	['ulsərɐ]
measles	**sarampo** (m)	[sɐr'ãpu]
German measles	**rubéola** (f)	[ʀub'ɛulɐ]
jaundice	**iterícia** (f)	[itər'isiɐ]
hepatitis	**hepatite** (f)	[epɐt'itə]
schizophrenia	**esquizofrenia** (f)	[əʃkizɔfrən'iɐ]
rabies (hydrophobia)	**raiva** (f)	[ʀ'ajvɐ]
neurosis	**neurose** (f)	[neur'ɔzə]
concussion	**comoção** (f) **cerebral**	[kumus'ãu sərəbr'al]
cancer	**cancro** (m)	[k'ãkru]
sclerosis	**esclerose** (f)	[əʃklər'ɔzə]
multiple sclerosis	**esclerose** (f) **múltipla**	[əʃklər'ɔzə m'ultiplɐ]
alcoholism	**alcoolismo** (m)	[alkuul'iʒmu]
alcoholic (n)	**alcoólico** (m)	[alku'ɔliku]
syphilis	**sífilis** (f)	[s'ifiliʃ]
AIDS	**SIDA** (f)	[s'idɐ]
tumor	**tumor** (m)	[tum'or]
malignant (adj)	**maligno**	[mɐl'ignu]
benign (adj)	**benigno**	[bən'ignu]
fever	**febre** (f)	[f'ɛbrə]
malaria	**malária** (f)	[mɐl'ariɐ]
gangrene	**gangrena** (f)	[gãgr'enɐ]
seasickness	**enjoo** (m)	[ẽʒ'ou]
epilepsy	**epilepsia** (f)	[epilɛps'iɐ]
epidemic	**epidemia** (f)	[epidəm'iɐ]
typhus	**tifo** (m)	[t'ifu]
tuberculosis	**tuberculose** (f)	[tubɛrkul'ɔzə]
cholera	**cólera** (f)	[k'ɔlərɐ]
plague (bubonic ~)	**peste** (f)	[p'ɛʃtə]

69. Symptoms. Treatments. Part 1

symptom	**sintoma** (m)	[sĩt'omɐ]
temperature	**temperatura** (f)	[tẽpərɐt'urɐ]
high temperature	**febre** (f)	[f'ɛbrə]
pulse	**pulso** (m)	[p'ulsu]
giddiness	**vertigem** (f)	[vərt'iʒẽj]
hot (adj)	**quente**	[k'ẽtə]

shivering **calafrio** (m) [kɐlɐfr'iu]
pale (e.g., ~ face) **pálido** [p'alidu]

cough **tosse** (f) [t'ɔsə]
to cough (vi) **tossir** (vi) [tɔs'ir]
to sneeze (vi) **espirrar** (vi) [əʃpiʀ'ar]
faint **desmaio** (m) [dəʒm'aju]
to faint (vi) **desmaiar** (vi) [dəʒmɐj'ar]

bruise (hématome) **nódoa** (f) **negra** [n'ɔduɐ n'egrɐ]
bump (lump) **galo** (m) [g'alu]
to bruise oneself **magoar-se** (vp) [mɐgu'arsə]
bruise (contusion) **pisadura** (f) [pizɐd'urɐ]
to get bruised **aleijar-se** (vp) [ɐlɐjʒ'arsə]

to limp (vi) **coxear** (vi) [kɔksj'ar]
dislocation **deslocação** (f) [dəʒlukɐs'ãu]
to dislocate (vt) **deslocar** (vt) [dəʒluk'ar]
fracture **fratura** (f) [frat'urɐ]
to have a fracture **fraturar** (vt) [frɐtur'ar]

cut (e.g., paper ~) **corte** (m) [k'ɔrtə]
to cut oneself **cortar-se** (vp) [kurt'arsə]
bleeding **hemorragia** (f) [emuʀɐʒ'iɐ]

burn (injury) **queimadura** (f) [kɐjmɐd'urɐ]
to scald oneself **queimar-se** (vp) [kɐjm'arsə]

to prick (vt) **picar** (vt) [pik'ar]
to prick oneself **picar-se** (vp) [pik'arsə]
to injure (vt) **lesionar** (vt) [ləziun'ar]
injury **lesão** (m) [ləz'ãu]
wound **ferida** (f), **ferimento** (m) [fər'idɐ], [fərim'ẽtu]
trauma **trauma** (m) [tr'aumɐ]

to be delirious **delirar** (vi) [dəlir'ar]
to stutter (vi) **gaguejar** (vi) [gɐgəʒ'ar]
sunstroke **insolação** (f) [ĩsulɐs'ãu]

70. Symptoms. Treatments. Part 2

pain **dor** (f) [dor]
splinter (in foot, etc.) **farpa** (f) [f'arpɐ]

sweat (perspiration) **suor** (m) [su'ɔr]
to sweat (perspire) **suar** (vi) [su'ar]
vomiting **vómito** (m) [v'ɔmitu]
convulsions **convulsões** (f pl) [kõvuls'ojʃ]
pregnant (adj) **grávida** [gr'avidɐ]
to be born **nascer** (vi) [nɐʃs'er]

delivery, labor	**parto** (m)	[p'artu]
to deliver (~ a baby)	**dar à luz**	[dar a luʃ]
abortion	**aborto** (m)	[ɐb'ortu]
breathing, respiration	**respiração** (f)	[ʀəʃpirɐs'ãu]
inhalation	**inspiração** (f)	[ĩʃpirɐs'ãu]
exhalation	**expiração** (f)	[əʃpirɐs'ãu]
to exhale (vi)	**expirar** (vi)	[əʃpir'ar]
to inhale (vi)	**inspirar** (vi)	[ĩʃpir'ar]
disabled person	**inválido** (m)	[ĩv'alidu]
cripple	**aleijado** (m)	[ɐlɐjʒ'adu]
drug addict	**toxicodependente** (m)	[tɔksikɔdəpẽd'ẽtə]
deaf (adj)	**surdo**	[s'urdu]
dumb, mute	**mudo**	[m'udu]
deaf-and-dumb (adj)	**surdo-mudo**	[s'urdu m'udu]
mad, insane (adj)	**louco**	[l'oku]
madman	**louco** (m)	[l'oku]
madwoman	**louca** (f)	[l'okɐ]
to go insane	**ficar louco**	[fik'ar l'oku]
gene	**gene** (m)	[ʒ'ɛnə]
immunity	**imunidade** (f)	[imunid'adə]
hereditary (adj)	**hereditário**	[erədit'ariu]
congenital (adj)	**congénito**	[kõʒ'ɛnitu]
virus	**vírus** (m)	[v'iruʃ]
microbe	**micróbio** (m)	[mikr'ɔbiu]
bacterium	**bactéria** (f)	[bakt'ɛriɐ]
infection	**infeção** (f)	[ĩfɛs'ãu]

71. Symptoms. Treatments. Part 3

hospital	**hospital** (m)	[ɔʃpit'al]
patient	**paciente** (m)	[pɐsj'ẽtə]
diagnosis	**diagnóstico** (m)	[diɐgn'ɔʃtiku]
cure	**cura** (f)	[k'urɐ]
medical treatment	**tratamento** (m) **médico**	[trɐtɐm'ẽtu m'ɛdiku]
to get treatment	**curar-se** (vp)	[kur'arsə]
to treat (vt)	**tratar** (vt)	[trɐt'ar]
to nurse (look after)	**cuidar** (vt)	[kuid'ar]
care (nursing ~)	**cuidados** (m pl)	[kuid'aduʃ]
operation, surgery	**operação** (f)	[ɔpərɐs'ãu]
to bandage (head, limb)	**pôr uma ligadura**	[por 'umɐ ligɐd'urɐ]
bandaging	**ligadura** (f)	[ligɐd'urɐ]
vaccination	**vacinação** (f)	[vɐsinɐs'ãu]

to vaccinate (vt)	**vacinar** (vt)	[vesin'ar]
injection, shot	**injeção** (f)	[ĩʒɛs'ãu]
to give an injection	**dar uma injeção**	[dar 'ume ĩʒɛs'ãu]
attack	**ataque** (m)	[ɐt'akə]
amputation	**amputação** (f)	[ãputɐs'ãu]
to amputate (vt)	**amputar** (vt)	[ãput'ar]
coma	**coma** (m)	[k'omɐ]
to be in a coma	**estar em coma**	[əʃt'ar ẽ k'omɐ]
intensive care	**reanimação** (f)	[ʀienimɐs'ãu]
to recover (~ from flu)	**recuperar-se** (vp)	[ʀəkupər'arsə]
state (patient's ~)	**estado** (m)	[əʃt'adu]
consciousness	**consciência** (f)	[kõʃsj'ẽsiɐ]
memory (faculty)	**memória** (f)	[məm'ɔriɐ]
to extract (tooth)	**tirar** (vt)	[tir'ar]
filling	**chumbo** (m), **obturação** (f)	[ʃ'ũbu], [ɔbturɐs'ãu]
to fill (a tooth)	**chumbar, obturar** (vt)	[ʃũb'ar], [ɔbtur'ar]
hypnosis	**hipnose** (f)	[ipn'ɔzə]
to hypnotize (vt)	**hipnotizar** (vt)	[ipnutiz'ar]

72. Doctors

doctor	**médico** (m)	[m'ɛdiku]
nurse	**enfermeira** (f)	[ẽfərm'ɐjrɐ]
private physician	**médico** (m) **pessoal**	[m'ɛdiku pəsu'al]
dentist	**dentista** (m)	[dẽt'iʃtɐ]
ophthalmologist	**oculista** (m)	[ɔkul'iʃtɐ]
internist	**terapeuta** (m)	[tərɐp'eutɐ]
surgeon	**cirurgião** (m)	[sirurʒj'ãu]
psychiatrist	**psiquiatra** (m)	[psiki'atrɐ]
pediatrician	**pediatra** (m)	[pədj'atrɐ]
psychologist	**psicólogo** (m)	[psik'ɔlugu]
gynecologist	**ginecologista** (m)	[ʒinɛkuluʒ'iʃtɐ]
cardiologist	**cardiologista** (m)	[kɐrdiuluʒ'iʃtɐ]

73. Medicine. Drugs. Accessories

medicine, drug	**medicamento** (m)	[mədikɐm'ẽtu]
remedy	**remédio** (m)	[ʀəm'ɛdiu]
to prescribe (vt)	**receitar** (vt)	[ʀəsɐjt'ar]
prescription	**receita** (f)	[ʀəs'ɐjtɐ]
tablet, pill	**comprimido** (m)	[kõprim'idu]
ointment	**pomada** (f)	[pum'adɐ]

ampule	**ampola** (f)	[ãp'ɔlɐ]
mixture	**preparado** (m)	[prəpɐr'adu]
syrup	**xarope** (m)	[ʃɐr'ɔpə]
pill	**cápsula** (f)	[k'apsulɐ]
powder	**remédio** (m) **em pó**	[ʀəm'ɛdiu ẽ pɔ]
bandage	**ligadura** (f)	[ligɐd'urɐ]
cotton wool	**algodão** (m)	[algud'ãu]
iodine	**iodo** (m)	[j'odu]
Band-Aid	**penso** (m) **rápido**	[p'ẽsu ʀ'apidu]
eyedropper	**conta-gotas** (f)	[k'õtɐ g'otɐʃ]
thermometer	**termómetro** (m)	[tərm'ɔmətru]
syringe	**seringa** (f)	[sər'ĩgɐ]
wheelchair	**cadeira** (m) **de rodas**	[kɐd'ɐjrɐ də ʀ'ɔdɐʃ]
crutches	**muletas** (f pl)	[mul'etɐʃ]
painkiller	**analgésico** (m)	[ɐnalʒ'ɛziku]
laxative	**laxante** (m)	[laʃ'ãtə]
spirit (ethanol)	**álcool** (m)	['alkuɔl]
medicinal herbs	**ervas** (f pl) **medicinais**	['ɛrvɐʃ mədisin'ajʃ]
herbal (~ tea)	**de ervas**	[də 'ɛrvɐʃ]

74. Smoking. Tobacco products

tobacco	**tabaco** (m)	[tɐb'aku]
cigarette	**cigarro** (m)	[sig'aʀu]
cigar	**charuto** (m)	[ʃɐr'utu]
pipe	**cachimbo** (m)	[kɐʃ'ĩbu]
pack (of cigarettes)	**maço** (m)	[m'asu]
matches	**fósforos** (m pl)	[f'ɔʃfuruʃ]
matchbox	**caixa** (f) **de fósforos**	[k'ajʃɐ də f'ɔʃfuruʃ]
lighter	**isqueiro** (m)	[iʃk'ɐjru]
ashtray	**cinzeiro** (m)	[sĩz'ɐjru]
cigarette case	**cigarreira** (f)	[sigɐʀ'ɐjrɐ]
cigarette holder	**boquilha** (f)	[buk'iʎɐ]
filter (cigarette tip)	**filtro** (m)	[f'iltru]
to smoke (vi, vt)	**fumar** (vi, vt)	[fum'ar]
to light a cigarette	**acender um cigarro**	[ɐsẽd'er ũ sig'aʀu]
smoking	**tabagismo** (m)	[tɐbɐʒ'iʒmu]
smoker	**fumador** (m)	[fumɐd'or]
stub, butt (of cigarette)	**beata** (f)	[bj'atɐ]
smoke, fumes	**fumo** (m)	[f'umu]
ash	**cinza** (f)	[s'ĩzɐ]

HUMAN HABITAT

City

75. City. Life in the city

city, town	**cidade** (f)	[sid'adə]
capital city	**capital** (f)	[kɐpit'al]
village	**aldeia** (f)	[ald'ɐjɐ]
city map	**mapa** (m) **da cidade**	[m'apɐ dɐ sid'adə]
downtown	**centro** (m) **da cidade**	[s'ẽtru dɐ sid'adə]
suburb	**subúrbio** (m)	[sub'urbiu]
suburban (adj)	**suburbano**	[suburb'ɐnu]
outskirts	**periferia** (f)	[pərifər'iɐ]
environs (suburbs)	**arredores** (m pl)	[ɐʀəd'orəʃ]
city block	**quarteirão** (m)	[kuɐrtɐjr'ãu]
residential block	**quarteirão** (m) **residencial**	[kuɐrtɐjr'ãu ʀəzidẽsj'al]
traffic	**tráfego** (m)	[tr'afəgu]
traffic lights	**semáforo** (m)	[səm'afuru]
public transportation	**transporte** (m) **público**	[trɐ̃ʃp'ɔrtə p'ubliku]
intersection	**cruzamento** (m)	[kruzɐm'ẽtu]
crosswalk	**passadeira** (f) **para peões**	[pɐsɐd'ɐjrɐ p'ɐrɐ pi'ojʃ]
pedestrian underpass	**passagem** (f) **subterrânea**	[pɐs'aʒẽj subtəʀ'ɐniɐ]
to cross (vt)	**cruzar, atravessar** (vt)	[kruz'ar], [ɐtrɐvəs'ar]
pedestrian	**peão** (m)	[pj'ãu]
sidewalk	**passeio** (m)	[pɐs'ɐju]
bridge	**ponte** (f)	[p'õtə]
bank (riverbank)	**marginal** (f)	[mɐrʒin'al]
fountain	**fonte** (f)	[f'õtə]
allée	**alameda** (f)	[ɐlɐm'edɐ]
park	**parque** (m)	[p'arkə]
boulevard	**bulevar** (m)	[buləv'ar]
square	**praça** (f)	[pr'asɐ]
avenue (wide street)	**avenida** (f)	[ɐvən'idɐ]
street	**rua** (f)	[ʀ'uɐ]
side street	**travessa** (f)	[trɐv'ɛsɐ]
dead end	**beco** (m) **sem saída**	[b'eku sẽ sɐ'idɐ]
house	**casa** (f)	[k'azɐ]
building	**edifício, prédio** (m)	[edif'isiu], [pr'ɛdiu]

skyscraper	**arranha-céus** (m)	[ɐʀ'ɐɲɐ s'ɛuʃ]
facade	**fachada** (f)	[fɐʃ'adɐ]
roof	**telhado** (m)	[təʎ'adu]
window	**janela** (f)	[ʒɐn'ɛlɐ]
arch	**arco** (m)	['arku]
column	**coluna** (f)	[kul'unɐ]
corner	**esquina** (f)	[əʃk'inɐ]
store window	**montra** (f)	[m'õtrɐ]
store sign	**letreiro** (m)	[lətr'ɐjru]
poster	**cartaz** (m)	[kɐrt'aʃ]
advertising poster	**cartaz** (m) **publicitário**	[kɐrt'aʃ publisit'ariu]
billboard	**painel** (m) **publicitário**	[pajn'ɛl publisit'ariu]
garbage, trash	**lixo** (m)	[l'iʃu]
garbage can	**cesta** (f) **do lixo**	[s'eʃtɐ du l'iʃu]
to litter (vi)	**jogar lixo na rua**	[ʒug'ar l'iʃu nɐ ʀ'uɐ]
garbage dump	**aterro** (m) **sanitário**	[ɐt'eʀu sɐnit'ariu]
phone booth	**cabine** (f) **telefónica**	[kɐb'inə tələf'ɔnikɐ]
lamppost	**candeeiro** (m) **de rua**	[kɐ̃dj'ɐjru də ʀ'uɐ]
bench (park ~)	**banco** (m)	[b'ɐ̃ku]
police officer	**polícia** (m)	[pul'isiɐ]
police	**polícia** (f)	[pul'isiɐ]
beggar	**mendigo** (m)	[mẽd'igu]
homeless, bum	**sem-abrigo** (m)	[sɛnɐbr'igu]

76. Urban institutions

store	**loja** (f)	[l'ɔʒɐ]
drugstore, pharmacy	**farmácia** (f)	[fɐrm'asiɐ]
optical store	**ótica** (f)	['ɔtikɐ]
shopping mall	**centro** (m) **comercial**	[s'ẽtru kumərsj'al]
supermarket	**supermercado** (m)	[supɛrmərk'adu]
bakery	**padaria** (f)	[pɐdɐr'iɐ]
baker	**padeiro** (m)	[pɐd'ɐjru]
candy store	**pastelaria** (f)	[pɐʃtəlɐr'iɐ]
grocery store	**mercearia** (f)	[mərsiɐr'iɐ]
butcher shop	**talho** (m)	[t'aʎu]
produce store	**loja** (f) **de legumes**	[l'ɔʒɐ də ləg'uməʃ]
market	**mercado** (m)	[mərk'adu]
coffee house	**café** (m)	[kɐf'ɛ]
restaurant	**restaurante** (m)	[ʀəʃtaur'ɐ̃tə]
pub	**cervejaria** (f)	[sərvəʒɐr'iɐ]
pizzeria	**pizzaria** (f)	[pitzɐr'iɐ]
hair salon	**salão** (m) **de cabeleireiro**	[sɐl'ɐ̃u də kɐbəlɐjr'ɐjru]

post office	**correios** (m pl)	[kuʀ'ɐjuʃ]
dry cleaners	**lavandaria** (f)	[lɐvãdɐr'iɐ]
photo studio	**estúdio** (m) **fotográfico**	[əʃt'udiu futugr'afiku]
shoe store	**sapataria** (f)	[sɐpɐtɐr'iɐ]
bookstore	**livraria** (f)	[livrɐr'iɐ]
sporting goods store	**loja** (f) **de artigos de desporto**	[l'ɔʒɐ də ɐrt'iguʃ də dəʃp'ortu]
clothes repair	**reparação** (f) **de roupa**	[ʀəpɐrɐs'ãu də ʀ'opɐ]
formal wear rental	**aluguer** (m) **de roupa**	[ɐlug'ɛr də ʀ'opɐ]
movie rental store	**aluguer** (m) **de filmes**	[ɐlug'ɛr də f'ilməʃ]
circus	**circo** (m)	[s'irku]
zoo	**jardim** (m) **zoológico**	[ʒɐrd'ĩ zuul'ɔʒiku]
movie theater	**cinema** (m)	[sin'emɐ]
museum	**museu** (m)	[muz'eu]
library	**biblioteca** (f)	[bibliut'ɛkɐ]
theater	**teatro** (m)	[tə'atru]
opera	**ópera** (f)	['ɔpərɐ]
nightclub	**clube** (m) **noturno**	[kl'ubə nɔt'urnu]
casino	**casino** (m)	[kɐz'inu]
mosque	**mesquita** (f)	[məʃk'itɐ]
synagogue	**sinagoga** (f)	[sinɐg'ɔgɐ]
cathedral	**catedral** (f)	[kɐtədr'al]
temple	**templo** (m)	[t'ẽplu]
church	**igreja** (f)	[igr'ɐʒɐ]
college	**instituto** (m)	[ĩʃtit'utu]
university	**universidade** (f)	[univərsid'adə]
school	**escola** (f)	[əʃk'ɔlɐ]
prefecture	**prefeitura** (f)	[prəfɐjt'urɐ]
city hall	**câmara** (f) **municipal**	[k'ɐmɐrɐ munisip'al]
hotel	**hotel** (m)	[ɔt'ɛl]
bank	**banco** (m)	[b'ãku]
embassy	**embaixada** (f)	[ẽbajʃ'adɐ]
travel agency	**agência** (f) **de viagens**	[ɐʒ'ẽsiɐ də vj'aʒẽjʃ]
information office	**agência** (f) **de informações**	[ɐʒ'ẽsiɐ də ĩfurmɐs'ojʃ]
money exchange	**casa** (f) **de câmbio**	[k'azɐ də k'ãbiu]
subway	**metro** (m)	[m'ɛtru]
hospital	**hospital** (m)	[ɔʃpit'al]
gas station	**posto** (m) **de gasolina**	[p'oʃtu də gɐzul'inɐ]
parking lot	**parque** (m) **de estacionamento**	[p'arkə də əʃtɐsiunɐm'ẽtu]

77. Urban transportation

bus	**autocarro** (m)	[autɔk'aʀu]
streetcar	**elétrico** (m)	[el'ɛtriku]
trolley	**troleicarro** (m)	[trulɛik'aʀu]
route (of bus)	**itinerário** (m)	[itinər'ariu]
number (e.g., bus ~)	**número** (m)	[n'uməru]
to go by ...	**ir de ...**	[ir də]
to get on (~ the bus)	**entrar em ...**	[ẽtr'ar ẽj]
to get off ...	**descer de ...**	[dəʃs'er də]
stop (e.g., bus ~)	**paragem** (f)	[pɐr'aʒẽj]
next stop	**próxima paragem** (f)	[pr'ɔsimɐ pɐr'aʒẽj]
terminus	**ponto** (m) **final**	[p'õtu fin'al]
schedule	**horário** (m)	[ɔr'ariu]
to wait (vt)	**esperar** (vt)	[əʃpər'ar]
ticket	**bilhete** (m)	[biʎ'etə]
fare	**custo** (m) **do bilhete**	[k'uʃtu du biʎ'etə]
cashier (ticket seller)	**bilheteiro** (m)	[biʎət'ɐjru]
ticket inspection	**controlo** (m) **dos bilhetes**	[kõtr'olu duʃ biʎ'etəʃ]
conductor	**revisor** (m)	[ʀəviz'or]
to be late (for ...)	**atrasar-se** (vp)	[ɐtrɐz'arsə]
to miss (~ the train, etc.)	**perder** (vt)	[pərd'er]
to be in a hurry	**estar com pressa**	[əʃt'ar kõ pr'ɛsɐ]
taxi, cab	**táxi** (m)	[t'aksi]
taxi driver	**taxista** (m)	[taks'iʃtɐ]
by taxi	**de táxi**	[də t'aksi]
taxi stand	**praça** (f) **de táxis**	[pr'asɐ də t'aksiʃ]
to call a taxi	**chamar um táxi**	[ʃɐm'ar ũ t'aksi]
to take a taxi	**apanhar um táxi**	[ɐpɐɲ'ar ũ t'aksi]
traffic	**tráfego** (m)	[tr'afəgu]
traffic jam	**engarrafamento** (m)	[ẽgɐʀɐfɐm'ẽtu]
rush hour	**horas** (f pl) **de ponta**	['ɔrɐʃ də p'õtɐ]
to park (vi)	**estacionar** (vi)	[əʃtɐsiun'ar]
to park (vt)	**estacionar** (vt)	[əʃtɐsiun'ar]
parking lot	**parque** (m) **de estacionamento**	[p'arkə də əʃtɐsiunɐm'ẽtu]
subway	**metro** (m)	[m'ɛtru]
station	**estação** (f)	[əʃtɐs'ãu]
to take the subway	**ir de metro**	[ir də m'ɛtru]
train	**comboio** (m)	[kõb'ɔju]
train station	**estação** (f)	[əʃtɐs'ãu]

78. Sightseeing

monument	**monumento** (m)	[munum'ẽtu]
fortress	**fortaleza** (f)	[furtɐl'ezɐ]
palace	**palácio** (m)	[pɐl'asiu]
castle	**castelo** (m)	[kɐʃt'ɛlu]
tower	**torre** (f)	[t'ORə]
mausoleum	**mausoléu** (m)	[mauzul'ɛu]
architecture	**arquitetura** (f)	[ɐrkitɛt'urɐ]
medieval (adj)	**medieval**	[mədiɛv'al]
ancient (adj)	**antigo**	[ɐ̃t'igu]
national (adj)	**nacional**	[nɐsiun'al]
well-known (adj)	**conhecido**	[kuɲəs'idu]
tourist	**turista** (m)	[tur'iʃtɐ]
guide (person)	**guia** (m)	[g'iɐ]
excursion, guided tour	**excursão** (f)	[əʃkurs'ãu]
to show (vt)	**mostrar** (vt)	[muʃtr'ar]
to tell (vt)	**contar** (vt)	[kõt'ar]
to find (vt)	**encontrar** (vt)	[ẽkõtr'ar]
to get lost (lose one's way)	**perder-se** (vp)	[pərd'ersə]
map (e.g., subway ~)	**mapa** (m)	[m'apɐ]
map (e.g., city ~)	**mapa** (m)	[m'apɐ]
souvenir, gift	**lembrança** (f), **presente** (m)	[lẽbr'ãsɐ], [prəz'ẽtə]
gift shop	**loja** (f) **de presentes**	[l'ɔʒɐ də prəz'ẽtəʃ]
to take pictures	**fotografar** (vt)	[futugrɐf'ar]
to be photographed	**fotografar-se**	[futugrɐf'arsə]

79. Shopping

to buy (purchase)	**comprar** (vt)	[kõpr'ar]
purchase	**compra** (f)	[k'õprɐ]
to go shopping	**fazer compras**	[fɐz'er k'õprɐʃ]
shopping	**compras** (f pl)	[k'õprɐʃ]
to be open (ab. store)	**estar aberta**	[əʃt'ar ɐb'ɛrtɐ]
to be closed	**estar fechada**	[əʃt'ar fəʃ'adɐ]
footwear	**calçado** (m)	[kals'adu]
clothes, clothing	**roupa** (f)	[R'opɐ]
cosmetics	**cosméticos** (m pl)	[kuʒm'ɛtikuʃ]
food products	**alimentos** (m pl)	[ɐlim'ẽtuʃ]
gift, present	**presente** (m)	[prəz'ẽtə]
salesman	**vendedor** (m)	[vẽdəd'or]
saleswoman	**vendedora** (f)	[vẽdəd'orɐ]

check out, cash desk	**caixa** (f)	[k'ajʃɐ]
mirror	**espelho** (m)	[əʃp'ɐʎu]
counter (in shop)	**balcão** (m)	[balk'ãu]
fitting room	**cabine** (f) **de provas**	[kɐb'inə də pɾ'ɔvɐʃ]
to try on	**provar** (vt)	[pɾuv'aɾ]
to fit (ab. dress, etc.)	**servir** (vi)	[səɾv'iɾ]
to like (I like ...)	**gostar** (vt)	[guʃt'aɾ]
price	**preço** (m)	[pɾ'esu]
price tag	**etiqueta** (f) **de preço**	[etik'etɐ də pɾ'esu]
to cost (vt)	**custar** (vt)	[kuʃt'aɾ]
How much?	**Quanto?**	[ku'ãtu]
discount	**desconto** (m)	[dəʃk'õtu]
inexpensive (adj)	**não caro**	[n'ãu k'aɾu]
cheap (adj)	**barato**	[bɐɾ'atu]
expensive (adj)	**caro**	[k'aɾu]
It's expensive	**É caro**	[ɛ k'aɾu]
rental (n)	**aluguer** (m)	[ɐlug'ɛɾ]
to rent (~ a tuxedo)	**alugar** (vt)	[ɐlug'aɾ]
credit	**crédito** (m)	[kɾ'ɛditu]
on credit (adv)	**a crédito**	[ɐ kɾ'ɛditu]

80. Money

money	**dinheiro** (m)	[diɲ'ɐjɾu]
currency exchange	**câmbio** (m)	[k'ãbiu]
exchange rate	**taxa** (f) **de câmbio**	[t'aʃɐ də k'ãbiu]
ATM	**Caixa Multibanco** (m)	[k'ajʃɐ multib'ãku]
coin	**moeda** (f)	[mu'ɛdɐ]
dollar	**dólar** (m)	[d'ɔlaɾ]
euro	**euro** (m)	['euɾu]
lira	**lira** (f)	[l'iɾɐ]
Deutschmark	**marco** (m)	[m'aɾku]
franc	**franco** (m)	[fɾ'ãku]
pound sterling	**libra** (f) **esterlina**	[l'ibɾɐ əʃtəɾl'inɐ]
yen	**iene** (m)	[j'ɛnə]
debt	**dívida** (f)	[d'ividɐ]
debtor	**devedor** (m)	[dəvəd'oɾ]
to lend (money)	**emprestar** (vt)	[ẽpɾəʃt'aɾ]
to borrow (vi, vt)	**pedir emprestado**	[pəd'iɾ ẽpɾəʃt'adu]
bank	**banco** (m)	[b'ãku]
account	**conta** (f)	[k'õtɐ]
to deposit (vt)	**depositar** (vt)	[dəpuzit'aɾ]

to deposit into the account	**depositar na conta**	[dəpuzit'ar nɐ k'õtɐ]
to withdraw (vt)	**levantar** (vt)	[ləvãt'ar]
credit card	**cartão** (m) **de crédito**	[kɐrt'ãu də kr'ɛditu]
cash	**dinheiro** (m) **vivo**	[diɲ'ɐjru v'ivu]
check	**cheque** (m)	[ʃ'ɛkə]
to write a check	**passar um cheque**	[pɐs'ar ũ ʃ'ɛkə]
checkbook	**livro** (m) **de cheques**	[l'ivru də ʃ'ɛkəʃ]
wallet	**carteira** (f)	[kɐrt'ɐjrɐ]
change purse	**porta-moedas** (m)	[p'ɔrtɐ mu'ɛdɐʃ]
billfold	**carteira** (f)	[kɐrt'ɐjrɐ]
safe	**cofre** (m)	[k'ɔfrə]
heir	**herdeiro** (m)	[erd'ɐjru]
inheritance	**herança** (f)	[er'ãsɐ]
fortune (wealth)	**fortuna** (f)	[furt'unɐ]
lease, rent	**arrendamento** (m)	[ɐʀẽdɐm'ẽtu]
rent money	**renda** (f) **de casa**	[ʀ'ẽdɐ də k'azɐ]
to rent (sth from sb)	**alugar** (vt)	[ɐlug'ar]
price	**preço** (m)	[pr'esu]
cost	**custo** (m)	[k'uʃtu]
sum	**soma** (f)	[s'omɐ]
to spend (vt)	**gastar** (vt)	[gɐʃt'ar]
expenses	**gastos** (m pl)	[g'aʃtuʃ]
to economize (vi, vt)	**economizar** (vi)	[ekɔnumiz'ar]
economical	**económico**	[ekun'ɔmiku]
to pay (vi, vt)	**pagar** (vt)	[pɐg'ar]
payment	**pagamento** (m)	[pɐgɐm'ẽtu]
change (give the ~)	**troco** (m)	[tr'oku]
tax	**imposto** (m)	[ĩp'oʃtu]
fine	**multa** (f)	[m'ultɐ]
to fine (vt)	**multar** (vt)	[mult'ar]

81. Post. Postal service

post office	**correios** (m pl)	[kuʀ'ɐjuʃ]
mail (letters, etc.)	**correio** (m)	[kuʀ'ɐju]
mailman	**carteiro** (m)	[kɐrt'ɐjru]
opening hours	**horário** (m)	[ɔr'ariu]
letter	**carta** (f)	[k'artɐ]
registered letter	**carta** (f) **registada**	[k'artɐ ʀəʒiʃt'adɐ]
postcard	**postal** (m)	[puʃt'al]
telegram	**telegrama** (m)	[tələgr'emɐ]

parcel	**encomenda** (f) **postal**	[ẽkum'ẽdɐ puʃt'al]
money transfer	**remessa** (f) **de dinheiro**	[ʀəm'ɛsɐ də diɲ'ɐjɾu]
to receive (vt)	**receber** (vt)	[ʀəsəb'eɾ]
to send (vt)	**enviar** (vt)	[ẽvj'aɾ]
sending	**envio** (m)	[ẽv'iu]
address	**endereço** (m)	[ẽdər'esu]
ZIP code	**código** (m) **postal**	[k'ɔdigu puʃt'al]
sender	**remetente** (m)	[ʀəmət'ẽtə]
receiver, addressee	**destinatário** (m)	[dəʃtinɐt'aɾiu]
name	**nome** (m)	[n'omə]
family name	**apelido** (m)	[ɐpəl'idu]
rate (of postage)	**tarifa** (f)	[tɐr'ifɐ]
standard (adj)	**normal**	[nɔɾm'al]
economical (adj)	**económico**	[ekun'ɔmiku]
weight	**peso** (m)	[p'ezu]
to weigh up (vt)	**pesar** (vt)	[pəz'aɾ]
envelope	**envelope** (m)	[ẽvəl'ɔpə]
postage stamp	**selo** (m)	[s'elu]
to stamp an envelope	**colar o selo**	[kul'aɾ u s'elu]

Dwelling. House. Home

82. House. Dwelling

house	**casa** (f)	[k'azɐ]
at home (adv)	**em casa**	[ẽ k'azɐ]
courtyard	**pátio** (m)	[p'atiu]
fence	**cerca** (f)	[s'erkɐ]
brick (n)	**tijolo** (m)	[tiʒ'olu]
brick (as adj)	**de tijolos**	[də tiʒ'ɔluʃ]
stone (n)	**pedra** (f)	[p'ɛdrɐ]
stone (as adj)	**de pedra**	[də p'ɛdrɐ]
concrete (n)	**betão** (m)	[bət'ãu]
concrete (as adj)	**de betão**	[də bət'ãu]
new (new-built)	**novo**	[n'ovu]
old (adj)	**velho**	[v'ɛʎu]
decrepit (house)	**decrépito**	[dəkr'ɛpitu]
modern (adj)	**moderno**	[mud'ɛrnu]
multistory (adj)	**de muitos andares**	[də m'ujtuʃ ãd'arəʃ]
high (adj)	**alto**	['altu]
floor, story	**andar** (m)	[ãd'ar]
single-story (adj)	**de um andar**	[də ũ ãd'ar]
ground floor	**andar** (m) **de baixo**	[ãdar də b'ajʃu]
top floor	**andar** (m) **de cima**	[ãdar də s'imɐ]
roof	**telhado** (m)	[təʎ'adu]
chimney (stack)	**chaminé** (f)	[ʃɐmin'ɛ]
roof tiles	**telha** (f)	[t'ɐʎɐ]
tiled (adj)	**de telha**	[də t'ɐʎɐ]
loft (attic)	**sótão** (m)	[s'ɔtãu]
window	**janela** (f)	[ʒɐn'ɛlɐ]
glass	**vidro** (m)	[v'idru]
window ledge	**parapeito** (m)	[pɐrɐp'ɐjtu]
shutters	**portadas** (f pl)	[purt'adɐʃ]
wall	**parede** (f)	[pɐr'edə]
balcony	**varanda** (f)	[vɐr'ãdɐ]
downspout	**tubo** (m) **de queda**	[t'ubu də k'ɛdɐ]
upstairs (to be ~)	**em cima**	[ẽ s'imɐ]
to go upstairs	**subir** (vi)	[sub'ir]
to come down	**descer** (vi)	[dəʃs'er]
to move (to new premises)	**mudar-se** (vp)	[mud'arsə]

83. House. Entrance. Lift

entrance	**entrada** (f)	[ẽtr'adɐ]
stairs (stairway)	**escada** (f)	[əʃk'adɐ]
steps	**degraus** (m pl)	[dəgr'auʃ]
banisters	**corrimão** (m)	[kuʀim'ãu]
lobby (hotel ~)	**hall** (m)	[ɔl]
mailbox	**caixa** (f) **de correio**	[k'ajʃɐ də kuʀ'ɐju]
trash container	**caixote** (m) **do lixo**	[kajʃ'ɔtə du l'iʃu]
trash chute	**conduta** (f) **do lixo**	[kõd'utɐ du l'iʃu]
elevator	**elevador** (m)	[eləvɐd'or]
freight elevator	**elevador** (m) **de carga**	[eləvɐd'or də k'argɐ]
elevator cage	**cabine** (f)	[kɐb'inə]
to take the elevator	**pegar o elevador**	[pəg'ar u eləvɐd'or]
apartment	**apartamento** (m)	[ɐpɐrtɐm'ẽtu]
residents, inhabitants	**moradores** (m pl)	[murɐd'orəʃ]
neighbor (masc.)	**vizinho** (m)	[viz'iɲu]
neighbor (fem.)	**vizinha** (f)	[viz'iɲɐ]
neighbors	**vizinhos** (pl)	[viz'iɲuʃ]

84. House. Doors. Locks

door	**porta** (f)	[p'ɔrtɐ]
vehicle gate	**portão** (m)	[purt'ãu]
handle, doorknob	**maçaneta** (f)	[mɐsɐn'etɐ]
to unlock (unbolt)	**destrancar** (vt)	[dəʃtrãk'ar]
to open (vt)	**abrir** (vt)	[ɐbr'ir]
to close (vt)	**fechar** (vt)	[fəʃ'ar]
key	**chave** (f)	[ʃ'avə]
bunch (of keys)	**molho** (m)	[m'oʎu]
to creak (door hinge)	**ranger** (vi)	[ʀãʒ'er]
creak	**rangido** (m)	[ʀãʒ'idu]
hinge (of door)	**dobradiça** (f)	[dubrɐd'isɐ]
doormat	**tapete** (m) **de entrada**	[tɐp'etə də ẽtr'adɐ]
door lock	**fechadura** (f)	[fəʃɐd'urɐ]
keyhole	**buraco** (m) **da fechadura**	[bur'aku dɐ fəʃɐd'urɐ]
bolt (sliding bar)	**ferrolho** (m)	[fəʀ'ɔʎu]
door latch	**ferrolho, fecho** (m)	[fəʀ'ɔʎu], [f'ɐʃu]
padlock	**cadeado** (m)	[kɐdj'adu]
to ring (~ the door bell)	**tocar** (vt)	[tuk'ar]
ringing (sound)	**toque** (m)	[t'ɔkə]
doorbell	**campainha** (f)	[kãpɐ'iɲɐ]
doorbell button	**botão** (m)	[but'ãu]

knock (at the door)	**batida** (f)	[bɐt'idɐ]
to knock (vi)	**bater** (vi)	[bɐt'er]
code	**código** (m)	[k'ɔdigu]
code lock	**fechadura** (f) **de código**	[fəʃɐd'urɐ də k'ɔdigu]
door phone	**telefone** (m) **de porta**	[tələf'ɔnə də p'ɔrtɐ]
number (on the door)	**número** (m)	[n'uməru]
doorplate	**placa** (f) **de porta**	[pl'akɐ də p'ɔrtɐ]
peephole	**vigia** (f), **olho** (m) **mágico**	[viʒ'iɐ], ['oʎu m'aʒiku]

85. Country house

village	**aldeia** (f)	[ald'ɐjɐ]
vegetable garden	**horta** (f)	['ɔrtɐ]
fence	**cerca** (f)	[s'erkɐ]
picket fence	**paliçada** (f)	[pɐlis'adɐ]
wicket gate	**cancela** (f)	[kɐ̃s'ɛlɐ]
granary	**celeiro** (m)	[səl'ɐjru]
cellar	**adega** (f)	[ɐd'ɛgɐ]
shed (in garden)	**galpão, barracão** (m)	[galp'ɐ̃u], [bɐʀɐk'ɐ̃u]
well (water)	**poço** (m)	[p'osu]
stove (wood-fired ~)	**fogão** (f)	[fug'ɐ̃u]
to stoke the stove	**atiçar o fogo**	[ɐtis'ar u f'ogu]
firewood	**lenha** (f)	[l'ɐɲɐ]
log (firewood)	**acha, lenha** (f)	[aʃɐ], [l'ɐɲɐ]
veranda, stoop	**varanda** (f)	[vɐr'ɐ̃dɐ]
terrace (patio)	**alpendre** (m)	[alp'ẽdrə]
front steps	**degraus** (m pl) **de entrada**	[dəgr'auʃ də ẽtr'adɐ]
swing (hanging seat)	**balouço** (m)	[bɐl'osu]

86. Castle. Palace

castle	**castelo** (m)	[kɐʃt'ɛlu]
palace	**palácio** (m)	[pɐl'asiu]
fortress	**fortaleza** (f)	[furtɐl'ezɐ]
wall (round castle)	**muralha** (f)	[mur'aʎɐ]
tower	**torre** (f)	[t'oʀə]
keep, donjon	**torre** (f) **de menagem**	[t'oʀə də mən'aʒẽj]
portcullis	**grade** (f)	[gr'adə]
underground passage	**passagem** (f) **subterrânea**	[pɐs'aʒẽj subtəʀ'ɐniɐ]
moat	**fosso** (m)	[f'osu]
chain	**corrente, cadeia** (f)	[kuʀ'ẽtə], [kɐd'ɐjɐ]
arrow loop	**seteira** (f)	[sət'ɐjrɐ]

magnificent (adj)	**magnífico**	[magn'ifiku]
majestic (adj)	**majestoso**	[mɐʒəʃt'ozu]
impregnable (adj)	**inexpugnável**	[inəʃpugn'avɛl]
medieval (adj)	**medieval**	[mədiɛv'al]

87. Apartment

apartment	**apartamento** (m)	[ɐpɐrtɐm'ẽtu]
room	**quarto** (m)	[ku'artu]
bedroom	**quarto** (m) **de dormir**	[ku'artu də durm'ir]
dining room	**sala** (f) **de jantar**	[s'alɐ də ʒɐ̃t'ar]
living room	**sala** (f) **de estar**	[s'alɐ də əʃt'ar]
study (home office)	**escritório** (m)	[əʃkrit'ɔriu]
entry room	**antessala** (f)	[ɐ̃təs'alɐ]
bathroom	**quarto** (m) **de banho**	[ku'artu də b'ɐɲu]
half bath	**quarto** (m) **de banho**	[ku'artu də b'ɐɲu]
ceiling	**teto** (m)	[t'ɛtu]
floor	**chão, soalho** (m)	[ʃ'ɐ̃u], [su'aʎu]
corner	**canto** (m)	[k'ɐ̃tu]

88. Apartment. Cleaning

to clean (vi, vt)	**arrumar, limpar** (vt)	[ɐʀum'ar], [lĩp'ar]
to put away (to stow)	**arrumar, guardar** (vt)	[ɐʀum'ar], [guɐrd'ar]
dust	**pó** (m)	[pɔ]
dusty (adj)	**empoeirado**	[ẽpɔɐjr'adu]
to dust (vt)	**limpar o pó**	[lĩp'ar u pɔ]
vacuum cleaner	**aspirador** (m)	[ɐʃpirɐd'or]
to vacuum (vt)	**aspirar** (vt)	[ɐʃpir'ar]
to sweep (vi, vt)	**varrer** (vt)	[vɐʀ'er]
sweepings	**varredura** (f), **cisco** (m)	[vɐʀəd'urɐ], [s'iʃku]
order	**arrumação** (f), **ordem** (f)	[ɐʀumɐs'ɐ̃u], ['ɔrdẽj]
disorder, mess	**desordem** (f)	[dəz'ɔrdẽj]
mop	**esfregona** (f)	[əʃfrəg'onɐ]
dust cloth	**pano** (m), **trapo** (m)	[p'ɐnu], [tr'apu]
broom	**vassoura** (f)	[vɐs'orɐ]
dustpan	**pá** (f) **de lixo**	[pa də l'iʃu]

89. Furniture. Interior

furniture	**mobiliário** (m)	[mubilj'ariu]
table	**mesa** (f)	[m'ezɐ]

chair	**cadeira** (f)	[kɐd'ɐjrɐ]
bed	**cama** (f)	[k'ɐmɐ]
couch, sofa	**divã** (m)	[div'ã]
armchair	**cadeirão** (m)	[kɐdɐjr'ãu]
bookcase	**biblioteca** (f)	[bibliut'ɛkɐ]
shelf	**prateleira** (f)	[prɐtəl'ɐjrɐ]
set of shelves	**estante** (f)	[əʃt'ãtə]
wardrobe	**guarda-vestidos** (m)	[gu'ardɐ vəʃt'iduʃ]
coat rack	**cabide** (m) **de parede**	[kɐb'idə də pɐr'edə]
coat stand	**cabide** (m) **de pé**	[kɐb'idə də pɛ]
dresser	**cómoda** (f)	[k'ɔmudɐ]
coffee table	**mesinha** (f) **de centro**	[məz'iɲɐ də s'ẽtru]
mirror	**espelho** (m)	[əʃp'ɐʎu]
carpet	**tapete** (m)	[tɐp'etə]
rug, small carpet	**tapete** (m) **pequeno**	[tɐp'etə pək'enu]
fireplace	**lareira** (f)	[lɐr'ɐjrɐ]
candle	**vela** (f)	[v'ɛlɐ]
candlestick	**castiçal** (m)	[kɐʃtis'al]
drapes	**cortinas** (f pl)	[kurt'inɐʃ]
wallpaper	**papel** (m) **de parede**	[pɐp'ɛl də pɐr'edə]
blinds (jalousie)	**estores** (f pl)	[əʃt'orəʃ]
table lamp	**candeeiro** (m) **de mesa**	[kãdj'ɐjru də m'ezɐ]
wall lamp (sconce)	**candeeiro** (m) **de parede**	[kãdj'ɐjru də pɐr'edə]
floor lamp	**candeeiro** (m) **de pé**	[kãdj'ɐjru də pɛ]
chandelier	**lustre** (m)	[l'uʃtrə]
leg (of chair, table)	**perna** (f)	[p'ɛrnɐ]
armrest	**braço** (m)	[br'asu]
back (backrest)	**costas** (f pl)	[k'ɔʃtɐʃ]
drawer	**gaveta** (f)	[gɐv'etɐ]

90. Bedding

bedclothes	**roupa** (f) **de cama**	[ʀ'opɐ də k'ɐmɐ]
pillow	**almofada** (f)	[almuf'adɐ]
pillowcase	**fronha** (f)	[fr'oɲɐ]
blanket (comforter)	**cobertor** (m)	[kubərt'or]
sheet	**lençol** (m)	[lẽs'ɔl]
bedspread	**colcha** (f)	[k'olʃɐ]

91. Kitchen

kitchen	**cozinha** (f)	[kuz'iɲɐ]
gas	**gás** (m)	[gaʃ]
gas cooker	**fogão** (m) **a gás**	[fug'ãu ɐ gaʃ]
electric cooker	**fogão** (m) **elétrico**	[fug'ãu el'ɛtriku]
oven	**forno** (m)	[f'ornu]
microwave oven	**forno** (m) **de micro-ondas**	[f'ornu də mikrɔ'õdɐʃ]
refrigerator	**frigorífico** (m)	[frigur'ifiku]
freezer	**congelador** (m)	[kõʒəlɐd'or]
dishwasher	**máquina** (f) **de lavar louça**	[m'akinɐ də lɐv'ar l'osɐ]
meat grinder	**moedor** (m) **de carne**	[muəd'or də k'arnə]
juicer	**espremedor** (m)	[əʃprəməd'or]
toaster	**torradeira** (f)	[tuʀɐd'ɐjrɐ]
mixer	**batedeira** (f)	[bɐtəd'ɐjrɐ]
coffee maker	**máquina** (f) **de café**	[m'akinɐ də kɐf'ɛ]
coffee pot	**cafeteira** (f)	[kɐfət'ɐjrɐ]
coffee grinder	**moinho** (m) **de café**	[mu'iɲu də kɐf'ɛ]
kettle	**chaleira** (f)	[ʃɐl'ɐjrɐ]
teapot	**bule** (m)	[b'ulə]
lid	**tampa** (f)	[t'ãpɐ]
tea strainer	**coador** (f) **de chá**	[kuɐd'or də ʃa]
spoon	**colher** (f)	[kuʎ'ɛr]
teaspoon	**colher** (f) **de chá**	[kuʎ'ɛr də ʃa]
tablespoon	**colher** (f) **de sopa**	[kuʎ'ɛr də s'opɐ]
fork	**garfo** (m)	[g'arfu]
knife	**faca** (f)	[f'akɐ]
tableware (dishes)	**louça** (f)	[l'osɐ]
plate (dinner ~)	**prato** (m)	[pr'atu]
saucer	**pires** (m)	[p'irəʃ]
shot glass	**cálice** (m)	[k'alisə]
glass (~ of water)	**copo** (m)	[k'ɔpu]
cup	**chávena** (f)	[ʃ'avənɐ]
sugar bowl	**açucareiro** (m)	[ɐsukɐr'ɐjru]
salt shaker	**saleiro** (m)	[sɐl'ɐjru]
pepper shaker	**pimenteiro** (m)	[pimẽt'ɐjru]
butter dish	**manteigueira** (f)	[mãtiig'ɐjrɐ]
saucepan	**panela** (f)	[pɐn'ɛlɐ]
frying pan	**frigideira** (f)	[friʒid'ɐjrɐ]
ladle	**concha** (f)	[k'õʃɐ]
colander	**passador** (m)	[pɐsɐd'or]

tray	**bandeja** (f)	[bãd'eʒɐ]
bottle	**garrafa** (f)	[gɐʀ'afɐ]
jar (glass)	**boião** (m) **de vidro**	[boj'ãu də v'idru]
can	**lata** (f)	[l'atɐ]
bottle opener	**abridor** (m) **de garrafas**	[ɐbrid'or də gɐʀ'afɐʃ]
can opener	**abre-latas** (m)	[abrə l'atɐʃ]
corkscrew	**saca-rolhas** (m)	[s'akɐ ʀ'oʎɐʃ]
filter	**filtro** (m)	[f'iltru]
to filter (vt)	**filtrar** (vt)	[filtr'ar]
trash	**lixo** (m)	[l'iʃu]
trash can	**balde** (m) **do lixo**	[b'aldə du l'iʃu]

92. Bathroom

bathroom	**quarto** (m) **de banho**	[ku'artu də b'ɐɲu]
water	**água** (f)	['aguɐ]
tap, faucet	**torneira** (f)	[turn'ɐjrɐ]
hot water	**água** (f) **quente**	['aguɐ k'ẽtə]
cold water	**água** (f) **fria**	['aguɐ fr'iɐ]
toothpaste	**pasta** (f) **de dentes**	[p'aʃtɐ də d'ẽtəʃ]
to brush one's teeth	**escovar os dentes**	[əʃkuv'ar uʃ d'ẽtəʃ]
toothbrush	**escova** (f) **de dentes**	[əʃk'ovɐ də d'ẽtəʃ]
to shave (vi)	**barbear-se** (vp)	[bɐrbj'arsə]
shaving foam	**espuma** (f) **de barbear**	[əʃp'umɐ də bɐrbj'ar]
razor	**máquina** (f) **de barbear**	[m'akinɐ də bɐrbi'ar]
to wash (one's hands, etc.)	**lavar** (vt)	[lɐv'ar]
to take a bath	**lavar-se** (vp)	[lɐv'arsə]
shower	**duche** (m)	[d'uʃə]
to take a shower	**tomar um duche**	[tum'ar ũ d'uʃə]
bathtub	**banheira** (f)	[bɐɲ'ɐjrɐ]
toilet (toilet bowl)	**sanita** (f)	[sɐn'itɐ]
sink (washbasin)	**lavatório** (m)	[lɐvɐt'ɔriu]
soap	**sabonete** (m)	[sɐbun'etə]
soap dish	**saboneteira** (f)	[sɐbunət'ɐjrɐ]
sponge	**esponja** (f)	[əʃp'õʒɐ]
shampoo	**champô** (m)	[ʃãp'o]
towel	**toalha** (f)	[tu'aʎɐ]
bathrobe	**roupão** (m) **de banho**	[ʀop'ãu də b'ɐɲu]
laundry (process)	**lavagem** (f)	[lɐv'aʒẽj]
washing machine	**máquina** (f) **de lavar**	[m'akinɐ də lɐv'ar]
to do the laundry	**lavar a roupa**	[lɐv'ar ɐ ʀ'opɐ]
laundry detergent	**detergente** (m)	[dətərʒ'ẽtə]

93. Household appliances

TV set	**televisor** (m)	[təleviz'or]
tape recorder	**gravador** (m)	[grɐvɐd'or]
video, VCR	**videogravador** (m)	[vidiɔgrɐvɐd'or]
radio	**rádio** (m)	[ʀ'adiu]
player (CD, MP3, etc.)	**leitor** (m)	[ləjt'or]
video projector	**projetor** (m)	[pruʒɛt'or]
home movie theater	**cinema** (m) **em casa**	[sin'emɐ ẽ k'azɐ]
DVD player	**leitor** (m) **de DVD**	[ləjt'or də dɛvɛd'e]
amplifier	**amplificador** (m)	[ãplifikɐd'or]
video game console	**console** (f) **de jogos**	[kõs'ɔlə də ʒ'ɔguʃ]
video camera	**câmara** (f) **de vídeo**	[k'ɐmɐrɐ də v'idiu]
camera (photo)	**máquina** (f) **fotográfica**	[m'akinɐ futugr'afikɐ]
digital camera	**câmara** (f) **digital**	[k'ɐmɐrɐ diʒit'al]
vacuum cleaner	**aspirador** (m)	[ɐʃpirɐd'or]
iron (e.g., steam ~)	**ferro** (m) **de engomar**	[f'ɛʀu də ẽgum'ar]
ironing board	**tábua** (f) **de engomar**	[t'abuɐ də ẽgum'ar]
telephone	**telefone** (m)	[tələf'ɔnə]
mobile phone	**telemóvel** (m)	[tɛlɛm'ɔvɛl]
typewriter	**máquina** (f) **de escrever**	[m'akinɐ də əʃkrəv'er]
sewing machine	**máquina** (f) **de costura**	[m'akinɐ də kuʃt'urɐ]
microphone	**microfone** (m)	[mikrɔf'ɔnə]
headphones	**auscultadores** (m pl)	[auʃkultɐd'orəʃ]
remote control (TV)	**controlo remoto** (m)	[kõtr'olu ʀəm'ɔtu]
CD, compact disc	**CD** (m)	[s'ɛdɛ]
cassette	**cassete** (f)	[kas'ɛtə]
vinyl record	**disco** (m) **de vinil**	[d'iʃku də vin'il]

94. Repairs. Renovation

renovations	**renovação** (f)	[ʀənuvɐs'ãu]
to renovate (vt)	**renovar** (vt), **fazer obras**	[ʀənuv'ar], [fɐz'er 'ɔbrɐʃ]
to repair (vt)	**reparar** (vt)	[ʀəpɐr'ar]
to put in order	**arranjar** (vt)	[ɐʀãʒ'ar]
to redo (do again)	**refazer** (vt)	[ʀəfɐz'er]
paint	**tinta** (f)	[t'ĩtɐ]
to paint (~ a wall)	**pintar** (vt)	[pĩt'ar]
house painter	**pintor** (m)	[pĩt'or]
paintbrush	**pincel** (m)	[pĩs'ɛl]
whitewash	**cal** (f)	[kal]
to whitewash (vt)	**caiar** (vt)	[kaj'ar]

wallpaper	**papel** (m) **de parede**	[pɐp'ɛl də pər'edə]
to wallpaper (vt)	**colar o papel**	[kul'ar u pɐp'ɛl]
varnish	**verniz** (m)	[vərn'iʒ]
to varnish (vt)	**envernizar** (vt)	[ẽvərniz'ar]

95. Plumbing

water	**água** (f)	['aguɐ]
hot water	**água** (f) **quente**	['aguɐ k'ẽtə]
cold water	**água** (f) **fria**	['aguɐ fr'iɐ]
tap, faucet	**torneira** (f)	[turn'ɐjrɐ]
drop (of water)	**gota** (f)	[g'otɐ]
to drip (vi)	**gotejar** (vi)	[gɔtəʒ'ar]
to leak (ab. pipe)	**vazar** (vt)	[vɐz'ar]
leak (pipe ~)	**vazamento** (m)	[vɐzɐm'ẽtu]
puddle	**poça** (f)	[p'ɔsɐ]
pipe	**tubo** (m)	[t'ubu]
stop valve	**válvula** (f)	[v'alvulɐ]
to be clogged up	**entupir-se** (vp)	[ẽtup'irsə]
tools	**ferramentas** (f pl)	[fəʀɐm'ẽtɐʃ]
adjustable wrench	**chave** (f) **inglesa**	[ʃ'avə ĩgl'ezɐ]
to unscrew, untwist (vt)	**desenroscar** (vt)	[dəzẽʀuʃk'ar]
to screw (tighten)	**enroscar** (vt)	[ẽʀuʃk'ar]
to unclog (vt)	**desentupir** (vt)	[dəzẽtup'ir]
plumber	**canalizador** (m)	[kɐnɐlizɐd'or]
basement	**cave** (f)	[k'avə]
sewerage (system)	**sistema** (m) **de esgotos**	[siʃt'emɐ də əʒg'ɔtuʃ]

96. Fire. Conflagration

fire (to catch ~)	**fogo** (m)	[f'ogu]
flame	**chama** (f)	[ʃ'ɐmɐ]
spark	**faísca** (f)	[fɐ'iʃkɐ]
smoke (from fire)	**fumo** (m)	[f'umu]
torch (flaming stick)	**tocha** (f)	[t'ɔʃɐ]
campfire	**fogueira** (f)	[fug'ɐjrɐ]
gas, gasoline	**gasolina** (f)	[gɐzul'inɐ]
kerosene (for aircraft)	**querosene** (m)	[kəruz'ɛnə]
flammable (adj)	**inflamável**	[ĩflɐm'avɛl]
explosive (adj)	**explosivo**	[əʃpluz'ivu]
NO SMOKING	**PROIBIDO FUMAR!**	[pruib'idu fum'ar]
safety	**segurança** (f)	[səgur'ãsɐ]
danger	**perigo** (m)	[pər'igu]

dangerous (adj)	**perigoso**	[pərig'ozu]
to catch fire	**incendiar-se** (vp)	[ĩsẽdj'arsə]
explosion	**explosão** (f)	[əʃpluz'ãu]
to set fire	**incendiar** (vt)	[ĩsẽdj'ar]
incendiary (arsonist)	**incendiário** (m)	[ĩsẽdj'ariu]
arson	**incêndio** (m) **criminoso**	[ĩs'ẽdiu krimin'ozu]
to blaze (vi)	**arder** (vi)	[ɐrd'er]
to burn (be on fire)	**queimar** (vi)	[kɐjm'ar]
to burn down	**queimar tudo** (vi)	[kɐjm'ar t'udu]
to call the fire department	**chamar os bombeiros**	[ʃɐm'ar uʃ bõb'ɐjruʃ]
fireman	**bombeiro** (m)	[bõb'ɐjru]
fire truck	**carro** (m) **de bombeiros**	[k'aʀu də bõb'ɐjruʃ]
fire department	**corpo** (m) **de bombeiros**	[k'orpu də bõb'ɐjruʃ]
fire truck ladder	**escada** (f) **extensivel**	[əʃk'adɐ əʃtẽsiv'ɛl]
fire hose	**mangueira** (f)	[mãg'ɐjrɐ]
fire extinguisher	**extintor** (m)	[əʃtĩt'or]
helmet	**capacete** (m)	[kɐpɐs'etə]
siren	**sirene** (f)	[sir'ɛnə]
to call out	**gritar** (vi)	[grit'ar]
to call for help	**chamar por socorro**	[ʃɐm'ar pur suk'oʀu]
rescuer	**salvador** (m)	[salvɐd'or]
to rescue (vt)	**salvar, resgatar** (vt)	[salv'ar], [ʀəʒgɐt'ar]
to arrive (vi)	**chegar** (vi)	[ʃəg'ar]
to extinguish (vt)	**apagar** (vt)	[ɐpɐg'ar]
water	**água** (f)	['agwɐ]
sand	**areia** (f)	[ɐr'ɐjɐ]
ruins (destruction)	**ruínas** (f pl)	[ʀu'inɐʃ]
to collapse (building, etc.)	**ruir** (vi)	[ʀu'ir]
to fall down (vi)	**desmoronar** (vi),	[dəʒmurun'ar]
to cave in (ceiling, floor)	**ir abaixo**	[ir ɐb'ajʃu]
piece of wreckage	**fragmento** (m)	[fragm'ẽtu]
ash	**cinza** (f)	[s'ĩzɐ]
to suffocate (die)	**sufocar** (vi)	[sufuk'ar]
to be killed (perish)	**ser morto, morrer** (vi)	[ser m'ortu], [muʀ'er]

HUMAN ACTIVITIES

Job. Business. Part 1

97. Banking

bank	**banco** (m)	[b'ãku]
branch (of bank, etc.)	**sucursal, balcão** (f)	[sukurs'al], [balk'ãu]
bank clerk, consultant	**consultor** (m)	[kõsult'or]
manager (director)	**gerente** (m)	[ʒər'ẽtə]
banking account	**conta** (f)	[k'õtɐ]
account number	**número** (m) **da conta**	[n'uməru dɐ k'õtɐ]
checking account	**conta** (f) **corrente**	[k'õtɐ kuʀ'ẽtə]
savings account	**conta** (f) **poupança**	[k'õtɐ pop'ãsɐ]
to open an account	**abrir uma conta**	[ɐbr'ir 'umɐ k'õtɐ]
to close the account	**fechar uma conta**	[fəʃ'ar 'umɐ k'õtɐ]
to deposit into the account	**depositar na conta**	[dəpuzit'ar nɐ k'õtɐ]
to withdraw (vt)	**levantar** (vt)	[ləvãt'ar]
deposit	**depósito** (m)	[dəp'ɔzitu]
to make a deposit	**fazer um depósito**	[fɐz'er ũ dəp'ɔzitu]
wire transfer	**transferência** (f) **bancária**	[trãʃfər'ẽsiɐ bãk'ariɐ]
to wire, to transfer	**transferir** (vt)	[trãʃfər'ir]
sum	**soma** (f)	[s'omɐ]
How much?	**Quanto?**	[ku'ãtu]
signature	**assinatura** (f)	[ɐsinɐt'urɐ]
to sign (vt)	**assinar** (vt)	[ɐsin'ar]
credit card	**cartão** (m) **de crédito**	[kɐrt'ãu də kr'ɛditu]
code	**código** (m)	[k'ɔdigu]
credit card number	**número** (m) **do cartão de crédito**	[n'uməru du kɐrt'ãu də kr'ɛditu]
ATM	**Caixa Multibanco** (m)	[k'ajʃɐ multib'ãku]
check	**cheque** (m)	[ʃ'ɛkə]
to write a check	**passar um cheque**	[pɐs'ar ũ ʃ'ɛkə]
checkbook	**livro** (m) **de cheques**	[l'ivru də ʃ'ɛkəʃ]
loan (bank ~)	**empréstimo** (m)	[ẽpr'ɛʃtimu]
to apply for a loan	**pedir um empréstimo**	[pəd'ir un ẽpr'ɛʃtimu]

to get a loan	**obter um empréstimo**	[ɔbt'er un ẽpr'ɛʃtimu]
to give a loan	**conceder um empréstimo**	[kõsəd'er un ẽpr'ɛʃtimu]
guarantee	**garantia** (f)	[gɐrãt'iɐ]

98. Telephone. Phone conversation

telephone	**telefone** (m)	[tələf'ɔnə]
mobile phone	**telemóvel** (m)	[tɛlɛm'ɔvɛl]
answering machine	**atendedor** (m) **de chamadas**	[ɐtẽdəd'or də ʃɐm'adɐʃ]
to call (telephone)	**fazer uma chamada**	[fɐz'er 'umɐ ʃɐm'adɐ]
phone call	**chamada** (f)	[ʃɐm'adɐ]
to dial a number	**marcar um número**	[mɐrk'ar ũ n'uməru]
Hello!	**Alô!**	[ɐl'o]
to ask (vt)	**perguntar** (vt)	[pərgũt'ar]
to answer (vi, vt)	**responder** (vt)	[ʀəʃpõd'er]
to hear (vt)	**ouvir** (vt)	[ov'ir]
well (adv)	**bem**	[bẽj]
not well (adv)	**mal**	[mal]
noises (interference)	**ruído** (m)	[ʀu'idu]
receiver	**auscultador** (m)	[auʃkultɐd'or]
to pick up (~ the phone)	**pegar o telefone**	[pəg'ar u tələf'ɔnə]
to hang up (~ the phone)	**desligar** (vi)	[dəʒlig'ar]
busy (adj)	**ocupado**	[ɔkup'adu]
to ring (ab. phone)	**tocar** (vi)	[tuk'ar]
telephone book	**lista** (f) **telefónica**	[l'iʃtɐ tələf'ɔnikɐ]
local (adj)	**local**	[luk'al]
local call	**chamada** (f) **local**	[ʃɐm'adɐ luk'al]
long distance (~ call)	**para outra cidade**	[p'ɐrɐ 'otrɐ sid'adə]
long-distance call	**chamada** (f) **para outra cidade**	[ʃɐm'adɐ p'ɐrɐ 'otrɐ sid'adə]
international (adj)	**internacional**	[ĩtərnɐsiun'al]
international call	**chamada** (f) **internacional**	[ʃɐm'adɐ ĩtərnɐsiun'al]

99. Mobile telephone

mobile phone	**telemóvel** (m)	[tɛlɛm'ɔvɛl]
display	**ecrã** (m)	[ɛkr'ã]
button	**botão** (m)	[but'ãu]
SIM card	**cartão SIM** (m)	[kɐrt'ãu sim]
battery	**bateria** (f)	[bɐtər'iɐ]

to be dead (battery)	**descarregar-se**	[dəʃkɐʀəg'arsə]
charger	**carregador** (m)	[kɐʀəgɐd'or]
menu	**menu** (m)	[mɛn'u]
settings	**definições** (f pl)	[dəfinis'ojʃ]
tune (melody)	**melodia** (f)	[məlud'iɐ]
to select (vt)	**escolher** (vt)	[əʃkuʎ'er]
calculator	**calculadora** (f)	[kalkulɐd'orɐ]
voice mail	**atendedor de chamadas** (m)	[ɐtẽdəd'or də ʃɐm'adɐʃ]
alarm clock	**despertador** (m)	[dəʃpərtɐd'or]
contacts	**contatos** (m pl)	[kõt'atuʃ]
SMS (text message)	**mensagem** (f) **de texto**	[mẽs'aʒẽj də t'ɛʃtu]
subscriber	**assinante** (m)	[ɐsin'ãtə]

100. Stationery

ballpoint pen	**caneta** (f)	[kɐn'etɐ]
fountain pen	**caneta** (f) **tinteiro**	[kɐn'etɐ tĩt'ɐjru]
pencil	**lápis** (m)	[l'apiʃ]
highlighter	**marcador** (m)	[mɐrkɐd'or]
felt-tip pen	**caneta** (f) **de feltro**	[kɐn'etɐ də f'eltru]
notepad	**bloco** (m) **de notas**	[bl'ɔku də n'ɔtɐʃ]
agenda (diary)	**agenda** (f)	[ɐʒ'ẽdɐ]
ruler	**régua** (f)	[ʀ'ɛguɐ]
calculator	**calculadora** (f)	[kalkulɐd'orɐ]
eraser	**borracha** (f)	[buʀ'aʃɐ]
thumbtack	**pionés** (m)	[piun'ɛʃ]
paper clip	**clipe** (m)	[kl'ipə]
glue	**cola** (f)	[k'ɔlɐ]
stapler	**agrafador** (m)	[ɐgrɐfɐd'or]
hole punch	**furador** (m)	[furɐd'or]
pencil sharpener	**afia-lápis** (m)	[ɐf'iɐ l'apiʃ]

Job. Business. Part 2

101. Mass Media

newspaper	**jornal** (m)	[ʒurn'al]
magazine	**revista** (f)	[Rəv'iʃtɐ]
press (printed media)	**imprensa** (f)	[ĩpr'ẽsɐ]
radio	**rádio** (m)	[R'adiu]
radio station	**estação** (f) **de rádio**	[əʃtes'ãu də R'adiu]
television	**televisão** (f)	[tələviz'ãu]
presenter, host	**apresentador** (m)	[ɐprəzẽted'or]
newscaster	**locutor** (m)	[lukut'or]
commentator	**comentador** (m)	[kumẽted'or]
journalist	**jornalista** (m)	[ʒurnɐl'iʃtɐ]
correspondent (reporter)	**correspondente** (m)	[kuRəʃpõd'ẽtə]
press photographer	**repórter** (m) **fotográfico**	[Rəp'ɔrtɛr futugr'afiku]
reporter	**repórter** (m)	[Rəp'ɔrtɛr]
editor	**redator** (m)	[Rədat'or]
editor-in-chief	**redator-chefe** (m)	[Rədat'or ʃ'ɛfə]
to subscribe (to ...)	**assinar a ...**	[ɐsin'ar ɐ]
subscription	**assinatura** (f)	[ɐsinɐt'urɐ]
subscriber	**assinante** (m)	[ɐsin'ãtə]
to read (vi, vt)	**ler** (vt)	[ler]
reader	**leitor** (m)	[ləjt'or]
circulation (of newspaper)	**tiragem** (f)	[tir'aʒẽj]
monthly (adj)	**mensal**	[mẽs'al]
weekly (adj)	**semanal**	[səmɐn'al]
issue (edition)	**número** (m)	[n'umәru]
new (~ issue)	**recente**	[Rəs'ẽtə]
headline	**título** (m)	[t'itulu]
short article	**pequeno artigo** (m)	[pək'enu ɐrt'igu]
column (regular article)	**rubrica** (f)	[Rubr'ikɐ]
article	**artigo** (m)	[ɐrt'igu]
page	**página** (f)	[p'aʒinɐ]
reportage, report	**reportagem** (f)	[Rəpurt'aʒẽj]
event (happening)	**evento** (m)	[ev'ẽtu]
sensation (news)	**sensação** (f)	[sẽsɐs'ãu]
scandal	**escândalo** (m)	[əʃk'ãdɐlu]
scandalous (adj)	**escandaloso**	[əʃkãdɐl'ozu]

great (~ scandal)	**grande**	[gr'ãdə]
program	**programa** (m) **de TV**	[prugr'emɐ də tɛv'ɛ]
interview	**entrevista** (f)	[ẽtrəv'iʃtɐ]
live broadcast	**transmissão** (f) **em direto**	[trãʒmis'ãu ẽ dir'ɛtu]
channel	**canal** (m)	[kɐn'al]

102. Agriculture

agriculture	**agricultura** (f)	[ɐgrikult'urɐ]
peasant (masc.)	**camponês** (m)	[kãpun'eʃ]
peasant (fem.)	**camponesa** (f)	[kãpun'ezɐ]
farmer	**agricultor** (m)	[ɐgrikult'or]
tractor	**trator** (m)	[trat'or]
combine, harvester	**ceifeira-debulhadora** (f)	[sɐjfɐjrɐ dəbuʎɐd'orɐ]
plow	**arado** (m)	[ɐr'adu]
to plow (vi, vt)	**arar** (vt)	[ɐr'ar]
plowland	**campo** (m) **lavrado**	[k'ãpu lɐvr'adu]
furrow (in field)	**rego** (m)	[ʀ'egu]
to sow (vi, vt)	**semear** (vt)	[səmj'ar]
seeder	**semeadora** (f)	[səmiɐd'orɐ]
sowing (process)	**semeação** (f)	[səmiɐs'ãu]
scythe	**gadanha** (m)	[gɐd'ɐɲɐ]
to mow, to scythe	**gadanhar** (vt)	[gɐdɐɲ'ar]
spade (tool)	**pá** (f)	[pa]
to dig (to till)	**cavar** (vt)	[kɐv'ar]
hoe	**enxada** (f)	[ẽʃ'adɐ]
to hoe, to weed	**carpir** (vt)	[kɐrp'ir]
weed (plant)	**erva** (f) **daninha**	['ɛrvɐ dɐn'iɲɐ]
watering can	**regador** (m)	[ʀəgɐd'or]
to water (plants)	**regar** (vt)	[ʀəg'ar]
watering (act)	**rega** (f)	[ʀ'ɛgɐ]
pitchfork	**forquilha** (f)	[fɔrk'iʎɐ]
rake	**ancinho** (m)	[ãs'iɲu]
fertilizer	**fertilizante** (m)	[fərtiliz'ãtə]
to fertilize (vt)	**fertilizar** (vt)	[fərtiliz'ar]
manure (fertilizer)	**estrume** (m)	[əʃtr'umə]
field	**campo** (m)	[k'ãpu]
meadow	**prado** (m)	[pr'adu]
vegetable garden	**horta** (f)	['ɔrtɐ]
orchard (e.g., apple ~)	**pomar** (m)	[pum'ar]

to pasture (vt)	**pastar** (vt)	[pɐʃt'ar]
herdsman	**pastor** (m)	[pɐʃt'or]
pastureland	**pastagem** (f)	[pɐʃt'aʒẽj]
cattle breeding	**pecuária** (f)	[pəku'ariɐ]
sheep farming	**criação** (f) **de ovelhas**	[kriɐs'ãu də ɔv'ɐʎɐʃ]
plantation	**plantação** (f)	[plãtɐs'ãu]
row (garden bed ~s)	**canteiro** (m)	[kãt'ɐjru]
hothouse	**invernadouro** (m)	[ĩvərnɐd'oru]
drought (lack of rain)	**seca** (f)	[s'ekɐ]
dry (~ summer)	**seco**	[s'eku]
grain	**cereal** (m)	[sərj'al]
cereal crops	**cereais** (m pl)	[sərj'ajʃ]
to harvest, to gather	**colher** (vt)	[kuʎ'ɛr]
miller (person)	**moleiro** (m)	[mul'ɐjru]
mill (e.g., gristmill)	**moinho** (m)	[mu'iɲu]
to grind (grain)	**moer** (vt)	[mu'ɛr]
flour	**farinha** (f)	[fɐr'iɲɐ]
straw	**palha** (f)	[p'aʎɐ]

103. Building. Building process

construction site	**canteiro** (m) **de obras**	[kãt'ɐjru də 'ɔbrɐʃ]
to build (vt)	**construir** (vt)	[kõʃtru'ir]
construction worker	**construtor** (m)	[kõʃtrut'or]
project	**projeto** (m)	[pruʒ'ɛtu]
architect	**arquiteto** (m)	[ɐrkit'ɛtu]
worker	**operário** (m)	[ɔpər'ariu]
foundation (of building)	**fundação** (f)	[fũdɐs'ãu]
roof	**telhado** (m)	[təʎ'adu]
foundation pile	**estaca** (f)	[əʃt'akɐ]
wall	**parede** (f)	[pɐr'edə]
reinforcing bars	**varões** (m pl) **para betão**	[vɐr'ojʃ p'ɐrɐ bət'ãu]
scaffolding	**andaime** (m)	[ãd'ajmə]
concrete	**betão** (m)	[bət'ãu]
granite	**granito** (m)	[grɐn'itu]
stone	**pedra** (f)	[p'ɛdrɐ]
brick	**tijolo** (m)	[tiʒ'olu]
sand	**areia** (f)	[ɐr'ɐjɐ]
cement	**cimento** (m)	[sim'ẽtu]
plaster (for walls)	**emboço** (m)	[ẽb'ɔsu]

to plaster (vt) | **emboçar** (vt) | [ẽbus'aɾ]
paint | **tinta** (f) | [t'ĩtɐ]
to paint (~ a wall) | **pintar** (vt) | [pĩt'aɾ]
barrel | **barril** (m) | [bɐʀ'il]

crane | **grua** (f), **guindaste** (m) | [gɾ'uɐ], [gĩd'aʃtə]
to lift (vt) | **erguer** (vt) | [erg'eɾ]
to lower (vt) | **baixar** (vt) | [bajʃ'aɾ]

bulldozer | **buldózer** (m) | [buld'ɔzəɾ]
excavator | **escavadora** (f) | [əʃkɐvɐd'oɾɐ]
scoop, bucket | **caçamba** (f) | [kɐs'ãbɐ]
to dig (excavate) | **escavar** (vt) | [əʃkɐv'aɾ]
hard hat | **capacete** (m) **de proteção** | [kɐpɐs'etə də prutɛs'ãu]

Professions and occupations

104. Job search. Dismissal

job	**trabalho** (m)	[trɐb'aʎu]
staff (work force)	**equipa** (f)	[ek'ipɐ]
personnel	**pessoal** (m)	[pəsu'al]
career	**carreira** (f)	[kɐʀ'ɐjrɐ]
prospects	**perspetivas** (f pl)	[pərʃpɛt'ivɐʃ]
skills (mastery)	**mestria** (f)	[mɛʃtr'iɐ]
selection (screening)	**seleção** (f)	[səlɛs'ãu]
employment agency	**agência** (f) **de emprego**	[ɐʒ'ẽsiɐ də ẽpr'egu]
résumé	**CV, currículo** (m)	[sɛv'ɛ], [kuʀ'ikulu]
interview (for job)	**entrevista** (f)	[ẽtrəv'iʃtɐ]
vacancy, opening	**vaga** (f)	[v'agɐ]
salary, pay	**salário** (m)	[sɐl'ariu]
fixed salary	**salário** (m) **fixo**	[sɐl'ariu f'iksu]
pay, compensation	**pagamento** (m)	[pɐgɐm'ẽtu]
position (job)	**posto** (m)	[p'oʃtu]
duty (of employee)	**dever** (m)	[dəv'er]
range of duties	**gama** (f) **de deveres**	[g'ɐmɐ də dəv'erəʃ]
busy (I'm ~)	**ocupado**	[ɔkup'adu]
to fire (dismiss)	**despedir, demitir** (vt)	[dəʃpəd'ir], [dəmit'ir]
dismissal	**demissão** (f)	[dəmis'ãu]
unemployment	**desemprego** (m)	[dəzẽpr'egu]
unemployed (n)	**desempregado** (m)	[dəzẽprəg'adu]
retirement	**reforma** (f)	[ʀəf'ɔrmɐ]
to retire (from job)	**reformar-se**	[ʀəfurm'arsə]

105. Business people

director	**diretor** (m)	[dirɛt'or]
manager (director)	**gerente** (m)	[ʒər'ẽtə]
boss	**patrão, chefe** (m)	[pɐtr'ãu], [ʃ'ɛfə]
superior	**superior** (m)	[supərj'or]
superiors	**superiores** (m pl)	[supərj'orəʃ]
president	**presidente** (m)	[prəzid'ẽtə]

chairman	**presidente** (m) **de direção**	[prəzid'ẽtə də dirɛs'ãu]
deputy (substitute)	**substituto** (m)	[subʃtit'utu]
assistant	**assistente** (m)	[ɐsiʃt'ẽtə]
secretary	**secretário** (m)	[səkrət'ariu]
personal assistant	**secretário** (m) **pessoal**	[səkrət'ariu pəsu'al]
businessman	**homem** (m) **de negócios**	['ɔmẽj də nəg'ɔsiuʃ]
entrepreneur	**empresário** (m)	[ẽprəz'ariu]
founder	**fundador** (m)	[fũdɐd'or]
to found (vt)	**fundar** (vt)	[fũd'ar]
incorporator	**fundador, sócio** (m)	[fũdɐd'or], [s'ɔsiu]
partner	**parceiro, sócio** (m)	[pɐrs'ɐjru], [s'ɔsiu]
stockholder	**acionista** (m)	[ɐsiun'iʃtɐ]
millionaire	**milionário** (m)	[miliun'ariu]
billionaire	**bilionário** (m)	[biliun'ariu]
owner, proprietor	**proprietário** (m)	[pruprieɛt'ariu]
landowner	**proprietário** (m) **de terras**	[pruprieɛt'ariu də t'ɛʀɐʃ]
client	**cliente** (m)	[klj'ẽtə]
regular client	**cliente** (m) **habitual**	[klj'ẽtə ɐbitu'al]
buyer (customer)	**comprador** (m)	[kõprɐd'or]
visitor	**visitante** (m)	[vizit'ãtə]
professional (n)	**profissional** (m)	[prufisiun'al]
expert	**perito** (m)	[pər'itu]
specialist	**especialista** (m)	[əʃpəsiɐl'iʃtɐ]
banker	**banqueiro** (m)	[bãk'ɐjru]
broker	**corretor** (m)	[kuʀɛt'or]
cashier, teller	**caixa** (m, f)	[k'ajʃɐ]
accountant	**contabilista** (m)	[kõtɐbil'iʃtɐ]
security guard	**guarda** (m)	[gu'ardɐ]
investor	**investidor** (m)	[ĩvəʃtid'or]
debtor	**devedor** (m)	[dəvəd'or]
creditor	**credor** (m)	[krɛd'or]
borrower	**mutuário** (m)	[mutu'ariu]
importer	**importador** (m)	[ĩpurtɐd'or]
exporter	**exportador** (m)	[əʃpurtɐd'or]
manufacturer	**produtor** (m)	[prudut'or]
distributor	**distribuidor** (m)	[diʃtribuid'or]
middleman	**intermediário** (m)	[ĩtərmədj'ariu]
consultant	**consultor** (m)	[kõsult'or]
sales representative	**representante** (m)	[ʀəprəzẽt'ãtə]
agent	**agente** (m)	[ɐʒ'ẽtə]
insurance agent	**agente** (m) **de seguros**	[ɐʒ'ẽtə də səg'uruʃ]

106. Service professions

cook	**cozinheiro** (m)	[kuziɲ'ejɾu]
chef (kitchen chef)	**cozinheiro chefe** (m)	[kuziɲ'ejɾu ʃ'ɛfə]
baker	**padeiro** (m)	[pad'ejɾu]
bartender	**barman** (m)	[b'armɐn]
waiter	**empregado** (m) **de mesa**	[ẽprəg'adu də m'ezɐ]
waitress	**empregada** (f) **de mesa**	[ẽprəg'adɐ də m'ezɐ]
lawyer, attorney	**advogado** (m)	[ɐdvug'adu]
lawyer (legal expert)	**jurista** (m)	[ʒuɾ'iʃtɐ]
notary	**notário** (m)	[nut'ariu]
electrician	**eletricista** (m)	[elɛtris'iʃtɐ]
plumber	**canalizador** (m)	[kɐnɐlizɐd'oɾ]
carpenter	**carpinteiro** (m)	[kɐrpĩt'ejɾu]
masseur	**massagista** (m)	[mɐsɐʒ'iʃtɐ]
masseuse	**massagista** (f)	[mɐsɐʒ'iʃtɐ]
doctor	**médico** (m)	[m'ɛdiku]
taxi driver	**taxista** (m)	[taks'iʃtɐ]
driver	**condutor** (m)	[kõdut'oɾ]
delivery man	**entregador** (m)	[ẽtrəgɐd'oɾ]
chambermaid	**camareira** (f)	[kɐmɐɾ'ejɾɐ]
security guard	**guarda** (m)	[gu'ardɐ]
flight attendant	**hospedeira** (f) **de bordo**	[ɔʃpəd'ejɾɐ də b'ɔrdu]
teacher (in primary school)	**professor** (m)	[prufəs'oɾ]
librarian	**bibliotecário** (m)	[bibliutək'ariu]
translator	**tradutor** (m)	[trɐdut'oɾ]
interpreter	**intérprete** (m)	[ĩt'ɛrprətə]
guide	**guia** (m)	[g'iɐ]
hairdresser	**cabeleireiro** (m)	[kɐbəlejɾ'ejɾu]
mailman	**carteiro** (m)	[kɐrt'ejɾu]
salesman (store staff)	**vendedor** (m)	[vẽdəd'oɾ]
gardener	**jardineiro** (m)	[ʒɐrdin'ejɾu]
domestic servant	**criado** (m)	[krj'adu]
maid	**criada** (f)	[krj'adɐ]
cleaner (cleaning lady)	**empregada** (f) **de limpeza**	[ẽprəg'adɐ də lĩp'ezɐ]

107. Military professions and ranks

private	**soldado** (m) **raso**	[sold'adu ʀ'azu]
sergeant	**sargento** (m)	[sɐrʒ'ẽtu]

lieutenant	**tenente** (m)	[tən'ẽtə]
captain	**capitão** (m)	[kɐpit'ãu]
major	**major** (m)	[mɐʒ'ɔr]
colonel	**coronel** (m)	[kurun'ɛl]
general	**general** (m)	[ʒənər'al]
marshal	**marechal** (m)	[mɐrəʃ'al]
admiral	**almirante** (m)	[almir'ãtə]
military man	**militar** (m)	[milit'ar]
soldier	**soldado** (m)	[sold'adu]
officer	**oficial** (m)	[ɔfisj'al]
commander	**comandante** (m)	[kumãd'ãtə]
border guard	**guarda** (m) **fronteiriço**	[gu'ardɐ frõtɐjr'isu]
radio operator	**operador** (m) **de rádio**	[ɔpərɐd'or də ʀ'adiu]
scout (searcher)	**explorador** (m)	[əʃplurɐd'or]
pioneer (sapper)	**sapador** (m)	[sɐpɐd'or]
marksman	**atirador** (m)	[ɐtirɐd'or]
navigator	**navegador** (m)	[nɐvəgɐd'or]

108. Officials. Priests

king	**rei** (m)	[ʀɐj]
queen	**rainha** (f)	[ʀɐ'iɲɐ]
prince	**príncipe** (m)	[pr'ĩsipə]
princess	**princesa** (f)	[prĩs'ezɐ]
tsar, czar	**czar** (m)	[kz'ar]
czarina	**czarina** (f)	[kzɐr'inɐ]
president	**presidente** (m)	[prəzid'ẽtə]
Secretary (~ of State)	**ministro** (m)	[min'iʃtru]
prime minister	**primeiro-ministro** (m)	[prim'ɐjru min'iʃtru]
senator	**senador** (m)	[sənɐd'or]
diplomat	**diplomata** (m)	[diplum'atɐ]
consul	**cônsul** (m)	[k'õsul]
ambassador	**embaixador** (m)	[ẽbajʃɐd'or]
advisor (military ~)	**conselheiro** (m)	[kõsəʎ'ɐjru]
official (civil servant)	**funcionário** (m)	[fũsiun'ariu]
prefect	**prefeito** (m)	[prəf'ɐjtu]
mayor	**Presidente** (m) **da Câmara**	[prəzid'ẽtə dɐ k'ɐmɐrɐ]
judge	**juiz** (m)	[ʒu'iʃ]
district attorney (prosecutor)	**procurador** (m)	[prɔkurɐd'or]
missionary	**missionário** (m)	[misiun'ariu]

monk	**monge** (m)	[m'õʒə]
abbot	**abade** (m)	[ɐb'adə]
rabbi	**rabino** (m)	[ʀɐb'inu]
vizier	**vizir** (m)	[viz'iɾ]
shah	**xá** (m)	[ʃa]
sheikh	**xeque** (m)	[ʃ'ɛkə]

109. Agricultural professions

beekeeper	**apicultor** (m)	[ɐpikult'oɾ]
herder, shepherd	**pastor** (m)	[pɐʃt'oɾ]
agronomist	**agrónomo** (m)	[ɐgɾ'ɔnumu]
cattle breeder	**criador** (m) **de gado**	[kriɐd'or də g'adu]
veterinarian	**veterinário** (m)	[vətəɾin'ariu]
farmer	**agricultor** (m)	[ɐgrikult'oɾ]
winemaker	**vinicultor** (m)	[vinikult'oɾ]
zoologist	**zoólogo** (m)	[zu'ɔlugu]
cowboy	**cowboy** (m)	[kɔb'ɔj]

110. Art professions

actor	**ator** (m)	[at'oɾ]
actress	**atriz** (f)	[ɐtɾ'iʃ]
singer (masc.)	**cantor** (m)	[kãt'oɾ]
singer (fem.)	**cantora** (f)	[kãt'orɐ]
dancer (masc.)	**bailarino** (m)	[bajlɐr'inu]
dancer (fem.)	**bailarina** (f)	[bajlɐr'inɐ]
performing artist (masc.)	**artista** (m)	[ɐrt'iʃtɐ]
performing artist (fem.)	**artista** (f)	[ɐrt'iʃtɐ]
musician	**músico** (m)	[m'uziku]
pianist	**pianista** (m)	[piɐn'iʃtɐ]
guitar player	**guitarrista** (m)	[gitɐʀ'iʃtɐ]
conductor (orchestra ~)	**maestro** (m)	[mɐ'ɛʃtru]
composer	**compositor** (m)	[kõpuzit'oɾ]
impresario	**empresário** (m)	[ẽprəz'ariu]
movie director	**realizador** (m)	[ʀiɐlizɐd'oɾ]
producer	**produtor** (m)	[prudut'oɾ]
scriptwriter	**argumentista** (m)	[ɐrgumẽt'iʃtɐ]
critic	**crítico** (m)	[kr'itiku]
writer	**escritor** (m)	[əʃkrit'oɾ]

poet	**poeta** (m)	[pu'ɛtɐ]
sculptor	**escultor** (m)	[əʃkult'or]
artist (painter)	**pintor** (m)	[pĩt'or]
juggler	**malabarista** (m)	[mɐlɐbɐr'iʃtɐ]
clown	**palhaço** (m)	[pɐʎ'asu]
acrobat	**acrobata** (m)	[ɐkrub'atɐ]
magician	**mágico** (m)	[m'aʒiku]

111. Various professions

doctor	**médico** (m)	[m'ɛdiku]
nurse	**enfermeira** (f)	[ẽfərm'ɐjrɐ]
psychiatrist	**psiquiatra** (m)	[psiki'atrɐ]
dentist	**estomatologista** (m)	[əʃtumɐtuluʒ'iʃtɐ]
surgeon	**cirurgião** (m)	[sirurʒj'ãu]
astronaut	**astronauta** (m)	[ɐʃtrɔn'autɐ]
astronomer	**astrónomo** (m)	[ɐʃtr'ɔnumu]
pilot	**piloto** (m)	[pil'otu]
driver (of taxi, etc.)	**motorista** (m)	[mutur'iʃtɐ]
engineer (train driver)	**maquinista** (m)	[mɐkin'iʃtɐ]
mechanic	**mecânico** (m)	[mək'ɐniku]
miner	**mineiro** (m)	[min'ɐjru]
worker	**operário** (m)	[ɔpər'ariu]
metalworker	**serralheiro** (m)	[səʀɐʎ'ɐjru]
joiner (carpenter)	**marceneiro** (m)	[mɐrsən'ɐjru]
turner	**torneiro** (m)	[turn'ɐjru]
construction worker	**construtor** (m)	[kõʃtrut'or]
welder	**soldador** (m)	[soldɐd'or]
professor (title)	**professor** (m) **catedrático**	[prufəs'or kɐtədr'atiku]
architect	**arquiteto** (m)	[ɐrkit'ɛtu]
historian	**historiador** (m)	[iʃturiɐd'or]
scientist	**cientista** (m)	[siẽt'iʃtɐ]
physicist	**físico** (m)	[f'iziku]
chemist (scientist)	**químico** (m)	[k'imiku]
archeologist	**arqueólogo** (m)	[ɐrkj'ɔlugu]
geologist	**geólogo** (m)	[ʒj'ɔlugu]
researcher	**investigador** (m)	[ĩvəʃtigɐd'or]
babysitter	**babysitter** (f)	[bɐbisit'er]
teacher, educator	**professor** (m)	[prufəs'or]
editor	**redator** (m)	[ʀədat'or]
editor-in-chief	**redator-chefe** (m)	[ʀədat'or ʃ'ɛfə]
correspondent	**correspondente** (m)	[kuʀəʃpõd'ẽtə]

typist (fem.)	**datilógrafa** (f)	[detil'ɔgrefe]
designer	**designer** (m)	[diz'ajner]
computer expert	**especialista em informática** (m)	[əʃpəsiel'iʃte ən ĩfurm'atike]
programmer	**programador** (m)	[prugremed'or]
engineer (designer)	**engenheiro** (m)	[ẽʒəɲ'ejru]
sailor	**marujo** (m)	[mer'uʒu]
seaman	**marinheiro** (m)	[meriɲ'ejru]
rescuer	**salvador** (m)	[salved'or]
fireman	**bombeiro** (m)	[bõb'ejru]
policeman	**polícia** (m)	[pul'isie]
watchman	**guarda-noturno** (m)	[gu'arde nɔt'urnu]
detective	**detetive** (m)	[dətɛt'ivə]
customs officer	**funcionário da alfândega** (m)	[fũsiun'ariu de alf'ãdəge]
bodyguard	**guarda-costas** (m)	[gu'arde k'ɔʃteʃ]
prison guard	**guarda** (m) **prisional**	[gu'arde priziun'al]
inspector	**inspetor** (m)	[ĩʃpɛt'or]
sportsman	**desportista** (m)	[dəʃpurt'iʃte]
trainer, coach	**treinador** (m)	[trejned'or]
butcher	**carniceiro** (m)	[kernis'ejru]
cobbler	**sapateiro** (m)	[sepet'ejru]
merchant	**comerciante** (m)	[kumərsj'ãtə]
loader (person)	**carregador** (m)	[keʀəged'or]
fashion designer	**estilista** (m)	[əʃtil'iʃte]
model (fem.)	**modelo** (f)	[mud'elu]

112. Occupations. Social status

schoolboy	**escolar** (m)	[əʃkul'ar]
student (college ~)	**estudante** (m)	[əʃtud'ãtə]
philosopher	**filósofo** (m)	[fil'ɔzufu]
economist	**economista** (m)	[ekɔnum'iʃte]
inventor	**inventor** (m)	[ĩvẽt'or]
unemployed (n)	**desempregado** (m)	[dəzẽprəg'adu]
retiree	**reformado** (m)	[ʀəfurm'adu]
spy, secret agent	**espião** (m)	[əʃpj'ãu]
prisoner	**preso** (m)	[pr'ezu]
striker	**grevista** (m)	[grɛv'iʃte]
bureaucrat	**burocrata** (m)	[burukr'ate]
traveler	**viajante** (m)	[vieʒ'ãtə]
homosexual	**homossexual** (m)	[ɔmɔsɛksu'al]

hacker	**hacker** (m)	['akɛr]
hippie	**hippie**	['ipi]
bandit	**bandido** (m)	[bãd'idu]
hit man, killer	**assassino** (m) **a soldo**	[ɐsɐs'inu ɐ s'oldu]
drug addict	**toxicodependente** (m)	[tɔksikɔdəpẽd'ẽtə]
drug dealer	**traficante** (m)	[trɐfik'ãtə]
prostitute (fem.)	**prostituta** (f)	[pruʃtit'utɐ]
pimp	**chulo** (m)	[ʃ'ulu]
sorcerer	**bruxo** (m)	[br'uʃu]
sorceress	**bruxa** (f)	[br'uʃɐ]
pirate	**pirata** (m)	[pir'atɐ]
slave	**escravo** (m)	[əʃkr'avu]
samurai	**samurai** (m)	[sɐmur'aj]
savage (primitive)	**selvagem** (m)	[sɛlv'aʒẽj]

Sports

113. Kinds of sports. Sportspersons

sportsman	**desportista** (m)	[dəʃpurt'iʃtɐ]
kind of sports	**tipo** (m) **de desporto**	[t'ipu də dəʃp'ortu]
basketball	**basquetebol** (m)	[bɐʃkɛtəb'ɔl]
basketball player	**jogador** (m) **de basquetebol**	[ʒugɐd'or də bɐʃkɛtəb'ɔl]
baseball	**beisebol** (m)	[b'ɛjzbɔl]
baseball player	**jogador** (m) **de beisebol**	[ʒugɐd'or də b'ɛjzbɔl]
soccer	**futebol** (m)	[futəb'ɔl]
soccer player	**futebolista** (m)	[futəbul'iʃtɐ]
goalkeeper	**guarda-redes** (m)	[gu'ardɐ ʀ'edəʃ]
hockey	**hóquei** (m)	['ɔkɐj]
hockey player	**jogador** (m) **de hóquei**	[ʒugɐd'or də 'ɔkɐj]
volleyball	**voleibol** (m)	[vɔlɐjb'ɔl]
volleyball player	**jogador** (m) **de voleibol**	[ʒugɐd'or də vɔlɐjb'ɔl]
boxing	**boxe** (m)	[b'ɔksə]
boxer	**boxeador, pugilista** (m)	[boʃied'or], [puʒil'iʃtɐ]
wrestling	**luta** (f)	[l'utɐ]
wrestler	**lutador** (m)	[lutɐd'or]
karate	**karaté** (m)	[karat'ɛ]
karate fighter	**karateca** (m)	[kɐrɐt'ɛkɐ]
judo	**judo** (m)	[ʒ'udu]
judo athlete	**judoca** (m)	[ʒud'ɔkɐ]
tennis	**ténis** (m)	[t'ɛniʃ]
tennis player	**tenista** (m)	[tɛn'iʃtɐ]
swimming	**natação** (f)	[nɐtɐs'ãu]
swimmer	**nadador** (m)	[nɐdɐd'or]
fencing	**esgrima** (f)	[əʒgr'imɐ]
fencer	**esgrimista** (m)	[əʒgrim'iʃtɐ]
chess	**xadrez** (m)	[ʃɐdr'eʃ]
chess player	**xadrezista** (m)	[ʃɐdrəz'iʃtɐ]

alpinism	**alpinismo** (m)	[alpin'iʒmu]
alpinist	**alpinista** (m)	[alpin'iʃtɐ]
running	**corrida** (f)	[kuʀ'idɐ]
runner	**corredor** (m)	[kuʀəd'or]
athletics	**atletismo** (m)	[ɐtlɛt'iʒmu]
athlete	**atleta** (m)	[ɐtl'ɛtɐ]
horseback riding	**hipismo** (m)	[ip'iʒmu]
horse rider	**cavaleiro** (m)	[kɐvɐl'ɐjru]
figure skating	**patinagem** (f) **artística**	[pɐtin'aʒẽj ɐrt'iʃtikɐ]
figure skater (masc.)	**patinador** (m)	[pɐtinɐd'or]
figure skater (fem.)	**patinadora** (f)	[pɐtinɐd'orɐ]
weightlifting	**halterofilismo** (m)	[altɛrɔfil'iʒmu]
weightlifter	**halterofilista** (m)	[altɛrɔfil'iʃtɐ]
car racing	**corrida** (f) **de carros**	[kuʀ'idɐ də k'aʀuʃ]
racing driver	**piloto** (m)	[pil'otu]
cycling	**ciclismo** (m)	[sikl'iʒmu]
cyclist	**ciclista** (m)	[sikl'iʃtɐ]
broad jump	**salto** (m) **em comprimento**	[s'altu ẽ kõprim'ẽtu]
pole vault	**salto** (m) **à vara**	[s'altu a v'arɐ]
jumper	**atleta** (m) **de saltos**	[ɐtl'ɛtɐ də s'altuʃ]

114. Kinds of sports. Miscellaneous

football	**futebol** (m) **americano**	[futəb'ɔl ɐmərik'ɐnu]
badminton	**badminton** (m)	[badm'ĩtɔn]
biathlon	**biatlo** (m)	[bj'atlu]
billiards	**bilhar** (m)	[biʎ'ar]
bobsled	**bobsleigh** (m)	[bɔbsl'ɐj]
bodybuilding	**musculação** (f)	[muʃkulɐs'ãu]
water polo	**pólo** (m) **aquático**	[p'ɔlu ɐku'atiku]
handball	**handebol** (m)	[ãdəb'ɔl]
golf	**golfe** (m)	[g'olfə]
rowing	**remo** (m)	[ʀ'ɛmu]
scuba diving	**mergulho** (m)	[mərg'uʎu]
cross-country skiing	**corrida** (f) **de esqui**	[kuʀ'idɐ də əʃk'i]
ping-pong	**ténis** (m) **de mesa**	[t'ɛniʃ də m'ezɐ]
sailing	**vela** (f)	[v'ɛlɐ]
rally racing	**rali** (m)	[ʀɐl'i]

rugby	**rugbi** (m)	[ʀ'ɐgbi]
snowboarding	**snowboard** (m)	[snoub'ɔrd]
archery	**tiro** (m) **com arco**	[t'iru kõ 'arku]

115. Gym

barbell	**barra** (f)	[b'aʀɐ]
dumbbells	**halteres** (m pl)	[alt'ɛrəʃ]
training machine	**aparelho** (m) **de musculaçao**	[ɐpɐr'ɐʎu də muʃkulɐs'ɐu]
bicycle trainer	**bicicleta** (f) **ergométrica**	[bisikl'ɛtɐ ergum'ɛtrikɐ]
treadmill	**passadeira** (f)	[pɐsɐd'ejrɐ]
horizontal bar	**barra** (f) **fixa**	[b'aʀɐ f'iksɐ]
parallel bars	**barras** (f) **paralelas**	[b'aʀɐʃ pɐrɐl'ɛlɐʃ]
vaulting horse	**cavalo** (m)	[kɐv'alu]
mat (in gym)	**tapete** (m) **de ginástica**	[tɐp'etə də ʒin'aʃtikɐ]
jump rope	**corda** (f) **de saltar**	[k'ɔrdɐ də salt'ar]
aerobics	**aeróbica** (f)	[ɐɛr'ɔbikɐ]
yoga	**ioga** (f)	[j'ɔgɐ]

116. Sports. Miscellaneous

Olympic Games	**Jogos** (m pl) **Olímpicos**	[ʒ'ɔguʃ ɔl'ĩpikuʃ]
winner	**vencedor** (m)	[vẽsəd'or]
to be winning	**vencer** (vi)	[vẽs'er]
to win (vi)	**ganhar** (vi)	[gaɲ'ar]
leader	**líder** (m)	[l'idɛr]
to lead (vi)	**liderar** (vt)	[lidər'ar]
first place	**primeiro lugar** (m)	[prim'ɐjru lug'ar]
second place	**segundo lugar** (m)	[səg'ũdu lug'ar]
third place	**terceiro lugar** (m)	[tərs'ɐjru lug'ar]
medal	**medalha** (f)	[məd'aʎɐ]
trophy	**troféu** (m)	[truf'ɛu]
prize cup (trophy)	**taça** (f)	[t'asɐ]
prize (in game)	**prémio** (m)	[pr'ɛmiu]
main prize	**prémio** (m) **principal**	[pr'ɛmiu prĩsip'al]
record	**recorde** (m)	[ʀək'ɔrdə]
to set a record	**estabelecer um recorde**	[əʃtəbələs'er ũ ʀək'ɔrdə]
final	**final** (m)	[fin'al]
final (adj)	**final**	[fin'al]

champion	**campeão** (m)	[kãpj'ãu]
championship	**campeonato** (m)	[kãpiun'atu]
stadium	**estádio** (m)	[əʃt'adiu]
stand (bleachers)	**bancadas** (f pl)	[bãk'adɐʃ]
fan, supporter	**fã, adepto** (m)	[fã], [ɐd'ɛptu]
opponent, rival	**adversário** (m)	[ɐdvərs'ariu]
start	**partida** (f)	[pɐrt'idɐ]
finish line	**chegada, meta** (f)	[ʃəg'adɐ], [m'ɛtɐ]
defeat	**derrota** (f)	[dəʀ'ɔtɐ]
to lose (not win)	**perder** (vt)	[pərd'er]
referee	**árbitro** (m)	['arbitru]
jury	**júri** (m)	[ʒ'uri]
score	**resultado** (m)	[ʀəzult'adu]
draw	**empate** (m)	[ẽp'atə]
to draw (vi)	**empatar** (vi)	[ẽpɐt'ar]
point	**ponto** (m)	[p'õtu]
result (final score)	**resultado** (m) **final**	[ʀəzult'adu fin'al]
period	**tempo, período** (m)	[t'ẽpu pər'iwdu]
half-time	**intervalo** (m)	[ĩtərv'alu]
doping	**doping** (m)	[d'ɔpĩg]
to penalize (vt)	**penalizar** (vt)	[pənɐliz'ar]
to disqualify (vt)	**desqualificar** (vt)	[dəʃkuɐlifik'ar]
apparatus	**aparelho** (m)	[ɐpɐr'ɐʎu]
javelin	**dardo** (m)	[d'ardu]
shot put ball	**peso** (m)	[p'ezu]
ball (snooker, etc.)	**bola** (f)	[b'ɔlɐ]
aim (target)	**alvo** (m)	['alvu]
target	**alvo** (m)	['alvu]
to shoot (vi)	**atirar, disparar** (vi)	[ɐtir'ar], [diʃpɐr'ar]
precise (~ shot)	**preciso**	[prəs'izu]
trainer, coach	**treinador** (m)	[trɐjnɐd'or]
to train (sb)	**treinar** (vt)	[trɐjn'ar]
to train (vi)	**treinar-se** (vp)	[trɐjn'arsə]
training	**treino** (m)	[tr'ɐjnu]
gym	**ginásio** (m)	[ʒin'aziu]
exercise (physical)	**exercício** (m)	[ezərs'isiu]
warm-up (of athlete)	**aquecimento** (m)	[ɐkɛsim'ẽtu]

Education

117. School

school	**escola** (f)	[əʃk'ɔlɐ]
headmaster	**diretor** (m) **de escola**	[dirɛt'or də əʃk'ɔlɐ]
pupil (boy)	**aluno** (m)	[ɐl'unu]
pupil (girl)	**aluna** (f)	[ɐl'unɐ]
schoolboy	**escolar** (m)	[əʃkul'ar]
schoolgirl	**escolar** (f)	[əʃkul'ar]
to teach (sb)	**ensinar** (vt)	[ẽsin'ar]
to learn (language, etc.)	**aprender** (vt)	[ɐprẽd'er]
to learn by heart	**aprender de cor**	[ɐprẽd'er də kor]
to study (work to learn)	**estudar** (vi)	[əʃtud'ar]
to be in school	**andar na escola**	[ãdar nɐ əʃk'ɔlɐ]
to go to school	**ir à escola**	[ir a əʃk'ɔlɐ]
alphabet	**alfabeto** (m)	[alfɐb'ɛtu]
subject (at school)	**disciplina** (f)	[diʃsipl'inɐ]
classroom	**sala** (f) **de aula**	[s'alɐ də 'aulɐ]
lesson	**lição, aula** (f)	[lis'ãu], ['aulɐ]
recess	**recreio** (m)	[ʀəkr'ɐju]
school bell	**toque** (m)	[t'ɔkə]
school desk	**carteira** (f)	[kɐrt'ɐjrɐ]
chalkboard	**quadro** (m) **negro**	[ku'adru n'egru]
grade	**nota** (f)	[n'ɔtɐ]
good grade	**boa nota** (f)	[b'oɐ n'ɔtɐ]
bad grade	**nota** (f) **baixa**	[n'ɔtɐ b'ajʃɐ]
to give a grade	**dar uma nota**	[dar 'umɐ n'ɔtɐ]
mistake, error	**erro** (m)	['eʀu]
to make mistakes	**fazer erros**	[fɐz'er 'eʀuʃ]
to correct (an error)	**corrigir** (vt)	[kuʀiʒ'ir]
cheat sheet	**cábula** (f)	[k'abulɐ]
homework	**trabalho** (m) **de casa**	[trɐb'aʎu də k'azɐ]
exercise (in education)	**exercício** (m)	[ezərs'isiu]
to be present	**estar presente**	[əʃt'ar prəz'ẽtə]
to be absent	**estar ausente**	[əʃt'ar auz'ẽtə]
to miss school	**faltar às aulas**	[falt'ar aʃ 'aulɐʃ]

to punish (vt)	**punir** (vt)	[pun'ir]
punishment	**punição** (f)	[punis'ãu]
conduct (behavior)	**comportamento** (m)	[kõpurtem'ẽtu]
report card	**boletim** (m) **escolar**	[bulət'ĩ əʃkul'ar]
pencil	**lápis** (m)	[l'apiʃ]
eraser	**borracha** (f)	[buʀ'aʃɐ]
chalk	**giz** (m)	[ʒiʃ]
pencil case	**estojo** (m)	[əʃt'oʒu]
schoolbag	**pasta** (f) **escolar**	[p'aʃtɐ əʃkul'ar]
pen	**caneta** (f)	[kɐn'etɐ]
school notebook	**caderno** (m)	[kɐd'ɛrnu]
textbook	**manual** (m) **escolar**	[mɐnu'al əʃkul'ar]
compasses	**compasso** (m)	[kõp'asu]
to draw (a blueprint, etc.)	**traçar** (vt)	[trɐs'ar]
technical drawing	**desenho** (m) **técnico**	[dəz'ɐɲu t'ɛkniku]
poem	**poesia** (f)	[puez'iɐ]
by heart (adv)	**de cor**	[də kor]
to learn by heart	**aprender de cor**	[ɐprẽd'er də kor]
school vacation	**férias** (f pl)	[f'ɛriɐʃ]
to be on vacation	**estar de férias**	[əʃt'ar də f'ɛriɐʃ]
to spend one's vacation	**passar as férias**	[pɐs'ar ɐʃ f'ɛriɐʃ]
test (written math ~)	**teste** (m)	[t'ɛʃtə]
essay (composition)	**composição, redação** (f)	[kõpuzis'ãu], [ʀədas'ãu]
dictation	**ditado** (m)	[dit'adu]
exam	**exame** (m)	[ez'ɐmə]
to take an exam	**fazer exame**	[fɐz'er ez'ɐmə]
experiment (chemical ~)	**experiência** (f)	[əʃpərj'ẽsiɐ]

118. College. University

academy	**academia** (f)	[ɐkɐdəm'iɐ]
university	**universidade** (f)	[univərsid'adə]
faculty (section)	**faculdade** (f)	[fɐkuld'adə]
student (masc.)	**estudante** (m)	[əʃtud'ãtə]
student (fem.)	**estudante** (f)	[əʃtud'ãtə]
lecturer (teacher)	**professor** (m)	[prufəs'or]
lecture hall, room	**sala** (f) **de palestras**	[s'alɐ də pɐl'ɛʃtrɐʃ]
graduate	**graduado** (m)	[grɐdu'adu]
diploma	**diploma** (m)	[dipl'omɐ]
dissertation	**tese** (f)	[t'ɛzə]
study (report)	**estudo** (m)	[əʃt'udu]
laboratory	**laboratório** (m)	[lɐburɐt'ɔriu]

lecture	**palestra** (f)	[pel'ɛʃtrɐ]
course mate	**colega** (m) **de curso**	[kul'ɛgɐ də k'ursu]
scholarship	**bolsa** (f) **de estudos**	[b'olsɐ də əʃt'uduʃ]
academic degree	**grau** (m) **académico**	[gr'au ɐkɐd'ɛmiku]

119. Sciences. Disciplines

mathematics	**matemática** (f)	[mɐtəm'atikɐ]
algebra	**álgebra** (f)	['alʒəbrɐ]
geometry	**geometria** (f)	[ʒiumətr'iɐ]
astronomy	**astronomia** (f)	[ɐʃtrunum'iɐ]
biology	**biologia** (f)	[biuluʒ'iɐ]
geography	**geografia** (f)	[ʒiugrɐf'iɐ]
geology	**geologia** (f)	[ʒiuluʒ'iɐ]
history	**história** (f)	[iʃt'ɔriɐ]
medicine	**medicina** (f)	[mədis'inɐ]
pedagogy	**pedagogia** (f)	[pədɐguʒ'iɐ]
law	**direito** (m)	[dir'ɐjtu]
physics	**física** (f)	[f'izikɐ]
chemistry	**química** (f)	[k'imikɐ]
philosophy	**filosofia** (f)	[filuzuf'iɐ]
psychology	**psicologia** (f)	[psikuluʒ'iɐ]

120. Writing system. Orthography

grammar	**gramática** (f)	[grɐm'atikɐ]
vocabulary	**léxico** (m)	[l'ɛksiku]
phonetics	**fonética** (f)	[fɔn'ɛtikɐ]
noun	**substantivo** (m)	[subʃtɐ̃t'ivu]
adjective	**adjetivo** (m)	[ɐdʒɛt'ivu]
verb	**verbo** (m)	[v'ɛrbu]
adverb	**advérbio** (m)	[ɐdv'ɛrbiu]
pronoun	**pronome** (m)	[prun'omə]
interjection	**interjeição** (f)	[ĩtɛrʒejs'ɐ̃u]
preposition	**preposição** (f)	[prəpuzis'ɐ̃u]
root	**raiz** (f) **da palavra**	[ʀɐ'iʃ dɐ pɐl'avrɐ]
ending	**terminação** (f)	[tərminɐs'ɐ̃u]
prefix	**prefixo** (m)	[prəf'iksu]
syllable	**sílaba** (f)	[s'ilɐbɐ]
suffix	**sufixo** (m)	[suf'iksu]
stress mark	**acento** (m)	[ɐs'ẽtu]
apostrophe	**apóstrofo** (m)	[ɐp'ɔʃtrɔfu]

period, dot	**ponto** (m)	[p'õtu]
comma	**vírgula** (f)	[v'irgulɐ]
semicolon	**ponto e vírgula** (m)	[p'õtu ə v'irgulɐ]
colon	**dois pontos** (m pl)	[d'ojʃ p'õtuʃ]
ellipsis	**reticências** (f pl)	[ʀətis'ẽsiɐʃ]
question mark	**ponto** (m) **de interrogação**	[p'õtu də ĩtəʀugɐs'ãu]
exclamation point	**ponto** (m) **de exclamação**	[p'õtu də əʃklɐmɐs'ãu]
quotation marks	**aspas** (f pl)	['aʃpɐʃ]
in quotation marks	**entre aspas**	[ẽtrə 'aʃpɐʃ]
parenthesis	**parênteses** (m pl)	[pɐr'ẽtəzəʃ]
in parenthesis	**entre parênteses**	[ẽtrə pɐr'ẽtəzəʃ]
hyphen	**hífen** (m)	['ifɛn]
dash	**travessão** (m)	[trɐvəs'ãu]
space (between words)	**espaço** (m)	[əʃp'asu]
letter	**letra** (f)	[l'etrɐ]
capital letter	**letra** (f) **maiúscula**	[l'etrɐ mɐj'uʃkulɐ]
vowel (n)	**vogal** (f)	[vug'al]
consonant (n)	**consoante** (f)	[kõsu'ãtə]
sentence	**frase** (f)	[fr'azə]
subject	**sujeito** (m)	[suʒ'ɐjtu]
predicate	**predicado** (m)	[prədik'adu]
line	**linha** (f)	[l'iɲɐ]
on a new line	**em uma nova linha**	[ɛn 'umɐ n'ɔvɐ l'iɲɐ]
paragraph	**parágrafo** (m)	[pɐr'agrɐfu]
word	**palavra** (f)	[pɐl'avrɐ]
group of words	**grupo** (m) **de palavras**	[gr'upu də pɐl'avrɐʃ]
expression	**expressão** (f)	[əʃprəs'ãu]
synonym	**sinónimo** (m)	[sin'ɔnimu]
antonym	**antónimo** (m)	[ãt'ɔnimu]
rule	**regra** (f)	[ʀ'ɛgrɐ]
exception	**exceção** (f)	[əʃsɛs'ãu]
correct (adj)	**correto**	[kuʀ'ɛtu]
conjugation	**conjugação** (f)	[kõʒugɐs'ãu]
declension	**declinação** (f)	[dəklinɐs'ãu]
nominal case	**caso** (m)	[k'azu]
question	**pergunta** (f)	[pərg'ũtɐ]
to underline (vt)	**sublinhar** (vt)	[subliɲ'ar]
dotted line	**linha** (f) **pontilhada**	[l'iɲɐ põtiʎ'adɐ]

121. Foreign languages

language	**língua** (f)	[l'ĩguɐ]
foreign (adj)	**estrangeiro**	[əʃtrãʒ'ɐjru]
foreign language	**língua** (f) **estrangeira**	[l'ĩguɐ əʃtrãʒ'ɐjrɐ]
to study (vt)	**estudar** (vt)	[əʃtud'ar]
to learn (language, etc.)	**aprender** (vt)	[ɐprẽd'er]
to read (vi, vt)	**ler** (vt)	[ler]
to speak (vi, vt)	**falar** (vi)	[fɐl'ar]
to understand (vt)	**compreender** (vt)	[kõpriẽd'er]
to write (vt)	**escrever** (vt)	[əʃkrəv'er]
fast (adv)	**rapidamente**	[ʀapidɐm'ẽtə]
slowly (adv)	**devagar**	[dəvɐg'ar]
fluently (adv)	**fluentemente**	[fluẽtəm'ẽtə]
rules	**regras** (f pl)	[ʀ'ɛgrɐʃ]
grammar	**gramática** (f)	[grɐm'atikɐ]
vocabulary	**léxico** (m)	[l'ɛksiku]
phonetics	**fonética** (f)	[fɔn'ɛtikɐ]
textbook	**manual** (m) **escolar**	[mɐnu'al əʃkul'ar]
dictionary	**dicionário** (m)	[disiun'ariu]
teach-yourself book	**manual** (m) **de autoaprendizagem**	[mɐnu'al də 'autɔɐprẽdiz'aʒẽj]
phrasebook	**guia** (m) **de conversação**	[g'iɐ də kõvərsɐs'ãu]
cassette	**cassete** (f)	[kas'ɛtə]
videotape	**cassete** (f) **de vídeo**	[kas'ɛtə də v'idiu]
CD, compact disc	**CD, disco** (m) **compacto**	[s'ɛdɛ], [d'iʃku kõp'aktu]
DVD	**DVD** (m)	[dɛvɛd'ɛ]
alphabet	**alfabeto** (m)	[alfɐb'ɛtu]
to spell (vt)	**soletrar** (vt)	[sulətr'ar]
pronunciation	**pronúncia** (f)	[prun'ũsiɐ]
accent	**sotaque** (m)	[sut'akə]
with an accent	**com sotaque**	[kõ sut'akə]
without an accent	**sem sotaque**	[sẽ sut'akə]
word	**palavra** (f)	[pɐl'avrɐ]
meaning	**sentido** (m)	[sẽt'idu]
course (e.g., a French ~)	**cursos** (m pl)	[k'ursuʃ]
to sign up	**inscrever-se** (vp)	[ĩʃkrəv'ersə]
teacher	**professor** (m)	[prufəs'or]
translation (process)	**tradução** (f)	[trɐdus'ãu]
translation (text, etc.)	**tradução** (f)	[trɐdus'ãu]
translator	**tradutor** (m)	[trɐdut'or]

interpreter	**intérprete** (m)	[ĩt'ɛrprətə]
polyglot	**poliglota** (m)	[pɔligl'ɔtɐ]
memory	**memória** (f)	[məm'ɔriɐ]

122. Fairy tale characters

Santa Claus	**Pai** (m) **Natal**	[paj nɐt'al]
Cinderella	**Cinderela** (f)	[sĩdər'ɛlɐ]
mermaid	**sereia** (f)	[sər'ɐjɐ]
Neptune	**Neptuno** (m)	[nɛpt'unu]
magician, wizard	**mago** (m)	[m'agu]
fairy	**fada** (f)	[f'adɐ]
magic (adj)	**mágico**	[m'aʒiku]
magic wand	**varinha** (f) **mágica**	[vɐr'iɲɐ m'aʒikɐ]
fairy tale	**conto** (m) **de fadas**	[k'õtu də f'adɐʃ]
miracle	**milagre** (m)	[mil'agrə]
dwarf	**anão** (m)	[ɐn'ãu]
to turn into ...	**transformar-se em ...**	[trãʃfurm'arsə ɛn]
ghost	**espetro** (m)	[əʃp'ɛtru]
phantom	**fantasma** (m)	[fãt'aʒmɐ]
monster	**monstro** (m)	[m'õʃtru]
dragon	**dragão** (m)	[drɐg'ãu]
giant	**gigante** (m)	[ʒig'ãtə]

123. Zodiac Signs

Aries	**Carneiro**	[kɐrn'ɐjru]
Taurus	**Touro**	[t'oru]
Gemini	**Gémeos**	[ʒ'ɛmiuʃ]
Cancer	**Caranguejo**	[kɐrãg'ɐʒu]
Leo	**Leão**	[lj'ãu]
Virgo	**Virgem**	[v'irʒẽj]
Libra	**Balança**	[bɐl'ãsɐ]
Scorpio	**Escorpião**	[əʃkurpj'ãu]
Sagittarius	**Sagitário**	[sɐʒit'ariu]
Capricorn	**Capricórnio**	[kɐprik'ɔrniu]
Aquarius	**Aquário**	[ɐku'ariu]
Pisces	**Peixes**	[p'ɐjʃəʃ]
character	**caráter** (m)	[kɐr'atɛr]
features of character	**traços** (m pl) **do caráter**	[tr'asuʃ du kɐr'atɛr]
behavior	**comportamento** (m)	[kõpurtɐm'ẽtu]
to tell fortunes	**predizer** (vt)	[prədiz'er]
fortune-teller	**adivinha** (f)	[ɐdiv'iɲɐ]
horoscope	**horóscopo** (m)	[ɔr'ɔʃkupu]

Arts

124. Theater

theater	**teatro** (m)	[tə'atru]
opera	**ópera** (f)	['ɔpərɐ]
operetta	**opereta** (f)	[ɔpər'etɐ]
ballet	**balé** (m)	[bɐl'ɛ]
theater poster	**cartaz** (m)	[kɐrt'aʃ]
theatrical company	**companhia** (f) **teatral**	[kõpɐɲ'iɐ tiɐtr'al]
tour	**turné** (f)	[turn'ɛ]
to be on tour	**estar em turné**	[əʃt'ar ẽ turn'ɛ]
to rehearse (vi, vt)	**ensaiar** (vt)	[ẽsaj'ar]
rehearsal	**ensaio** (m)	[ẽs'aju]
repertoire	**repertório** (m)	[ʀəpərt'ɔriu]
performance	**apresentação** (f)	[ɐprəzẽtɐs'ãu]
theatrical show	**espetáculo** (m)	[əʃpɛt'akulu]
play	**peça** (f)	[p'ɛsɐ]
ticket	**bilhete** (m)	[biʎ'etə]
Box office	**bilheteira** (f)	[biʎət'ɐjrɐ]
lobby, foyer	**hall** (m)	[ɔl]
coat check	**guarda-roupa** (m)	[guardɐ ʀ'opɐ]
coat check tag	**senha** (f) **numerada**	[s'ɐɲɐ numər'adɐ]
binoculars	**binóculo** (m)	[bin'ɔkulu]
usher	**lanterninha** (m)	[lãtərn'iɲɐ]
orchestra seats	**plateia** (f)	[plɐt'ɐjɐ]
balcony	**balcão** (m)	[balk'ãu]
dress circle	**primeiro balcão** (m)	[prim'ɐjru balk'ãu]
box	**camarote** (m)	[kɐmɐr'ɔtə]
row	**fila** (f)	[f'ilɐ]
seat	**assento** (m)	[ɐs'ẽtu]
audience	**público** (m)	[p'ubliku]
spectator	**espetador** (m)	[əʃpətɐd'or]
to clap (vi, vt)	**aplaudir** (vt)	[ɐplaud'ir]
applause	**aplausos** (m pl)	[ɐpl'auzuʃ]
ovation	**ovação** (f)	[ɔvɐs'ãu]
stage	**palco** (m)	[p'alku]
curtain	**pano** (m) **de boca**	[p'ɐnu də b'okɐ]
scenery	**cenário** (m)	[sən'ariu]
backstage	**bastidores** (m pl)	[bɐʃtid'orəʃ]

scene (e.g., the last ~)	**cena** (f)	[s'ene]
act	**ato** (m)	['atu]
intermission	**entreato** (m)	[ẽtrj'atu]

125. Cinema

actor	**ator** (m)	[at'or]
actress	**atriz** (f)	[etr'iʃ]
movies (industry)	**cinema** (m)	[sin'eme]
movie	**filme** (m)	[f'ilmə]
episode	**episódio** (m)	[epiz'ɔdiu]
detective	**filme** (m) **policial**	[f'ilmə pulisj'al]
action movie	**filme** (m) **de ação**	[f'ilmə də as'ãu]
adventure movie	**filme** (m) **de aventuras**	[f'ilmə də evẽt'ureʃ]
science fiction movie	**filme** (m) **de ficção científica**	[f'ilmə də fiks'ãu siẽt'ifike]
horror movie	**filme** (m) **de terror**	[f'ilmə də təʀ'or]
comedy movie	**comédia** (f)	[kum'ɛdie]
melodrama	**melodrama** (m)	[mɛlɔdr'eme]
drama	**drama** (m)	[dr'eme]
fictional movie	**filme** (m) **ficcional**	[f'ilmə fiksiun'al]
documentary	**documentário** (m)	[dukumẽt'ariu]
cartoon	**desenho** (m) **animado**	[dəz'eɲu enim'adu]
silent movies	**cinema** (m) **mudo**	[sin'eme m'udu]
role (part)	**papel** (m)	[pep'ɛl]
leading role	**papel** (m) **principal**	[pep'ɛl prĩsip'al]
to play (vi, vt)	**representar** (vt)	[ʀəprəzẽt'ar]
movie star	**estrela** (f) **de cinema**	[əʃtr'ele də sin'eme]
well-known (adj)	**conhecido**	[kuɲəs'idu]
famous (adj)	**famoso**	[fem'ozu]
popular (adj)	**popular**	[pupul'ar]
script (screenplay)	**argumento** (m)	[ergum'ẽtu]
scriptwriter	**argumentista** (m)	[ergumẽt'iʃte]
movie director	**realizador** (m)	[ʀielized'or]
producer	**produtor** (m)	[prudut'or]
assistant	**assistente** (m)	[esiʃt'ẽtə]
cameraman	**diretor** (m) **de fotografia**	[dirɛt'or də futugref'ie]
stuntman	**duplo** (m)	[d'uplu]
double	**duplo** (m)	[d'uplu]
to shoot a movie	**filmar** (vt)	[film'ar]
audition, screen test	**audição** (f)	[audis'ãu]
shooting	**filmagem** (f)	[film'aʒẽj]

movie crew	**equipe** (f) **de filmagem**	[ek'ipə də film'aʒẽj]
movie set	**set** (m) **de filmagem**	[s'ɛtə də film'aʒẽj]
camera	**câmara** (f)	[k'ɐmɐrɐ]
movie theater	**cinema** (m)	[sin'emɐ]
screen (e.g., big ~)	**ecrã, tela** (m)	[ɛkr'ã], [t'ɛlɐ]
to show a movie	**exibir um filme**	[ezib'ir ũ f'ilmə]
soundtrack	**pista** (f) **sonora**	[p'iʃtɐ sun'ɔrɐ]
special effects	**efeitos** (m pl) **especiais**	[ef'ejtuʃ əʃpəsj'ajʃ]
subtitles	**legendas** (f pl)	[ləʒ'ẽdɐʃ]
credits	**genérico** (m)	[ʒən'ɛriku]
translation	**tradução** (f)	[trɐdus'ãu]

126. Painting

art	**arte** (f)	['artə]
fine arts	**belas-artes** (f pl)	[bɛlez'artəʃ]
art gallery	**galeria** (f) **de arte**	[gelər'iɐ də 'artə]
art exhibition	**exposição** (f) **de arte**	[əʃpuzis'ãu də 'artə]
painting (art)	**pintura** (f)	[pĩt'urɐ]
graphic art	**arte** (f) **gráfica**	['artə gr'afikɐ]
abstract art	**arte** (f) **abstrata**	['artə ɐbʃtr'atɐ]
impressionism	**impressionismo** (m)	[ĩprəsiun'iʒmu]
picture (painting)	**pintura** (f), **quadro** (m)	[pĩt'urɐ], [ku'adru]
drawing	**desenho** (m)	[dəz'ɐɲu]
poster	**cartaz, póster** (m)	[kɐrt'aʃ], [p'ɔʃtɛr]
illustration (picture)	**ilustração** (f)	[iluʃtrɐs'ãu]
miniature	**miniatura** (f)	[miniɐt'urɐ]
copy (of painting, etc.)	**cópia** (f)	[k'ɔpiɐ]
reproduction	**reprodução** (f)	[ʀəprudus'ãu]
mosaic	**mosaico** (m)	[muz'ajku]
stained glass	**vitral** (m)	[vitr'al]
fresco	**fresco** (m)	[fr'eʃku]
engraving	**gravura** (f)	[grɐv'urɐ]
bust (sculpture)	**busto** (m)	[b'uʃtu]
sculpture	**escultura** (f)	[əʃkult'urɐ]
statue	**estátua** (f)	[əʃt'atuɐ]
plaster of Paris	**gesso** (m)	[ʒ'esu]
plaster (as adj)	**em gesso**	[ẽ ʒ'esu]
portrait	**retrato** (m)	[ʀətr'atu]
self-portrait	**autorretrato** (m)	[autɔʀətr'atu]
landscape painting	**paisagem** (f)	[pajz'aʒẽj]
still life	**natureza** (f) **morta**	[nɐtur'ezɐ m'ɔrtɐ]

caricature	**caricatura** (f)	[keriket'ure]
sketch	**esboço** (m)	[əʒb'osu]
paint	**tinta** (f)	[t'ĩte]
watercolor	**aguarela** (f)	[aguer'ɛle]
oil (paint)	**óleo** (m)	['ɔliu]
pencil	**lápis** (m)	[l'apiʃ]
Indian ink	**tinta da China** (f)	[tĩte de ʃ'ine]
charcoal	**carvão** (m)	[kerv'ãu]
to draw (vi, vt)	**desenhar** (vt)	[dəzəɲ'ar]
to paint (vi, vt)	**pintar** (vt)	[pĩt'ar]
to pose (vi)	**posar** (vi)	[poz'ar]
artist's model (masc.)	**modelo** (m)	[mud'elu]
artist's model (fem.)	**modelo** (f)	[mud'elu]
artist (painter)	**pintor** (m)	[pĩt'or]
work of art	**obra** (f)	['ɔbre]
masterpiece	**obra-prima** (f)	['ɔbre pr'ime]
artist's workshop	**estúdio** (m)	[əʃt'udiu]
canvas (cloth)	**tela** (f)	[t'ɛle]
easel	**cavalete** (m)	[kevel'etə]
palette	**paleta** (f)	[pel'ete]
frame (of picture, etc.)	**moldura** (f)	[mɔld'ure]
restoration	**restauração** (f)	[ʀəʃtaures'ãu]
to restore (vt)	**restaurar** (vt)	[ʀəʃtaur'ar]

127. Literature & Poetry

literature	**literatura** (f)	[litəret'ure]
author (writer)	**autor** (m)	[aut'or]
pseudonym	**pseudónimo** (m)	[pseud'ɔnimu]
book	**livro** (m)	[l'ivru]
volume	**volume** (m)	[vul'umə]
table of contents	**índice** (m)	['ĩdisə]
page	**página** (f)	[p'aʒine]
main character	**protagonista** (m)	[prutegun'iʃte]
autograph	**autógrafo** (m)	[aut'ɔgrefu]
short story	**conto** (m)	[k'õtu]
story (novella)	**novela** (f)	[nuv'ɛle]
novel	**romance** (m)	[ʀum'ãsə]
work (writing)	**obra** (f)	['ɔbre]
fable	**fábula** (m)	[f'abule]
detective novel	**romance** (m) **policial**	[ʀum'ãsə pulisj'al]
poem (verse)	**poesia** (f)	[puez'ie]

poetry	**poesia** (f)	[puez'iɐ]
poem (epic, ballad)	**poema** (m)	[pu'emɐ]
poet	**poeta** (m)	[pu'ɛtɐ]
fiction	**ficção** (f)	[fiks'ãu]
science fiction	**ficção** (f) **científica**	[fiks'ãu siẽt'ifikɐ]
adventures	**aventuras** (f pl)	[ɐvẽt'urɐʃ]
educational literature	**literatura** (f) **didática**	[litərɐt'urɐ did'atikɐ]
children's literature	**literatura** (f) **infantil**	[litərɐt'urɐ ĩfãt'il]

128. Circus

circus	**circo** (m)	[s'irku]
chapiteau circus	**circo** (m) **ambulante**	[s'irku ãbul'ãtə]
program	**programa** (m)	[prugr'ɐmɐ]
performance	**apresentação** (f)	[ɐprəzẽtɐs'ãu]
act (circus ~)	**número** (m)	[n'uməru]
circus ring	**arena** (f)	[ɐr'enɐ]
pantomime (act)	**pantomima** (f)	[pãtum'imɐ]
clown	**palhaço** (m)	[pɐʎ'asu]
acrobat	**acrobata** (m)	[ɐkrub'atɐ]
acrobatics	**acrobacia** (f)	[ɐkrubɐs'iɐ]
gymnast	**ginasta** (m)	[ʒin'aʃtɐ]
gymnastics	**ginástica** (f)	[ʒin'aʃtikɐ]
somersault	**salto** (m) **mortal**	[s'altu murt'al]
athlete (strongman)	**homem forte** (m)	[ɔmɛj f'ɔrtə]
animal-tamer	**domador** (m)	[dumɐd'or]
equestrian	**cavaleiro** (m) **equilibrista**	[kɐvɐl'ɐjru ekilibr'iʃtɐ]
assistant	**assistente** (m)	[ɐsiʃt'ẽtə]
stunt	**truque** (m)	[tr'ukə]
magic trick	**truque** (m) **de mágica**	[tr'ukə də m'aʒikɐ]
conjurer, magician	**mágico** (m)	[m'aʒiku]
juggler	**malabarista** (m)	[mɐlɐbɐr'iʃtɐ]
to juggle (vi, vt)	**fazer malabarismos**	[fɐz'er mɐlɐbɐr'iʒmuʃ]
animal trainer	**domador** (m)	[dumɐd'or]
animal training	**adestramento** (m)	[ɐdəʃtrɐm'ẽtu]
to train (animals)	**adestrar** (vt)	[ɐdəʃtr'ar]

129. Music. Pop music

music	**música** (f)	[m'uzikɐ]
musician	**músico** (m)	[m'uziku]

musical instrument	**instrumento** (m) **musical**	[ĩʃtrum'ẽtu muzik'al]
to play ...	**tocar ...**	[tuk'ar]
guitar	**guitarra** (f)	[git'aʀɐ]
violin	**violino** (m)	[viul'inu]
cello	**violoncelo** (m)	[viulõs'ɛlu]
double bass	**contrabaixo** (m)	[kõtrɐb'ajʃu]
harp	**harpa** (f)	['arpɐ]
piano	**piano** (m)	[pj'ɐnu]
grand piano	**piano** (m) **de cauda**	[pj'ɐnu də k'audɐ]
organ	**órgão** (m)	['ɔrgãu]
wind instruments	**instrumentos** (m pl) **de sopro**	[ĩʃtrum'ẽtuʃ də s'opru]
oboe	**oboé** (m)	[ɔbu'ɛ]
saxophone	**saxofone** (m)	[saksɔf'ɔnə]
clarinet	**clarinete** (m)	[klɐrin'etə]
flute	**flauta** (f)	[fl'autɐ]
trumpet	**trompete** (m)	[trõp'ɛtə]
accordion	**acordeão** (m)	[ɐkɔrdj'ãu]
drum	**tambor** (m)	[tãb'or]
duo	**duo, dueto** (m)	[d'uu], [du'etu]
trio	**trio** (m)	[tr'iu]
quartet	**quarteto** (m)	[kuɐrt'etu]
choir	**coro** (m)	[k'oru]
orchestra	**orquestra** (f)	[ɔrk'ɛʃtrɐ]
pop music	**música** (f) **pop**	[m'uzikɐ p'ɔpə]
rock music	**música** (f) **rock**	[m'uzikɐ ʀ'ɔk]
rock group	**grupo** (m) **de rock**	[gr'upu də ʀ'ɔkə]
jazz	**jazz** (m)	[ʒaz]
idol	**ídolo** (m)	['idulu]
admirer, fan	**fã, admirador** (m)	[fã], [ɐdmirɐd'or]
concert	**concerto** (m)	[kõs'ertu]
symphony	**sinfonia** (f)	[sĩfun'iɐ]
composition	**composição** (f)	[kõpuzis'ãu]
to compose (write)	**compor** (vt)	[kõp'or]
singing	**canto** (m)	[k'ãtu]
song	**canção** (f)	[kãs'ãu]
tune (melody)	**melodia** (f)	[məlud'iɐ]
rhythm	**ritmo** (m)	[ʀ'itmu]
blues	**blues** (m)	[bl'uz]
sheet music	**notas** (f pl)	[n'ɔtɐʃ]
baton	**batuta** (f)	[bɐt'utɐ]
bow	**arco** (m)	['arku]

string	**corda** (f)	[k'ɔrdɐ]
case (e.g., guitar ~)	**estojo** (m)	[əʃt'oʒu]

Rest. Entertainment. Travel

130. Trip. Travel

tourism	**turismo** (m)	[tur'iʒmu]
tourist	**turista** (m)	[tur'iʃtɐ]
trip, voyage	**viagem** (f)	[vj'aʒẽj]
adventure	**aventura** (f)	[ɐvẽt'urɐ]
trip, journey	**viagem** (f)	[vj'aʒẽj]
vacation	**férias** (f pl)	[f'ɛriɐʃ]
to be on vacation	**estar de férias**	[əʃt'ar də f'ɛriɐʃ]
rest	**descanso** (m)	[dəʃk'ãsu]
train	**comboio** (m)	[kõb'ɔju]
by train	**de comboio**	[də kõb'ɔju]
airplane	**avião** (m)	[ɐvj'ãu]
by airplane	**de avião**	[də ɐvj'ãu]
by car	**de carro**	[də k'aʀu]
by ship	**de navio**	[də nɐv'iu]
luggage	**bagagem** (f)	[bɐg'aʒẽj]
suitcase, luggage	**mala** (f)	[m'alɐ]
luggage cart	**carrinho** (m)	[kɐʀ'iɲu]
passport	**passaporte** (m)	[pasɐp'ɔrtə]
visa	**visto** (m)	[v'iʃtu]
ticket	**bilhete** (m)	[biʎ'etə]
air ticket	**bilhete** (m) **de avião**	[biʎ'etə də ɐvj'ãu]
guidebook	**guia** (m) **de viagem**	[g'iɐ də vi'aʒẽj]
map	**mapa** (m)	[m'apɐ]
area (rural ~)	**local** (m), **area** (f)	[luk'al], [ɐr'ɛɐ]
place, site	**lugar, sítio** (m)	[lug'ar], [s'itiu]
exotic (n)	**exotismo** (m)	[ezut'iʒmu]
exotic (adj)	**exótico**	[ez'ɔtiku]
amazing (adj)	**surpreendente**	[surpriẽd'ẽtə]
group	**grupo** (m)	[gr'upu]
excursion	**excursão** (f)	[əʃkurs'ãu]
guide (person)	**guia** (m)	[g'iɐ]

131. Hotel

hotel	**hotel** (m)	[ɔt'ɛl]
motel	**motel** (m)	[mut'ɛl]
three-star	**três estrelas**	[tr'eʃ əʃtr'eləʃ]
five-star	**cinco estrelas**	[s'ĩku əʃtr'eləʃ]
to stay (in hotel, etc.)	**ficar** (vi, vt)	[fik'ar]
room	**quarto** (m)	[ku'artu]
single room	**quarto** (m) **individual**	[ku'artu ĩdividu'al]
double room	**quarto** (m) **duplo**	[ku'artu d'uplu]
to book a room	**reservar um quarto**	[ʀəzərv'ar ũ ku'artu]
half board	**meia pensão** (f)	[m'ɐjɐ pẽs'ãu]
full board	**pensão** (f) **completa**	[pẽs'ãu kõpl'ɛtɐ]
with bath	**com banheira**	[kõ bɐɲ'ɐjrɐ]
with shower	**com duche**	[kõ d'uʃə]
satellite television	**televisão** (m) **satélite**	[tələviz'ãu sɐt'ɛlitə]
air-conditioner	**ar** (m) **condicionado**	[ar kõdisiun'adu]
towel	**toalha** (f)	[tu'aʎɐ]
key	**chave** (f)	[ʃ'avə]
administrator	**administrador** (m)	[ɐdminiʃtrɐd'or]
chambermaid	**camareira** (f)	[kɐmɐr'ɐjrɐ]
porter, bellboy	**bagageiro** (m)	[bɐgɐʒ'ɐjru]
doorman	**porteiro** (m)	[purt'ɐjru]
restaurant	**restaurante** (m)	[ʀəʃtaur'ãtə]
pub, bar	**bar** (m)	[bar]
breakfast	**pequeno-almoço** (m)	[pək'enu alm'osu]
dinner	**jantar** (m)	[ʒãt'ar]
buffet	**buffet** (m)	[buf'e]
lobby	**hall** (m) **de entrada**	[ɔl də ẽtr'adɐ]
elevator	**elevador** (m)	[eləvɐd'or]
DO NOT DISTURB	**NÃO PERTURBE**	[n'ãu pərt'urbə]
NO SMOKING	**PROIBIDO FUMAR!**	[pruib'idu fum'ar]

132. Books. Reading

book	**livro** (m)	[l'ivru]
author	**autor** (m)	[aut'or]
writer	**escritor** (m)	[əʃkrit'or]
to write (~ a book)	**escrever** (vt)	[əʃkrəv'er]
reader	**leitor** (m)	[ləjt'or]
to read (vi, vt)	**ler** (vt)	[ler]

reading (activity)	**leitura** (f)	[lɐjt'urɐ]
silently (to oneself)	**para si**	[p'ɐrɐ si]
aloud (adv)	**em voz alta**	[ẽ vɔʒ 'altɐ]
to publish (vt)	**publicar** (vt)	[publik'ar]
publishing (process)	**publicação** (f)	[publikɐs'ãu]
publisher	**editor** (m)	[edit'or]
publishing house	**editora** (f)	[edit'orɐ]
to come out (be released)	**sair** (vi)	[sɐ'ir]
release (of a book)	**lançamento** (m)	[lãsɐm'ẽtu]
print run	**tiragem** (f)	[tir'aʒẽj]
bookstore	**livraria** (f)	[livrɐr'iɐ]
library	**biblioteca** (f)	[bibliut'ɛkɐ]
story (novella)	**novela** (f)	[nuv'ɛlɐ]
short story	**conto** (m)	[k'õtu]
novel	**romance** (m)	[ʀum'ãsə]
detective novel	**romance** (m) **policial**	[ʀum'ãsə pulisj'al]
memoirs	**memórias** (f pl)	[məm'ɔriɐʃ]
legend	**lenda** (f)	[l'ẽdɐ]
myth	**mito** (m)	[m'itu]
poetry, poems	**poesia** (f)	[puez'iɐ]
autobiography	**autobiografia** (f)	[autɔbiugrɐf'iɐ]
selected works	**obras** (f pl) **escolhidas**	['ɔbrɐʃ əʃkuʎ'idɐʃ]
science fiction	**ficção** (f) **científica**	[fiks'ãu siẽt'ifikɐ]
title	**título** (m)	[t'itulu]
introduction	**introdução** (f)	[ĩtrudus'ãu]
title page	**folha** (f) **de rosto**	[f'oʎɐ də ʀ'oʃtu]
chapter	**capítulo** (m)	[kɐp'itulu]
extract	**excerto** (m)	[əʃs'ertu]
episode	**episódio** (m)	[epiz'ɔdiu]
plot (storyline)	**tema** (m)	[t'emɐ]
contents	**conteúdo** (m)	[kõtj'udu]
table of contents	**índice** (m)	['ĩdisə]
main character	**protagonista** (m)	[prutɐgun'iʃtɐ]
volume	**tomo, volume** (m)	[t'omu], [vul'umə]
cover	**capa** (f)	[k'apɐ]
binding	**encadernação** (f)	[ẽkɐdərnɐs'ãu]
bookmark	**marcador** (m)	[mɐrkɐd'or]
page	**página** (f)	[p'aʒinɐ]
to flick through	**folhear** (vt)	[fuʎe'ar]
margins	**margem** (f)	[m'arʒẽj]
annotation	**anotação** (f)	[ɐnutɐs'ãu]

footnote	**nota** (f) **de rodapé**	[n'ɔtɐ də ʀɔdɐp'ɛ]
text	**texto** (m)	[t'ɛʃtu]
type, font	**fonte** (f)	[f'õtə]
misprint, typo	**gralha** (f)	[gɾ'aʎɐ]
translation	**tradução** (f)	[tɾɐdus'ãu]
to translate (vt)	**traduzir** (vt)	[tɾɐduz'iɾ]
original (n)	**original** (m)	[ɔɾiʒin'al]
famous (adj)	**famoso**	[fɐm'ozu]
unknown (adj)	**desconhecido**	[dəʃkuɲəs'idu]
interesting (adj)	**interessante**	[ĩtəɾəs'ãtə]
bestseller	**best-seller** (m)	[bɛsts'ɛlɐɾ]
dictionary	**dicionário** (m)	[disiun'aɾiu]
textbook	**manual** (m) **escolar**	[mɐnu'al əʃkul'aɾ]
encyclopedia	**enciclopédia** (f)	[ẽsiklup'ɛdiɐ]

133. Hunting. Fishing

hunting	**caça** (f)	[k'asɐ]
to hunt (vi, vt)	**caçar** (vi)	[kɐs'aɾ]
hunter	**caçador** (m)	[kɐsɐd'oɾ]
to shoot (vi)	**atirar** (vi)	[ɐtiɾ'aɾ]
rifle	**caçadeira** (f)	[kɐsɐd'ɐjɾɐ]
bullet (shell)	**cartucho** (m)	[kɐɾt'uʃu]
shot (lead balls)	**chumbo** (m) **de caça**	[ʃ'ũbu də k'asɐ]
trap (e.g., bear ~)	**armadilha** (f)	[ɐɾmɐd'iʎɐ]
snare (for birds, etc.)	**armadilha** (f)	[ɐɾmɐd'iʎɐ]
to fall into the trap	**cair na armadilha**	[kɐ'iɾ nɐ ɐɾmɐd'iʎɐ]
to lay a trap	**pôr a armadilha**	[p'oɾ ɐ ɐɾmɐd'iʎɐ]
poacher	**caçador** (m) **furtivo**	[kɐsɐd'oɾ fuɾt'ivu]
game (in hunting)	**caça** (f)	[k'asɐ]
hound dog	**cão** (m) **de caça**	[k'ãu də k'asɐ]
safari	**safári** (m)	[saf'aɾi]
mounted animal	**animal** (m) **empalhado**	[ɐnim'al ẽpɐʎ'adu]
fisherman	**pescador** (m)	[pəʃkɐd'oɾ]
fishing	**pesca** (f)	[p'ɛʃkɐ]
to fish (vi)	**pescar** (vt)	[pəʃk'aɾ]
fishing rod	**cana** (f) **de pesca**	[k'ɐnɐ də p'ɛʃkɐ]
fishing line	**linha** (f) **de pesca**	[l'iɲɐ də p'ɛʃkɐ]
hook	**anzol** (m)	[ãz'ɔl]
float	**boia** (f), **flutuador** (m)	[b'ɔjɐ], [flutuɐd'oɾ]
bait	**isca** (f)	['iʃkɐ]
to cast a line	**lançar a linha**	[lãs'aɾ ɐ l'iɲɐ]

to bite (ab. fish)	**morder** (vt)	[murd'er]
catch (of fish)	**pesca** (f)	[p'ɛʃkɐ]
ice-hole	**buraco** (m) **no gelo**	[bur'aku nu ʒ'elu]
fishing net	**rede** (f)	[ʀ'edə]
boat	**barco** (m)	[b'arku]
to net (catch with net)	**pescar com rede**	[pəʃk'ar kõ ʀ'edə]
to cast the net	**lançar a rede**	[lãs'ar ɐ ʀ'edə]
to haul in the net	**puxar a rede**	[puʃ'ar ɐ ʀ'edə]
to fall into the net	**cair nas malhas**	[kɐ'ir nɐʃ m'aʎɐʃ]
whaler (person)	**baleeiro** (m)	[bɐlj'ɐjru]
whaleboat	**baleeira** (f)	[bɐlj'ɐjrɐ]
harpoon	**arpão** (m)	[ɐrp'ãu]

134. Games. Billiards

billiards	**bilhar** (m)	[biʎ'ar]
billiard room, hall	**sala** (f) **de bilhar**	[s'alɐ də biʎ'ar]
ball	**bola** (f) **de bilhar**	[b'ɔlɐ də biʎ'ar]
to pocket a ball	**embolsar uma bola**	[ẽbɔls'ar 'umɐ b'ɔlɐ]
cue	**taco** (m)	[t'aku]
pocket	**bolsa** (f)	[b'olsɐ]

135. Games. Playing cards

diamonds	**ouros** (m pl)	['oruʃ]
spades	**espadas** (f pl)	[əʃp'adɐʃ]
hearts	**copas** (f pl)	[k'ɔpɐʃ]
clubs	**paus** (m pl)	[p'auʃ]
ace	**ás** (m)	[aʃ]
king	**rei** (m)	[ʀɐj]
queen	**dama** (f)	[d'ɐmɐ]
jack, knave	**valete** (m)	[vɐl'etə]
playing card	**carta** (f) **de jogar**	[k'artɐ də ʒug'ar]
cards	**cartas** (f pl)	[k'artɐʃ]
trump	**trunfo** (m)	[tr'ũfu]
deck of cards	**baralho** (m)	[bɐr'aʎu]
point	**ponto** (m)	[p'õtu]
to deal (vi, vt)	**dar, distribuir** (vt)	[dar], [diʃtribu'ir]
to shuffle (cards)	**embaralhar** (vt)	[ẽbɐrɐʎ'ar]
lead, turn (n)	**vez, jogada** (f)	[veʒ], [ʒug'adɐ]
cardsharp	**batoteiro** (m)	[bɐtut'ɐjru]

136. Rest. Games. Miscellaneous

to walk, to stroll (vi)	**passear** (vi)	[pesj'ar]
walk, stroll	**passeio** (m)	[pes'eju]
road trip	**viagem** (f) **de carro**	[vj'aʒẽj də k'aʀu]
adventure	**aventura** (f)	[evẽt'ure]
picnic	**piquenique** (m)	[pikən'ikə]
game (chess, etc.)	**jogo** (m)	[ʒ'ogu]
player	**jogador** (m)	[ʒuged'or]
game (one ~ of chess)	**partida** (f)	[pert'ide]
collector (e.g., philatelist)	**colecionador** (m)	[kulɛsiuned'or]
to collect (vt)	**colecionar** (vt)	[kulɛsiun'ar]
collection	**coleção** (f)	[kulɛs'ãu]
crossword puzzle	**palavras** (f pl) **cruzadas**	[pel'avreʃ kruz'adeʃ]
racetrack (hippodrome)	**hipódromo** (m)	[ip'ɔdrumu]
discotheque	**discoteca** (f)	[diʃkut'ɛke]
sauna	**sauna** (f)	[s'eune]
lottery	**lotaria** (f)	[luter'ie]
camping trip	**viagem** (f) **de acampamento**	[vj'aʒẽj də ekãpem'ẽtu]
camp	**acampamento** (m)	[ekãpem'ẽtu]
tent (for camping)	**tenda** (f)	[t'ẽde]
compass	**bússola** (f)	[b'usule]
camper	**campista** (m)	[kãp'iʃte]
to watch (movie, etc.)	**ver** (vt), **assistir à ...**	[ver], [esiʃt'ir a]
viewer	**telespetador** (m)	[tɛlɛʃpɛted'or]
TV show	**programa** (m) **de TV**	[prugr'eme də tɛv'ɛ]

137. Photography

camera (photo)	**máquina** (f) **fotográfica**	[m'akine futugr'afike]
photo, picture	**foto, fotografia** (f)	[f'ɔtu], [futugref'ie]
photographer	**fotógrafo** (m)	[fut'ɔgrefu]
photo studio	**estúdio** (m) **fotográfico**	[əʃt'udiu futugr'afiku]
photo album	**álbum** (m) **de fotografias**	[albũ də futugref'ieʃ]
camera lens	**objetiva** (f)	[ɔbʒɛt'ive]
telephoto lens	**teleobjetiva** (f)	[tɛlɛɔbʒɛt'ive]
filter	**filtro** (m)	[f'iltru]
lens	**lente** (f)	[l'ẽtə]
optics (high-quality ~)	**ótica** (f)	['ɔtike]
diaphragm (aperture)	**abertura** (f)	[ebərt'ure]

exposure time	**exposição** (f)	[əʃpuzis'ãu]
viewfinder	**visor** (m)	[viz'or]
digital camera	**câmara** (f) **digital**	[k'ɐmɐrɐ diʒit'al]
tripod	**tripé** (m)	[trip'ɛ]
flash	**flash** (m)	[flaʃ]
to photograph (vt)	**fotografar** (vt)	[futugrɐf'ar]
to take pictures	**tirar fotos**	[tir'ar f'ɔtuʃ]
to be photographed	**fotografar-se**	[futugrɐf'arsə]
focus	**foco** (m)	[f'ɔku]
to adjust the focus	**focar** (vt)	[fuk'ar]
sharp, in focus (adj)	**nítido**	[n'itidu]
sharpness	**nitidez** (f)	[nitid'eʃ]
contrast	**contraste** (m)	[kõtr'aʃtə]
contrasty (adj)	**contrastante**	[kõtrɐʃt'ãtə]
picture (photo)	**retrato** (m)	[ʀətr'atu]
negative (n)	**negativo** (m)	[nəgɐt'ivu]
film (a roll of ~)	**filme** (m)	[f'ilmə]
frame (still)	**fotograma** (m)	[futugr'ɐmɐ]
to print (photos)	**imprimir** (vt)	[ĩprim'ir]

138. Beach. Swimming

beach	**praia** (f)	[pr'ajɐ]
sand	**areia** (f)	[ɐr'ɐjɐ]
deserted (beach)	**deserto**	[dəz'ɛrtu]
suntan	**bronzeado** (m)	[brõzj'adu]
to get a tan	**bronzear-se** (vp)	[brõzj'arsə]
tan (adj)	**bronzeado**	[brõzj'adu]
sunscreen	**protetor** (m) **solar**	[prutɛt'or sul'ar]
bikini	**biquíni** (m)	[bik'ini]
bathing suit	**fato** (m) **de banho**	[f'atu də b'ɐɲu]
swim briefs	**calção** (m) **de banho**	[kals'ãu də b'ɐɲu]
swimming pool	**piscina** (f)	[piʃs'inɐ]
to swim (vi)	**nadar** (vi)	[nɐd'ar]
shower	**duche** (m)	[d'uʃə]
to change (one's clothes)	**mudar de roupa**	[mudar də ʀ'opɐ]
towel	**toalha** (f)	[tu'aʎɐ]
boat	**barco** (m)	[b'arku]
motorboat	**lancha** (f)	[l'ãʃɐ]
water ski	**esqui** (m) **aquático**	[əʃk'i ɐku'atiku]
paddle boat	**barco** (m) **de pedais**	[b'arku də pəd'ajʃ]

surfing	**surf, surfe** (m)	[s'urfə]
surfer	**surfista** (m)	[surf'iʃtɐ]
scuba set	**scuba** (m)	[sk'ubɐ]
flippers (swimfins)	**barbatanas** (f pl)	[bɐrbɐt'ɐnɐʃ]
mask	**máscara** (f)	[m'aʃkɐrɐ]
diver	**mergulhador** (m)	[mərguʎɐd'or]
to dive (vi)	**mergulhar** (vi)	[mərguʎ'ar]
underwater (adv)	**debaixo d'água**	[dəb'ajʃu d'aguɐ]
beach umbrella	**guarda-sol** (m)	[gu'ardɐ s'ɔl]
beach chair	**espreguiçadeira** (f)	[əʃprəgisɐd'ɐjrɐ]
sunglasses	**óculos** (m pl) **de sol**	['ɔkuluʃ də s'ɔl]
air mattress	**colchão** (m) **de ar**	[kolʃ'ãu də 'ar]
to play (amuse oneself)	**brincar** (vi)	[brĩk'ar]
to go for a swim	**ir nadar**	[ir nɐd'ar]
beach ball	**bola** (f) **de praia**	[b'ɔlɐ də pr'ajɐ]
to inflate (vt)	**encher** (vt)	[ẽʃ'er]
inflatable, air- (adj)	**inflável, de ar**	[ĩfl'avɛl], [də 'ar]
wave	**onda** (f)	['õdɐ]
buoy	**boia** (f)	[b'ɔjɐ]
to drown (ab. person)	**afogar-se** (vp)	[ɐfug'arsə]
to save, to rescue	**salvar** (vt)	[salv'ar]
life vest	**colete** (m) **salva-vidas**	[kul'etə s'alvɐ v'idɐʃ]
to observe, to watch	**observar** (vt)	[ɔbsərv'ar]
lifeguard	**nadador-salvador** (m)	[nɐdɐd'or salvɐd'or]

TECHNICAL EQUIPMENT. TRANSPORTATION

Technical equipment

139. Computer

computer	**computador** (m)	[kõputɐd'or]
notebook, laptop	**portátil** (m)	[purt'atil]
to turn on	**ligar** (vt)	[lig'ar]
to turn off	**desligar** (vt)	[dəʒlig'ar]
keyboard	**teclado** (m)	[tɛkl'adu]
key	**tecla** (f)	[t'ɛklɐ]
mouse	**rato** (m)	[ʀ'atu]
mouse pad	**tapete** (m) **de rato**	[tɐp'etə də ʀ'atu]
button	**botão** (m)	[but'ãu]
cursor	**cursor** (m)	[kurs'or]
monitor	**monitor** (m)	[munit'or]
screen	**ecrã** (m)	[ɛkr'ã]
hard disk	**disco** (m) **rígido**	[d'iʃku ʀ'iʒidu]
hard disk volume	**capacidade** (f) **do disco rígido**	[kɐpɐsid'adə du d'iʃku ʀ'iʒidu]
memory	**memória** (f)	[məm'ɔriɐ]
random access memory	**memória** (f) **operativa**	[məm'ɔriɐ ɔpərɐt'ivɐ]
file	**ficheiro** (m)	[fiʃ'ɐjru]
folder	**pasta** (f)	[p'aʃtɐ]
to open (vt)	**abrir** (vt)	[ɐbr'ir]
to close (vt)	**fechar** (vt)	[fəʃ'ar]
to save (vt)	**guardar** (vt)	[guɐrd'ar]
to delete (vt)	**apagar, eliminar** (vt)	[ɐpɐg'ar], [elimin'ar]
to copy (vt)	**copiar** (vt)	[kupj'ar]
to sort (vt)	**ordenar** (vt)	[ɔrdən'ar]
to transfer (copy)	**copiar** (vt)	[kupj'ar]
program	**programa** (m)	[prugr'emɐ]
software	**software** (m)	[s'ɔftuɛr]
programmer	**programador** (m)	[prugrɐmɐd'or]
to program (vt)	**programar** (vt)	[prugrɐm'ar]
hacker	**hacker** (m)	['akɛr]

password	**senha** (f)	[s'ɐɲɐ]
virus	**vírus** (m)	[v'iruʃ]
to find, to detect	**detetar** (vt)	[dətɛt'ar]
byte	**byte** (m)	[b'ajtə]
megabyte	**megabyte** (m)	[mɛgɐb'ajtə]
data	**dados** (m pl)	[d'aduʃ]
database	**base** (f) **de dados**	[b'azə də d'aduʃ]
cable (USB, etc.)	**cabo** (m)	[k'abu]
to disconnect (vt)	**desconectar** (vt)	[dəʃkunɛt'ar]
to connect (sth to sth)	**conetar** (vt)	[kunɛt'ar]

140. Internet. E-mail

Internet	**internet** (f)	[ĩtɛrn'ɛtə]
browser	**browser** (m)	[br'auzer]
search engine	**motor** (m) **de busca**	[mut'or də b'uʃkɐ]
provider	**provedor** (m)	[pruvəd'or]
web master	**webmaster** (m)	[wɛbm'astɛr]
website	**website, sítio web** (m)	[wɛbsitə], [s'itiu wɛb]
web page	**página** (f) **web**	[p'aʒinɐ wɛb]
address	**endereço** (m)	[ẽdər'esu]
address book	**livro** (m) **de endereços**	[l'ivru də ẽdər'esuʃ]
mailbox	**caixa** (f) **de correio**	[k'ajʃɐ də kuʀ'ɐju]
mail	**correio** (m)	[kuʀ'ɐju]
full (adj)	**cheia**	[ʃ'ɐjɐ]
message	**mensagem** (f)	[mẽs'aʒẽj]
incoming messages	**mensagens recebidas**	[mẽs'aʒẽjʃ ʀəsəb'idɐʃ]
outgoing messages	**mensagens enviadas**	[mẽs'aʒẽjʃ ẽvj'adɐʃ]
sender	**remetente** (m)	[ʀəmət'ẽtə]
to send (vt)	**enviar** (vt)	[ẽvj'ar]
sending (of mail)	**envio** (m)	[ẽv'iu]
receiver	**destinatário** (m)	[dəʃtinɐt'ariu]
to receive (vt)	**receber** (vt)	[ʀəsəb'er]
correspondence	**correspondência** (f)	[kuʀəʃpõd'ẽsiɐ]
to correspond (vi)	**corresponder-se** (vp)	[kuʀəʃpõd'ersə]
file	**ficheiro** (m)	[fiʃ'ɐjru]
to download (vt)	**fazer download, baixar** (vt)	[fɐz'er daunl'oɐd], [bajʃ'ar]
to create (vt)	**criar** (vt)	[kri'ar]
to delete (vt)	**apagar, eliminar** (vt)	[ɐpɐg'ar], [elimin'ar]

deleted (adj)	**eliminado**	[elimin'adu]
connection (ADSL, etc.)	**ligação** (f)	[liges'ãu]
speed	**velocidade** (f)	[vəlusid'adə]
modem	**modem** (m)	[m'ɔdɛm]
access	**acesso** (m)	[ɐs'ɛsu]
port (e.g., input ~)	**porta** (f)	[p'ɔrtɐ]
connection (make a ~)	**conexão** (f)	[kunɛks'ãu]
to connect to ... (vi)	**conetar** (vi)	[kunɛt'aɾ]
to select (vt)	**escolher** (vt)	[əʃkuʎ'eɾ]
to search (for ...)	**buscar** (vt)	[buʃk'aɾ]

Transportation

141. Airplane

airplane	**avião** (m)	[ɐvj'ãu]
air ticket	**bilhete** (m) **de avião**	[biʎ'etə də ɐvj'ãu]
airline	**companhia** (f) **aérea**	[kõpɐɲ'iɐ ɐ'ɛriɐ]
airport	**aeroporto** (m)	[ɐɛrɔp'ortu]
supersonic (adj)	**supersónico**	[supərs'ɔniku]
captain	**comandante** (m) **do avião**	[kumãd'ãtə du ɐvj'ãu]
crew	**tripulação** (f)	[tripulɐs'ãu]
pilot	**piloto** (m)	[pil'otu]
flight attendant	**hospedeira** (f) **de bordo**	[ɔʃpəd'ɐjrɐ də b'ɔrdu]
navigator	**copiloto** (m)	[kopil'otu]
wings	**asas** (f pl)	['azɐʃ]
tail	**cauda** (f)	[k'audɐ]
cockpit	**cabine** (f)	[kɐb'inə]
engine	**motor** (m)	[mut'or]
undercarriage	**trem** (m) **de aterragem**	[trẽj də ɐtəʀ'aʒẽj]
turbine	**turbina** (f)	[turb'inɐ]
propeller	**hélice** (f)	['ɛlisə]
black box	**caixa** (f) **negra**	[k'ajʃɐ n'egrɐ]
control column	**coluna** (f) **de controle**	[kul'unɐ də kõtr'ɔlə]
fuel	**combustível** (m)	[kõbuʃt'ivɛl]
safety card	**instruções** (f pl) **de segurança**	[ĩʃtrus'ojʃ də səgur'ãsɐ]
oxygen mask	**máscara** (f) **de oxigénio**	[m'aʃkɐrɐ də ɔksiʒ'ɛniu]
uniform	**uniforme** (m)	[unif'ɔrmə]
life vest	**colete** (m) **salva-vidas**	[kul'etə s'alvɐ v'idɐʃ]
parachute	**paraquedas** (m)	[pɐrɐk'ɛdɐʃ]
takeoff	**descolagem** (f)	[dəʃkul'aʒẽj]
to take off (vi)	**descolar** (vi)	[dəʃkul'ar]
runway	**pista** (f) **de descolagem**	[p'iʃtɐ də dəʃkul'aʒẽj]
visibility	**visibilidade** (f)	[vizibilid'adə]
flight (act of flying)	**voo** (m)	[v'ou]
altitude	**altura** (f)	[alt'urɐ]
air pocket	**poço** (m) **de ar**	[p'osu də 'ar]
seat	**assento** (m)	[ɐs'ẽtu]
headphones	**auscultadores** (m pl)	[auʃkultɐd'orəʃ]

folding tray	**mesa** (f) **rebatível**	[m'eze Rəbet'ivɛl]
airplane window	**vigia** (f)	[viʒ'iɐ]
aisle	**passagem** (f)	[pes'aʒẽj]

142. Train

train	**comboio** (m)	[kõb'ɔju]
suburban train	**comboio** (m) **suburbano**	[kõb'ɔju suburb'enu]
express train	**comboio** (m) **rápido**	[kõb'ɔju R'apidu]
diesel locomotive	**locomotiva** (f) **diesel**	[lukumut'ive d'izɛl]
steam engine	**comboio** (m) **a vapor**	[kõb'ɔju ɐ vɐp'or]
passenger car	**carruagem** (f)	[kɐRu'aʒẽj]
dining car	**carruagem restaurante** (f)	[kɐRu'aʒẽj Rəʃtaur'ãtə]
rails	**trilhos** (m pl)	[tr'iʎuʃ]
railroad	**caminho de ferro** (m)	[kɐm'iɲu də f'ɛRu]
railway tie	**travessa** (f)	[trɐv'ɛsɐ]
platform (railway ~)	**plataforma** (f)	[plɐtɐf'ɔrmɐ]
track (~ 1, 2, etc.)	**linha** (f)	[l'iɲɐ]
semaphore	**semáforo** (m)	[səm'afuru]
station	**estação** (f)	[əʃtɐs'ãu]
engineer	**maquinista** (m)	[mɐkin'iʃtɐ]
porter (of luggage)	**bagageiro** (m)	[bɐgɐʒ'ɐjru]
train steward	**condutor** (m)	[kõdut'or]
passenger	**passageiro** (m)	[pɐsɐʒ'ɐjru]
conductor	**revisor** (m)	[Rəviz'or]
corridor (in train)	**corredor** (m)	[kuRəd'or]
emergency break	**freio** (m) **de emergência**	[fr'ɐju də emərʒ'ẽsiɐ]
compartment	**compartimento** (m)	[kõpɐrtim'ẽtu]
berth	**cama** (f)	[k'ɐmɐ]
upper berth	**cama** (f) **de cima**	[k'ɐmɐ də s'imɐ]
lower berth	**cama** (f) **de baixo**	[k'ɐmɐ də b'ajʃu]
bed linen	**roupa** (f) **de cama**	[R'opɐ də k'ɐmɐ]
ticket	**bilhete** (m)	[biʎ'etə]
schedule	**horário** (m)	[ɔr'ariu]
information display	**painel** (m) **de informação**	[pajn'ɛl də ĩfurmɐs'ãu]
to leave, to depart	**partir** (vt)	[pɐrt'ir]
departure (of train)	**partida** (f)	[pɐrt'idɐ]
to arrive (ab. train)	**chegar** (vi)	[ʃəg'ar]
arrival	**chegada** (f)	[ʃəg'adɐ]
to arrive by train	**chegar de comboio**	[ʃəg'ar də kõb'ɔju]
to get on the train	**apanhar o comboio**	[ɐpɐɲ'ar u kõb'ɔju]

to get off the train	**sair do comboio**	[sɐ'ir du kõb'ɔju]
train wreck	**acidente** (m) **ferroviário**	[ɐsid'ẽtə fɛʀɔvj'ariu]
to be derailed	**descarrilar** (vi)	[dəʃkɐʀil'ar]
steam engine	**comboio** (m) **a vapor**	[kõb'ɔju ɐ vɐp'or]
stoker, fireman	**fogueiro** (m)	[fug'ɐjru]
firebox	**fornalha** (f)	[furn'aʎɐ]
coal	**carvão** (m)	[kɐrv'ãu]

143. Ship

ship	**navio** (m)	[nɐv'iu]
vessel	**embarcação** (f)	[ẽbɐrkɐs'ãu]
steamship	**vapor** (m)	[vɐp'or]
riverboat	**navio** (m)	[nɐv'iu]
ocean liner	**transatlântico** (m)	[trãzɐtl'ãtiku]
cruiser	**cruzador** (m)	[kruzɐd'or]
yacht	**iate** (m)	[j'atə]
tugboat	**rebocador** (m)	[ʀəbukɐd'or]
barge	**barcaça** (f)	[bɐrk'asɐ]
ferry	**ferry** (m)	[f'ɛʀi]
sailing ship	**veleiro** (m)	[vəl'ɐjru]
brigantine	**bergantim** (m)	[bərgãt'ĩ]
ice breaker	**quebra-gelo** (m)	[k'ɛbrɐ ʒ'ɛlu]
submarine	**submarino** (m)	[submɐr'inu]
boat (flat-bottomed ~)	**bote, barco** (m)	[b'ɔtə], [b'arku]
dinghy	**bote, dingue** (m)	[b'ɔtə], [d'ĩgə]
lifeboat	**bote** (m) **salva-vidas**	[b'ɔtə s'alvɐ v'idɐʃ]
motorboat	**lancha** (f)	[l'ãʃɐ]
captain	**capitão** (m)	[kɐpit'ãu]
seaman	**marinheiro** (m)	[mɐriɲ'ɐjru]
sailor	**marujo** (m)	[mɐr'uʒu]
crew	**tripulação** (f)	[tripulɐs'ãu]
boatswain	**contramestre** (m)	[kõtrəm'ɛʃtrə]
ship's boy	**grumete** (m)	[grum'ɛtə]
cook	**cozinheiro** (m) **de bordo**	[kuziɲ'ɐjru də b'ɔrdu]
ship's doctor	**médico** (m) **de bordo**	[m'ɛdiku də b'ɔrdu]
deck	**convés** (m)	[kõv'ɛʃ]
mast	**mastro** (m)	[m'aʃtru]
sail	**vela** (f)	[v'ɛlɐ]
hold	**porão** (m)	[pur'ãu]
bow (prow)	**proa** (f)	[pr'oɐ]
stern	**popa** (f)	[p'opɐ]

oar	**remo** (m)	[ʀ'ɛmu]
screw propeller	**hélice** (f)	['ɛlisə]
cabin	**camarote** (m)	[kɐmɐr'ɔtə]
wardroom	**sala** (f) **dos oficiais**	[s'alɐ duʃ ɔfisj'ajʃ]
engine room	**sala** (f) **das máquinas**	[s'alɐ dɐʃ m'akinɐʃ]
bridge	**ponte** (m) **de comando**	[p'õtə də kum'ãdu]
radio room	**sala** (f) **de comunicações**	[s'alɐ də kumunikɐs'ojʃ]
wave (radio)	**onda** (f)	['õdɐ]
logbook	**diário** (m) **de bordo**	[dj'ariu də b'ɔrdu]
spyglass	**luneta** (f)	[lun'ɛtɐ]
bell	**sino** (m)	[s'inu]
flag	**bandeira** (f)	[bãd'ɐjrɐ]
rope (mooring ~)	**cabo** (m)	[k'abu]
knot (bowline, etc.)	**nó** (m)	[nɔ]
deckrail	**corrimão** (m)	[kuʀim'ãu]
gangway	**prancha** (f) **de embarque**	[pr'ãʃɐ də ẽb'arkə]
anchor	**âncora** (f)	['ãkurɐ]
to weigh anchor	**recolher a âncora**	[ʀəkuʎ'er ɐ 'ãkurɐ]
to drop anchor	**lançar a âncora**	[lãs'ar ɐ 'ãkurɐ]
anchor chain	**amarra** (f)	[ɐm'aʀɐ]
port (harbor)	**porto** (m)	[p'ortu]
berth, wharf	**cais, amarradouro** (m)	[kajʃ], [ɐmɐʀɐd'oru]
to berth (moor)	**atracar** (vi)	[ɐtrɐk'ar]
to cast off	**desatracar** (vi)	[dəzɐtrɐk'ar]
trip, voyage	**viagem** (f)	[vj'aʒẽj]
cruise (sea trip)	**cruzeiro** (m)	[kruz'ɐjru]
course (route)	**rumo** (m), **rota** (f)	[ʀ'umu], [ʀ'ɔtɐ]
route (itinerary)	**itinerário** (m)	[itinər'ariu]
fairway	**canal** (m) **navegável**	[kɐn'al nɐvəg'avɛl]
shallows (shoal)	**baixio** (m)	[bajʃ'iu]
to run aground	**encalhar** (vt)	[ẽkɐʎ'ar]
storm	**tempestade** (f)	[tẽpəʃt'adə]
signal	**sinal** (m)	[sin'al]
to sink (vi)	**afundar-se** (vp)	[ɐfũd'arsə]
Man overboard!	**Homem ao mar!**	['ɔmẽj 'au m'ar]
SOS	**SOS**	[ɛsəo 'ɛsə]
ring buoy	**boia** (f) **salva-vidas**	[b'ɔjɐ s'alvɐ v'idɐʃ]

144. Airport

airport	**aeroporto** (m)	[ɐɛrɔp'ortu]
airplane	**avião** (m)	[ɐvj'ãu]

airline	**companhia** (f) **aérea**	[kõpeɲ'ie e'ɛrie]
air-traffic controller	**controlador** (m) **de tráfego aéreo**	[kõtruled'or də tr'afəgu e'ɛriu]
departure	**partida** (f)	[pert'ide]
arrival	**chegada** (f)	[ʃəg'ade]
to arrive (by plane)	**chegar** (vi)	[ʃəg'ar]
departure time	**hora** (f) **de partida**	['ɔre də pert'ide]
arrival time	**hora** (f) **de chegada**	['ɔre də ʃəg'ade]
to be delayed	**estar atrasado**	[əʃt'ar etrez'adu]
flight delay	**atraso** (m) **de voo**	[etr'azu də v'ou]
information board	**painel** (m) **de informação**	[pajn'ɛl də ĩfurmes'ãu]
information	**informação** (f)	[ĩfurmes'ãu]
to announce (vt)	**anunciar** (vt)	[enũsj'ar]
flight (e.g., next ~)	**voo** (m)	[v'ou]
customs	**alfândega** (f)	[alf'ãdəge]
customs officer	**funcionário** (m) **da alfândega**	[fũsiun'ariu de alf'ãdəge]
customs declaration	**declaração** (f) **alfandegária**	[dəkleres'ãu alfãdəg'arie]
to fill out (vt)	**preencher** (vt)	[priẽʃ'er]
to fill out the declaration	**preencher a declaração**	[priẽʃ'er e dəkleres'ãu]
passport control	**controlo** (m) **de passaportes**	[kõtr'olu də pasep'ɔrtəʃ]
luggage	**bagagem** (f)	[beg'aʒẽj]
hand luggage	**bagagem** (f) **de mão**	[beg'aʒẽj də m'ãu]
Lost Luggage Desk	**Perdidos e Achados**	[pərd'iduʃ i eʃ'aduʃ]
luggage cart	**carrinho** (m)	[keʀ'iɲu]
landing	**aterragem** (f)	[etəʀ'aʒẽj]
landing strip	**pista** (f) **de aterragem**	[p'iʃte də etəʀ'aʒẽj]
to land (vi)	**aterrar** (vi)	[etəʀ'ar]
airstairs	**escada** (f) **de avião**	[əʃk'ade də evj'ãu]
check-in	**check-in** (m)	[ʃɛk'in]
check-in desk	**balcão** (m) **do check-in**	[balk'ãu du ʃɛk'in]
to check-in (vi)	**fazer o check-in**	[fez'er u ʃɛk'in]
boarding pass	**cartão** (m) **de embarque**	[kert'ãu də ẽb'arkə]
departure gate	**porta** (f) **de embarque**	[p'ɔrte də ẽb'arkə]
transit	**trânsito** (m)	[tr'ãzitu]
to wait (vt)	**esperar** (vi, vt)	[əʃpər'ar]
departure lounge	**sala** (f) **de espera**	[s'ale də əʃp'ɛre]
to see off	**despedir-se de ...**	[dəʃpəd'irsə də]
to say goodbye	**dizer adeus**	[diz'er ed'ewʃ]

145. Bicycle. Motorcycle

bicycle	**bicicleta** (f)	[bisikl'ɛtɐ]
scooter	**scotter, lambreta** (f)	[skut'eɾ], [lãbɾ'etɐ]
motorcycle, bike	**mota** (f)	[m'ɔtɐ]
to go by bicycle	**ir de bicicleta**	[iɾ də bisikl'ɛtɐ]
handlebars	**guiador** (m)	[giɐd'oɾ]
pedal	**pedal** (m)	[pəd'al]
brakes	**travões** (m pl)	[tɾɐv'ojʃ]
bicycle seat	**selim** (m)	[səl'ĩ]
pump	**bomba** (f) **de ar**	[b'õbɐ də 'aɾ]
luggage rack	**porta-bagagens** (m)	[p'ɔɾtɐ bɐg'aʒẽjʃ]
front lamp	**lanterna** (f)	[lãt'ɛɾnɐ]
helmet	**capacete** (m)	[kɐpɐs'etə]
wheel	**roda** (f)	[ʀ'ɔdɐ]
fender	**guarda-lamas** (m)	[guaɾdɐ l'ɐmɐʃ]
rim	**aro** (m)	['aɾu]
spoke	**raio** (m)	[ʀ'aju]

Cars

146. Types of cars

automobile, car	**carro, automóvel** (m)	[k'aʀu], [autum'ɔvɛl]
sports car	**carro** (m) **desportivo**	[k'aʀu dəʃpuɾt'ivu]
limousine	**limusine** (f)	[limuz'inə]
off-road vehicle	**todo o terreno** (m)	[t'odu u təʀ'enu]
convertible	**descapotável** (m)	[dəʃkɐput'avɛl]
minibus	**minibus** (m)	[m'inibɐz]
ambulance	**ambulância** (f)	[ãbul'ãsiɐ]
snowplow	**limpa-neve** (m)	[l'ĩpɐ n'ɛvə]
truck	**camião** (m)	[kamj'ãu]
tank truck	**camião-cisterna** (m)	[kamj'ãu siʃt'ɛrnɐ]
van (small truck)	**carrinha** (f)	[kɐʀ'iɲɐ]
tractor (big rig)	**caminhão-trator** (m)	[kɐmiɲ'ãu trɐt'oɾ]
trailer	**atrelado** (m)	[ɐtrəl'adu]
comfortable (adj)	**confortável**	[kõfuɾt'avɛl]
second hand (adj)	**usado**	[uz'adu]

147. Cars. Bodywork

hood	**capô** (m)	[kɐp'o]
fender	**guarda-lamas** (m)	[guardɐ l'ɐmɐʃ]
roof	**tejadilho** (m)	[təʒɐd'iʎu]
windshield	**para-brisa** (m)	[paɾɐbr'izɐ]
rear-view mirror	**espelho** (m) **retrovisor**	[əʃp'ɐʎu ʀɛtrɔviz'oɾ]
windshield washer	**lavador** (m)	[lɐvɐd'oɾ]
windshield wipers	**limpa-para-brisas** (m)	[l'ĩpɐ p'aɾɐ br'izɐʃ]
side window	**vidro** (m) **lateral**	[v'idɾu lɐtər'al]
window lift	**elevador** (m) **do vidro**	[eləvɐd'or du v'idɾu]
antenna	**antena** (f)	[ãt'enɐ]
sun roof	**teto solar** (m)	[t'ɛtu sul'aɾ]
bumper	**para-choques** (m pl)	[p'aɾɐ ʃ'ɔkəʃ]
trunk	**bagageira** (f)	[bɐgɐʒ'ɐjɾɐ]
roof luggage rack	**bagageira** (f) **de tejadilho**	[bɐgɐʒ'ɐjɾɐ də təʒɐd'iʎu]
door	**porta** (f)	[p'ɔɾtɐ]

door handle	**maçaneta** (f)	[mesen'ete]
door lock	**fechadura** (f)	[fəʃed'ure]
license plate	**matrícula** (f)	[metr'ikule]
muffler	**silenciador** (m)	[silẽsied'or]
gas tank	**tanque** (m) **de gasolina**	[t'ãkə də gezul'ine]
tail pipe	**tubo** (m) **de escape**	[t'ubu də əʃk'apə]
gas, accelerator	**acelerador** (m)	[esələred'or]
pedal	**pedal** (m)	[pəd'al]
gas pedal	**pedal** (m) **do acelerador**	[pəd'al du esələred'or]
brake	**travão** (m)	[trev'ãu]
brake pedal	**pedal** (m) **do travão**	[pəd'al du trev'ãu]
to slow down (to brake)	**travar** (vt)	[trev'ar]
parking brake	**travão** (m) **de mão**	[trev'ãu də m'ãu]
clutch	**embraiagem** (f)	[ẽbraj'aʒẽj]
clutch pedal	**pedal** (m) **da embraiagem**	[pəd'al de ẽbraj'aʒẽj]
clutch plate	**disco** (m) **de embraiagem**	[d'iʃku də ẽbraj'aʒẽj]
shock absorber	**amortecedor** (m)	[emurtəsəd'or]
wheel	**roda** (f)	[ʀ'ɔde]
spare tire	**pneu** (m) **sobresselente**	[pn'eu sobrəsəl'ẽtə]
tire	**pneu** (m)	[pn'eu]
hubcap	**tampão** (m) **de roda**	[tãp'ãu də ʀ'ɔde]
driving wheels	**rodas** (f pl) **motrizes**	[ʀ'ɔdeʃ mutr'izəʃ]
front-wheel drive (as adj)	**de tração dianteira**	[də tras'ãu diãt'ejre]
rear-wheel drive (as adj)	**de tração traseira**	[də tras'ãu trez'ejre]
all-wheel drive (as adj)	**de tração às 4 rodas**	[də tras'ãu aʃ ku'atru ʀ'ɔdeʃ]
gearbox	**caixa** (f) **de mudanças**	[k'ajʃe də mud'ãseʃ]
automatic (adj)	**automático**	[autum'atiku]
mechanical (adj)	**mecânico**	[mək'eniku]
gear shift	**alavanca** (f) **das mudanças**	[elev'ãke deʃ mud'ãseʃ]
headlight	**farol** (m)	[fer'ɔl]
headlights	**faróis** (m pl), **luzes** (f pl)	[fer'ɔjʃ], [l'uzəʃ]
low beam	**médios** (m pl)	[m'ɛdiuʃ]
high beam	**máximos** (m pl)	[m'asimuʃ]
brake light	**luzes** (f pl) **de stop**	[l'uzəʃ də st'ɔp]
parking lights	**mínimos** (m pl)	[m'inimuʃ]
hazard lights	**luzes** (f pl) **de emergência**	[l'uzəʃ də emərʒ'ẽsie]
fog lights	**faróis** (m pl) **antinevoeiro**	[fer'ɔjʃ ãtinəvu'ejru]
turn signal	**pisca-pisca** (m)	[p'iʃke p'iʃke]
back-up light	**luz** (f) **de marcha atrás**	[luʃ də m'arʃe etr'aʃ]

148. Cars. Passenger compartment

car inside	**interior** (m) **do carro**	[ĩtərj'or du k'aʀu]
leather (as adj)	**de couro, de pele**	[də k'oru], [də p'ɛlə]
velour (as adj)	**de veludo**	[də vəl'udu]
upholstery	**estofos** (m pl)	[əʃt'ɔfuʃ]
instrument (gage)	**indicador** (m)	[ĩdikɐd'or]
dashboard	**painel** (m) **de instrumentos**	[pajn'ɛl də ĩʃtrum'ẽtuʃ]
speedometer	**velocímetro** (m)	[vəlus'imətru]
needle (pointer)	**ponteiro** (m)	[põt'ɐjru]
odometer	**conta-quilómetros** (m)	[k'õtɐ kil'ɔmətruʃ]
indicator (sensor)	**sensor** (m)	[sẽs'or]
level	**nível** (m)	[n'ivɛl]
warning light	**luz** (f) **avisadora**	[luʃ ɐvizɐd'orɐ]
steering wheel	**volante** (m)	[vul'ãtə]
horn	**buzina** (f)	[buz'inɐ]
button	**botão** (m)	[but'ãu]
switch	**interruptor** (m)	[ĩtəʀupt'or]
seat	**assento** (m)	[ɐs'ẽtu]
backrest	**costas** (f pl) **do assento**	[k'ɔʃtɐʃ du ɐs'ẽtu]
headrest	**cabeceira** (f)	[kɐbəs'ɐjrɐ]
seat belt	**cinto** (m) **de segurança**	[s'ĩtu də səgur'ãsɐ]
to fasten the belt	**apertar o cinto**	[ɐpərt'ar u s'ĩtu]
adjustment (of seats)	**regulação** (f)	[ʀəgulɐs'ãu]
airbag	**airbag** (m)	[ɛrb'ɛg]
air-conditioner	**ar** (m) **condicionado**	[ar kõdisiun'adu]
radio	**rádio** (m)	[ʀ'adiu]
CD player	**leitor** (m) **de CD**	[lɛjt'or də s'ɛdɛ]
to turn on	**ligar** (vt)	[lig'ar]
antenna	**antena** (f)	[ãt'enɐ]
glove box	**porta-luvas** (m)	[p'ɔrtɐ l'uvɐʃ]
ashtray	**cinzeiro** (m)	[sĩz'ɐjru]

149. Cars. Engine

engine, motor	**motor** (m)	[mut'or]
diesel (as adj)	**diesel**	[d'izɛl]
gasoline (as adj)	**a gasolina**	[ɐ gɐzul'inɐ]
engine volume	**cilindrada** (f)	[silĩdr'adɐ]
power	**potência** (f)	[put'ẽsiɐ]
horsepower	**cavalo-vapor** (m)	[kɐv'alu vɐp'or]

piston	**pistão** (m)	[piʃt'ãu]
cylinder	**cilindro** (m)	[sil'ĩdru]
valve	**válvula** (f)	[v'alvulɐ]
injector	**injetor** (m)	[ĩʒɛt'or]
generator	**gerador** (m)	[ʒərɐd'or]
carburetor	**carburador** (m)	[kɐrburɐd'or]
engine oil	**óleo** (m) **para motor**	['ɔliu p'ɐrɐ mut'or]
radiator	**radiador** (m)	[ʀɐdiɐd'or]
coolant	**refrigerante** (m)	[ʀəfriʒər'ãtə]
cooling fan	**ventilador** (m)	[vẽtilɐd'or]
battery (accumulator)	**bateria** (f)	[bɐtər'iɐ]
starter	**dispositivo** (m) **de arranque**	[diʃpuzit'ivu də ɐʀ'ãkə]
ignition	**ignição** (f)	[ignis'ãu]
spark plug	**vela** (f) **de ignição**	[v'ɛlɐ də ignis'ãu]
terminal (of battery)	**borne** (m)	[b'ɔrnə]
positive terminal	**borne** (m) **positivo**	[b'ɔrnə puzit'ivu]
negative terminal	**borne** (m) **negativo**	[b'ɔrnə nəget'ivu]
fuse	**fusível** (m)	[fuz'ivɛl]
air filter	**filtro** (m) **de ar**	[f'iltru də 'ar]
oil filter	**filtro** (m) **de óleo**	[f'iltru də 'ɔliu]
fuel filter	**filtro** (m) **de combustível**	[f'iltru də kõbuʃt'ivɛl]

150. Cars. Crash. Repair

car accident	**acidente** (m) **de carro**	[ɐsid'ẽtə də k'aʀu]
road accident	**acidente** (m) **rodoviário**	[ɐsid'ẽtə ʀɔdɔvj'ariu]
to run into ...	**ir contra ...**	[ir k'õtrɐ]
to have an accident	**sofrer um acidente**	[sufr'er ũ ɐsid'ẽtə]
damage	**danos** (m pl)	[d'ɐnuʃ]
intact (adj)	**intato**	[ĩt'atu]
breakdown	**avaria** (f)	[ɐvɐr'iɐ]
to break down (vi)	**avariar** (vi)	[ɐvɐrj'ar]
towrope	**cabo** (m) **de reboque**	[k'abu də ʀəb'ɔkə]
puncture	**furo** (m)	[f'uru]
to be flat	**estar furado**	[əʃt'ar fur'adu]
to pump up	**encher** (vt)	[ẽʃ'er]
pressure	**pressão** (f)	[prəs'ãu]
to check (to examine)	**verificar** (vt)	[vərifik'ar]
repair	**reparação** (f)	[ʀəpɐrɐs'ãu]
auto repair shop	**oficina** (f) **de reparação de carros**	[ɔfis'inɐ də ʀəpɐrɐs'ãu də k'aʀuʃ]

spare part	**peça** (f) **sobresselente**	[p'ɛsɐ sobrəsəl'ẽtə]
part	**peça** (f)	[p'ɛsɐ]
bolt (with nut)	**parafuso** (m)	[pɐrɐf'uzu]
screw bolt (without nut)	**parafuso** (m) **autoroscante**	[pɐrɐf'uzu 'autɔʀɔʃk'ãtə]
nut	**porca** (f)	[p'ɔrkɐ]
washer	**anilha** (f)	[ɐn'iʎɐ]
bearing	**rolamento** (m)	[ʀulɐm'ẽtu]
tube	**tubo** (m)	[t'ubu]
gasket (head ~)	**junta** (f)	[ʒ'ũtɐ]
cable, wire	**fio** (m), **cabo** (m)	[f'iu], [k'abu]
jack	**macaco** (m)	[mɐk'aku]
wrench	**chave** (f) **de boca**	[ʃ'avə də b'okɐ]
hammer	**martelo** (m)	[mɐrt'ɛlu]
pump	**bomba** (f)	[b'õbɐ]
screwdriver	**chave** (f) **de fendas**	[ʃ'avə də f'ẽdɐʃ]
fire extinguisher	**extintor** (m)	[əʃtĩt'or]
warning triangle	**triângulo** (m) **de emergência**	[trj'ãgulu də emərʒ'ẽsiɐ]
to stall (vi)	**parar** (vi)	[pɐr'ar]
stalling	**paragem** (f)	[pɐr'aʒẽj]
to be broken	**estar quebrado**	[əʃt'ar kəbr'adu]
to overheat (vi)	**superaquecer-se** (vp)	[supɛrɐkəs'ersə]
to be clogged up	**entupir** (vi)	[ẽtup'ir]
to freeze up (pipes, etc.)	**congelar** (vi)	[kõʒəl'ar]
to burst (vi, ab. tube)	**rebentar** (vi)	[ʀəbẽt'ar]
pressure	**pressão** (f)	[prəs'ãu]
level	**nível** (m)	[n'ivɛl]
slack (~ belt)	**frouxo**	[fr'oʃu]
dent	**mossa** (f)	[m'ɔsɐ]
abnormal noise (motor)	**ruído** (m) **anormal**	[ʀu'idu ɐnɔrm'al]
crack	**fissura** (f)	[fis'urɐ]
scratch	**aranhão** (m)	[ɐrɐɲ'ãu]

151. Cars. Road

road	**estrada** (f)	[əʃtr'adɐ]
highway	**autoestrada** (f)	[autɔəʃtr'adɐ]
freeway	**rodovia** (f)	[ʀɔdɔv'iɐ]
direction (way)	**direção** (f)	[dirɛs'ãu]
distance	**distância** (f)	[diʃt'ãsiɐ]
bridge	**ponte** (f)	[p'õtə]

parking lot	**parque** (m) **de estacionamento**	[p'arkə də ɐʃtesiunɐm'ẽtu]
square	**praça** (f)	[pr'asɐ]
interchange	**nó** (m) **rodoviário**	[nɔ ʀɔdɔvj'ariu]
tunnel	**túnel** (m)	[t'unɛl]
gas station	**posto** (m) **de gasolina**	[p'oʃtu də gɐzul'inɐ]
parking lot	**parque** (m) **de estacionamento**	[p'arkə də ɐʃtesiunɐm'ẽtu]
gas pump	**bomba** (f) **de gasolina**	[b'õbɐ də gɐzul'inɐ]
auto repair shop	**oficina** (f) **de reparação de carros**	[ɔfis'inɐ də ʀəpɐrɐs'ãu də k'aʀuʃ]
to get gas	**abastecer** (vi)	[ɐbɐʃtəs'er]
fuel	**combustível** (m)	[kõbuʃt'ivɛl]
jerrycan	**bidão** (m) **de gasolina**	[bid'ãu də gɐzul'inɐ]
asphalt	**asfalto** (m)	[ɐʃf'altu]
road markings	**marcação** (f) **de estradas**	[mɐrkɐs'ãu də əʃtr'adɐʃ]
curb	**lancil** (m)	[lãs'il]
guardrail	**proteção** (f) **guard-rail**	[prutɛs'ãu guardʀɐ'il]
ditch	**valeta** (f)	[vɐl'etɐ]
roadside (shoulder)	**berma** (f) **da estrada**	[b'ɛrmɐ dɐ əʃtr'adɐ]
lamppost	**poste** (m) **de luz**	[p'ɔʃtə də l'uʃ]
to drive (a car)	**conduzir, guiar** (vt)	[kõduz'ir], [gi'ar]
to turn (~ to the left)	**virar** (vi)	[vir'ar]
to make a U-turn	**fazer inversão de marcha**	[fɐz'er ĩvərs'ãu də m'arʃɐ]
reverse (~ gear)	**marcha-atrás** (f)	[m'arʃɐ ɐtr'aʃ]
to honk (vi)	**buzinar** (vi)	[buzin'ar]
honk (sound)	**buzina** (f)	[buz'inɐ]
to get stuck	**atolar-se** (vp)	[ɐtul'arsə]
to spin (in mud)	**patinar** (vi)	[pɐtin'ar]
to cut, to turn off	**desligar** (vt)	[dəʒlig'ar]
speed	**velocidade** (f)	[vəlusid'adə]
to exceed the speed limit	**exceder a velocidade**	[əʃsəd'er ɐ vəlusid'adə]
to give a ticket	**multar** (vt)	[mult'ar]
traffic lights	**semáforo** (m)	[səm'afuru]
driver's license	**carta** (f) **de condução**	[k'artɐ də kõdus'ãu]
grade crossing	**passagem** (f) **de nível**	[pɐs'aʒẽj də n'ivɛl]
intersection	**cruzamento** (m)	[kruzɐm'ẽtu]
crosswalk	**passadeira** (f) **para peões**	[pɐsɐd'ejrɐ p'ɐrɐ pi'ojʃ]
bend, curve	**curva** (f)	[k'urvɐ]
pedestrian zone	**zona** (f) **pedonal**	[z'onɐ pədun'al]

PEOPLE. LIFE EVENTS

Life events

152. Holidays. Event

celebration, holiday	**festa** (f)	[f'ɛʃtɐ]
national day	**festa** (f) **nacional**	[f'ɛʃtɐ nɐsiun'al]
public holiday	**feriado** (m)	[fərj'adu]
to commemorate (vt)	**festejar** (vt)	[fəʃtəʒ'ar]
event (happening)	**evento** (m)	[ev'ẽtu]
event (organized activity)	**evento** (m)	[ev'ẽtu]
banquet (party)	**banquete** (m)	[bɐ̃k'etə]
reception (formal party)	**receção** (f)	[ʀəsɛs'ɐ̃u]
feast	**festim** (m)	[fəʃt'ĩ]
anniversary	**aniversário** (m)	[ɐnivərs'ariu]
jubilee	**jubileu** (m)	[ʒubil'eu]
to celebrate (vt)	**celebrar** (vt)	[sələbr'ar]
New Year	**Ano** (m) **Novo**	['ɐnu n'ovu]
Happy New Year!	**Feliz Ano Novo!**	[fəl'iʃ 'ɐnu n'ovu]
Santa Claus	**Pai** (m) **Natal**	[paj nɐt'al]
Christmas	**Natal** (m)	[nɐt'al]
Merry Christmas!	**Feliz Natal!**	[fəl'iʃ nɐt'al]
Christmas tree	**árvore** (f) **de Natal**	['arvurə də nɐt'al]
fireworks	**fogo** (m) **de artifício**	[f'ogu də ɐrtif'isiu]
wedding	**boda** (f)	[b'odɐ]
groom	**noivo** (m)	[n'ojvu]
bride	**noiva** (f)	[n'ojvɐ]
to invite (vt)	**convidar** (vt)	[kõvid'ar]
invitation card	**convite** (m)	[kõv'itə]
guest	**convidado** (m)	[kõvid'adu]
to visit (~ your parents, etc.)	**visitar** (vt)	[vizit'ar]
to greet the guests	**receber os hóspedes**	[ʀəsəb'er uʃ 'ɔʃpədəʃ]
gift, present	**presente** (m)	[prəz'ẽtə]
to give (sth as present)	**oferecer** (vt)	[ɔfərəs'er]
to receive gifts	**receber presentes**	[ʀəsəb'er prəz'ẽtəʃ]

bouquet (of flowers)	**ramo** (m) **de flores**	[ʀ'ɐmu də fl'orəʃ]
congratulations	**felicitações** (f pl)	[fəlisitɐs'oj̃ʃ]
to congratulate (vt)	**felicitar** (vt), **dar os parabéns**	[fəlisit'ar], [dar uʃ pɐrɐb'ẽjʃ]
greeting card	**cartão** (m) **de parabéns**	[kɐrt'ãu də pɐrɐb'ẽjʃ]
to send a postcard	**enviar um postal**	[ẽvj'ar ũ puʃt'al]
to get a postcard	**receber um postal**	[ʀəsəb'er ũ puʃt'al]
toast	**brinde** (m)	[br'ĩdə]
to offer (a drink, etc.)	**oferecer** (vt)	[ɔfərəs'er]
champagne	**champanhe** (m)	[ʃãp'ɐɲə]
to have fun	**divertir-se** (vp)	[divərt'irsə]
fun, merriment	**diversão** (f)	[divərs'ãu]
joy (emotion)	**alegria** (f)	[ɐləgr'iɐ]
dance	**dança** (f)	[d'ãsɐ]
to dance (vi, vt)	**dançar** (vi)	[dãs'ar]
waltz	**valsa** (f)	[v'alsɐ]
tango	**tango** (m)	[t'ãgu]

153. Funerals. Burial

cemetery	**cemitério** (m)	[səmit'ɛriu]
grave, tomb	**sepultura** (f), **túmulo** (m)	[səpult'urɐ], [t'umulu]
cross	**cruz** (f)	[kruʃ]
gravestone	**lápide** (f)	[l'apidə]
fence	**cerca** (f)	[s'erkɐ]
chapel	**capela** (f)	[kɐp'ɛlɐ]
death	**morte** (f)	[m'ɔrtə]
to die (vi)	**morrer** (vi)	[muʀ'er]
the deceased	**defunto** (m)	[dəf'ũtu]
mourning	**luto** (m)	[l'utu]
to bury (vt)	**enterrar, sepultar** (vt)	[ẽtəʀ'ar], [səpult'ar]
funeral home	**agência** (f) **funerária**	[ɐʒ'ẽsiɐ funər'ariɐ]
funeral	**funeral** (m)	[funər'al]
wreath	**coroa** (f) **de flores**	[kur'oɐ də fl'orəʃ]
casket	**caixão** (m)	[kajʃ'ãu]
hearse	**carro** (m) **funerário**	[k'aʀu funər'ariu]
shroud	**mortalha** (f)	[murt'aʎɐ]
funeral procession	**procissão** (f) **funerária**	[prusis'ãu funər'ariɐ]
cremation urn	**urna** (f) **funerária**	['urnɐ funər'ariɐ]
crematory	**crematório** (m)	[krəmɐt'ɔriu]
obituary	**obituário** (m), **necrologia** (f)	[ɔbitu'ariu], [nəkruluʒ'iɐ]

to cry (weep) **chorar** (vi) [ʃur'aɾ]
to sob (vi) **soluçar** (vi) [sulus'aɾ]

154. War. Soldiers

platoon **pelotão** (m) [pəlut'ãu]
company **companhia** (f) [kõpɐɲ'iɐ]
regiment **regimento** (m) [ʀəʒim'ẽtu]
army **exército** (m) [ez'ɛrsitu]
division **divisão** (f) [diviz'ãu]

section, squad **destacamento** (m) [dəʃtɐkɐm'ẽtu]
host (army) **hoste** (f) ['ɔʃtə]

soldier **soldado** (m) [sold'adu]
officer **oficial** (m) [ɔfisj'al]

private **soldado** (m) **raso** [sold'adu ʀ'azu]
sergeant **sargento** (m) [sɐɾʒ'ẽtu]
lieutenant **tenente** (m) [tən'ẽtə]
captain **capitão** (m) [kɐpit'ãu]
major **major** (m) [mɐʒ'ɔɾ]
colonel **coronel** (m) [kurun'ɛl]
general **general** (m) [ʒənəɾ'al]

sailor **marujo** (m) [mɐɾ'uʒu]
captain **capitão** (m) [kɐpit'ãu]
boatswain **contramestre** (m) [kõtɾɐm'ɛʃtɾə]

artilleryman **artilheiro** (m) [ɐɾtiʎ'ɐjɾu]
paratrooper **soldado** (m) **paraquedista** [sold'adu pɐɾɐkəd'iʃtɐ]
pilot **piloto** (m) [pil'otu]
navigator **navegador** (m) [nɐvəgɐd'oɾ]
mechanic **mecânico** (m) [mək'ɐniku]

pioneer (sapper) **sapador** (m) [sɐpɐd'oɾ]
parachutist **paraquedista** (m) [pɐɾɐkəd'iʃtɐ]
reconnaissance scout **explorador** (m) [əʃpluɾɐd'oɾ]
sniper **franco-atirador** (m) [fɾ'ãkɔ ɐtiɾɐd'oɾ]

patrol (group) **patrulha** (f) [pɐtɾ'uʎɐ]
to patrol (vt) **patrulhar** (vt) [pɐtɾuʎ'aɾ]
sentry, guard **sentinela** (f) [sẽtin'ɛlɐ]

warrior **guerreiro** (m) [gəʀ'ɐjɾu]
hero **herói** (m) [eɾ'ɔj]
heroine **heroína** (f) [eɾu'inɐ]
patriot **patriota** (m) [pɐtɾj'ɔtɐ]
traitor **traidor** (m) [tɾajd'oɾ]
to betray (vt) **trair** (vt) [tɾɐ'iɾ]

deserter	**desertor** (m)	[dəzərt'or]
to desert (vi)	**desertar** (vt)	[dəzərt'ar]
mercenary	**mercenário** (m)	[mərsən'ariu]
recruit	**recruta** (m)	[ʀəkr'utɐ]
volunteer	**voluntário** (m)	[vulũt'ariu]
dead (n)	**morto** (m)	[m'ortu]
wounded (n)	**ferido** (m)	[fər'idu]
prisoner of war	**prisioneiro** (m) **de guerra**	[priziun'ɐjru də g'ɛʀɐ]

155. War. Military actions. Part 1

war	**guerra** (f)	[g'ɛʀɐ]
to be at war	**guerrear** (vt)	[gɛʀə'ar]
civil war	**guerra** (f) **civil**	[g'ɛʀɐ siv'il]
treacherously (adv)	**perfidamente**	[pərfidɐm'ẽtə]
declaration of war	**declaração** (f) **de guerra**	[dəklɐrɐs'ãu də g'ɛʀɐ]
to declare (~ war)	**declarar** (vt) **guerra**	[dəklɐr'ar g'ɛʀɐ]
aggression	**agressão** (f)	[ɐgrəs'ãu]
to attack (invade)	**atacar** (vt)	[ɐtɐk'ar]
to invade (vt)	**invadir** (vt)	[ĩvad'ir]
invader	**invasor** (m)	[ĩvaz'or]
conqueror	**conquistador** (m)	[kõkiʃtɐd'or]
defense	**defesa** (f)	[dəf'ezɐ]
to defend (a country, etc.)	**defender** (vt)	[dəfẽd'er]
to defend oneself	**defender-se** (vp)	[dəfẽd'ersə]
enemy	**inimigo** (m)	[inim'igu]
foe, adversary	**adversário** (m)	[ɐdvərs'ariu]
enemy (as adj)	**inimigo**	[inim'igu]
strategy	**estratégia** (f)	[əʃtrɐt'ɛʒiɐ]
tactics	**tática** (f)	[t'atikɐ]
order	**ordem** (f)	['ɔrdẽj]
command (order)	**comando** (m)	[kum'ãdu]
to order (vt)	**ordenar** (vt)	[ɔrdən'ar]
mission	**missão** (f)	[mis'ãu]
secret (adj)	**secreto**	[səkr'ɛtu]
battle	**batalha** (f)	[bɐt'aʎɐ]
combat	**combate** (m)	[kõb'atə]
attack	**ataque** (m)	[ɐt'akə]
storming (assault)	**assalto** (m)	[ɐs'altu]
to storm (vt)	**assaltar** (vt)	[ɐsalt'ar]

siege (to be under ~)	**assédio, sítio** (m)	[ɐs'ɛdiu], [s'itiu]
offensive (n)	**ofensiva** (f)	[ɔfẽs'ivɐ]
to go on the offensive	**passar à ofensiva**	[pɐs'ar a ɔfẽs'ivɐ]
retreat	**retirada** (f)	[ʀətir'adɐ]
to retreat (vi)	**retirar-se** (vp)	[ʀətir'arsə]
encirclement	**cerco** (m)	[s'erku]
to encircle (vt)	**cercar** (vt)	[sərk'ar]
bombing (by aircraft)	**bombardeio** (m)	[bõbɐrd'ɐju]
to drop a bomb	**lançar uma bomba**	[lãs'ar 'umɐ b'õbɐ]
to bomb (vt)	**bombardear** (vt)	[bõbɐrdj'ar]
explosion	**explosão** (f)	[əʃpluz'ãu]
shot	**tiro** (m)	[t'iru]
to fire a shot	**disparar um tiro**	[diʃpɐr'ar ũ t'iru]
firing (burst of ~)	**tiroteio** (m)	[tirut'ɐju]
to take aim (at ...)	**apontar para ...**	[ɐpõt'ar p'ɐrɐ]
to point (a gun)	**apontar** (vt)	[ɐpõt'ar]
to hit (the target)	**acertar** (vt)	[ɐsərt'ar]
to sink (~ a ship)	**afundar** (vt)	[ɐfũd'ar]
hole (in a ship)	**brecha** (f)	[br'ɛʃɐ]
to founder, to sink (vi)	**afundar** (vi)	[ɐfũd'ar]
front (war ~)	**frente** (m)	[fr'ẽtə]
rear (homefront)	**retaguarda** (f)	[ʀɛtɐgu'ardɐ]
evacuation	**evacuação** (f)	[evɐkuɐs'ãu]
to evacuate (vt)	**evacuar** (vt)	[evɐku'ar]
trench	**trincheira** (f)	[trĩʃ'ɐjrɐ]
barbwire	**arame** (m) **farpado**	[ɐr'ɐmə fɐrp'adu]
barrier (anti tank ~)	**obstáculo** (m) **anticarro**	[ɔbʃt'akulu ãtik'aʀu]
watchtower	**torre** (f) **de vigia**	[t'oʀə də viʒ'iɐ]
hospital	**hospital** (m)	[ɔʃpit'al]
to wound (vt)	**ferir** (vt)	[fər'ir]
wound	**ferida** (f)	[fər'idɐ]
wounded (n)	**ferido** (m)	[fər'idu]
to be wounded	**ficar ferido**	[fik'ar fər'idu]
serious (wound)	**grave**	[gr'avə]

156. Weapons

weapons	**arma** (f)	['armɐ]
firearm	**arma** (f) **de fogo**	['armɐ də f'ogu]
cold weapons (knives, etc.)	**arma** (f) **branca**	['armɐ br'ãkɐ]

chemical weapons	**arma** (f) **química**	['armɐ k'imikɐ]
nuclear (adj)	**nuclear**	[nuklə'ar]
nuclear weapons	**arma** (f) **nuclear**	['armɐ nuklə'ar]
bomb	**bomba** (f)	[b'õbɐ]
atomic bomb	**bomba** (f) **atómica**	[b'õbɐ ɐt'ɔmikɐ]
pistol (gun)	**pistola** (f)	[piʃt'ɔlɐ]
rifle	**caçadeira** (f)	[kɐsɐd'ɐjrɐ]
submachine gun	**pistola-metralhadora** (f)	[piʃt'ɔlɐ mətrɐʎɐd'orɐ]
machine gun	**metralhadora** (f)	[mətrɐʎɐd'orɐ]
muzzle	**boca** (f)	[b'okɐ]
barrel	**cano** (m)	[k'ɐnu]
caliber	**calibre** (m)	[kɐl'ibrə]
trigger	**gatilho** (m)	[gɐt'iʎu]
sight (aiming device)	**mira** (f)	[m'irɐ]
magazine	**carregador** (m)	[kɐʀəgɐd'or]
butt (of rifle)	**coronha** (f)	[kur'oɲɐ]
hand grenade	**granada** (f) **de mão**	[grɐn'adɐ də m'ãu]
explosive	**explosivo** (m)	[əʃpluz'ivu]
bullet	**bala** (f)	[b'alɐ]
cartridge	**cartucho** (m)	[kɐrt'uʃu]
charge	**carga** (f)	[k'argɐ]
ammunition	**munições** (f pl)	[munis'ojʃ]
bomber (aircraft)	**bombardeiro** (m)	[bõbɐrd'ɐjru]
fighter	**avião** (m) **de caça**	[ɐvj'ãu də k'asɐ]
helicopter	**helicóptero** (m)	[elik'ɔptəru]
anti-aircraft gun	**canhão** (m) **antiaéreo**	[kɐɲ'ãu ãtiɐ'ɛriu]
tank	**tanque** (m)	[t'ãkə]
tank gun	**canhão** (m), **peça** (f)	[kɐɲ'ãu], [p'ɛsɐ]
artillery	**artilharia** (f)	[ɐrtiʎɐr'iɐ]
cannon	**canhão** (m)	[kɐɲ'ãu]
to lay (a gun)	**fazer a pontaria**	[fɐz'er ɐ põtɐr'iɐ]
shell (projectile)	**obus** (m)	[ɔb'uʃ]
mortar bomb	**granada** (f) **de morteiro**	[grɐn'adɐ də murt'ɐjru]
mortar	**morteiro** (m)	[murt'ɐjru]
splinter (shell fragment)	**estilhaço** (m)	[əʃtiʎ'asu]
submarine	**submarino** (m)	[submɐr'inu]
torpedo	**torpedo** (m)	[turp'ɛdu]
missile	**míssil** (m)	[m'isil]
to load (gun)	**carregar** (vt)	[kɐʀəg'ar]
to shoot (vi)	**atirar, disparar** (vi)	[ɐtir'ar], [diʃpɐr'ar]

to point at (the cannon)	**apontar para ...**	[ɐpõt'ar p'ɐrɐ]
bayonet	**baioneta** (f)	[bajun'etɐ]
epee	**espada** (f)	[əʃp'adɐ]
saber (e.g., cavalry ~)	**sabre** (m)	[s'abrə]
spear (weapon)	**lança** (f)	[l'ãsɐ]
bow	**arco** (m)	['arku]
arrow	**flecha** (f)	[fl'ɛʃɐ]
musket	**mosquete** (m)	[muʃk'etə]
crossbow	**besta** (f)	[b'eʃtɐ]

157. Ancient people

primitive (prehistoric)	**primitivo**	[primit'ivu]
prehistoric (adj)	**pré-histórico**	[prɛiʃt'ɔriku]
ancient (~ civilization)	**antigo**	[ãt'igu]
Stone Age	**Idade** (f) **da Pedra**	[id'adə dɐ p'ɛdrɐ]
Bronze Age	**Idade** (f) **do Bronze**	[id'adə du br'õzə]
Ice Age	**período** (m) **glacial**	[pər'iudu glɐsj'al]
tribe	**tribo** (f)	[tr'ibu]
cannibal	**canibal** (m)	[kɐnib'al]
hunter	**caçador** (m)	[kɐsɐd'or]
to hunt (vi, vt)	**caçar** (vi)	[kɐs'ar]
mammoth	**mamute** (m)	[mɐm'utə]
cave	**caverna** (f)	[kɐv'ɛrnɐ]
fire	**fogo** (m)	[f'ogu]
campfire	**fogueira** (f)	[fug'ɐjrɐ]
rock painting	**pintura** (f) **rupestre**	[pĩt'urɐ ʀup'ɛʃtrə]
tool (e.g., stone ax)	**ferramenta** (f)	[fəʀɐm'ẽtɐ]
spear	**lança** (f)	[l'ãsɐ]
stone ax	**machado** (m) **de pedra**	[mɐʃ'adu də p'ɛdrɐ]
to be at war	**guerrear** (vt)	[gɛʀə'ar]
to domesticate (vt)	**domesticar** (vt)	[duməʃtik'ar]
idol	**ídolo** (m)	['idulu]
to worship (vt)	**adorar, venerar** (vt)	[ɐdur'ar], [vənər'ar]
superstition	**superstição** (f)	[supərʃtis'ãu]
rite	**ritual** (m)	[ʀitu'al]
evolution	**evolução** (f)	[evulus'ãu]
development	**desenvolvimento** (m)	[dəzẽvɔlvim'ẽtu]
disappearance (extinction)	**desaparecimento** (m)	[dəzɐpɐrəsim'ẽtu]
to adapt oneself	**adaptar-se** (vp)	[ɐdɐpt'arsə]
archeology	**arqueologia** (f)	[ɐrkiuluʒ'iɐ]
archeologist	**arqueólogo** (m)	[ɐrkj'ɔlugu]

archeological (adj)	**arqueológico**	[ɐrkiul'ɔʒiku]
excavation site	**local** (m) **das escavações**	[luk'al deʃ əʃkɐvɐs'ojʃ]
excavations	**escavações** (f pl)	[əʃkɐvɐs'ojʃ]
find (object)	**achado** (m)	[ɐʃ'adu]
fragment	**fragmento** (m)	[fragm'ẽtu]

158. Middle Ages

people (ethnic group)	**povo** (m)	[p'ovu]
peoples	**povos** (m pl)	[p'ɔvuʃ]
tribe	**tribo** (f)	[tr'ibu]
tribes	**tribos** (f pl)	[tr'ibuʃ]
barbarians	**bárbaros** (m pl)	[b'arbɐruʃ]
Gauls	**gauleses** (m pl)	[gaul'ezəʃ]
Goths	**godos** (m pl)	[g'oduʃ]
Slavs	**eslavos** (m pl)	[əʒl'avuʃ]
Vikings	**vikings** (m pl)	[vikĩgəʃ]
Romans	**romanos** (m pl)	[ʀum'ɐnuʃ]
Roman (adj)	**romano**	[ʀum'ɐnu]
Byzantines	**bizantinos** (m pl)	[bizɐ̃t'inuʃ]
Byzantium	**Bizâncio**	[biz'ɐ̃siu]
Byzantine (adj)	**bizantino**	[bizɐ̃t'inu]
emperor	**imperador** (m)	[ĩpərɐd'or]
leader, chief	**líder** (m)	[l'idɛr]
powerful (~ king)	**poderoso**	[pudər'ozu]
king	**rei** (m)	[ʀɐj]
ruler (sovereign)	**governante** (m)	[guvərn'ɐ̃tə]
knight	**cavaleiro** (m)	[kɐvɐl'ɐjru]
feudal lord	**senhor feudal** (m)	[səɲ'or feud'al]
feudal (adj)	**feudal**	[feud'al]
vassal	**vassalo** (m)	[vɐs'alu]
duke	**duque** (m)	[d'ukə]
earl	**conde** (m)	[k'õdə]
baron	**barão** (m)	[bɐr'ɐ̃u]
bishop	**bispo** (m)	[b'iʃpu]
armor	**armadura** (f)	[ɐrmɐd'urɐ]
shield	**escudo** (m)	[ɛz'udu]
sword	**espada** (f)	[əʃp'adɐ]
visor	**viseira** (f)	[viz'ɐjrɐ]
chainmail	**cota** (f) **de malha**	[k'ɔtɐ də m'aʎɐ]
crusade	**cruzada** (f)	[kruz'adɐ]
crusader	**cruzado** (m)	[kruz'adu]

territory	**território** (m)	[təʀit'ɔriu]
to attack (invade)	**atacar** (vt)	[ɐtɐk'aɾ]
to conquer (vt)	**conquistar** (vt)	[kõkiʃt'aɾ]
to occupy (invade)	**ocupar, invadir** (vt)	[ɔkup'aɾ], [ĩvad'iɾ]
siege (to be under ~)	**assédio, sítio** (m)	[ɐs'ɛdiu], [s'itiu]
besieged (adj)	**sitiado**	[sitj'adu]
to besiege (vt)	**assediar, sitiar** (vt)	[ɐsədj'aɾ], [sitj'aɾ]
inquisition	**inquisição** (f)	[ĩkizis'ãu]
inquisitor	**inquisidor** (m)	[ĩkizid'oɾ]
torture	**tortura** (f)	[tuɾt'urɐ]
cruel (adj)	**cruel**	[kru'ɛl]
heretic	**herege** (m)	[eɾ'ɛʒə]
heresy	**heresia** (f)	[erəz'iɐ]
seafaring	**navegação** (f) **maritima**	[nɐvəgɐs'ãu mɐrit'imɐ]
pirate	**pirata** (m)	[piɾ'atɐ]
piracy	**pirataria** (f)	[piɾɐtɐɾ'iɐ]
boarding (attack)	**abordagem** (f)	[ɐburd'aʒẽj]
loot, booty	**saque, pulhagem** (f)	[s'akə], [puʎ'aʒẽj]
treasures	**tesouros** (m pl)	[təz'oruʃ]
discovery	**descobrimento** (m)	[dəʃkubrim'ẽtu]
to discover (new land, etc.)	**descobrir** (vt)	[dəʃkubɾ'iɾ]
expedition	**expedição** (f)	[əʃpədis'ãu]
musketeer	**mosqueteiro** (m)	[muʃkət'ɐjɾu]
cardinal	**cardeal** (m)	[kɐrdj'al]
heraldry	**heráldica** (f)	[er'aldikɐ]
heraldic (adj)	**heráldico**	[er'aldiku]

159. Leader. Chief. Authorities

king	**rei** (m)	[ʀɐj]
queen	**rainha** (f)	[ʀɐ'iɲɐ]
royal (adj)	**real**	[ʀə'al]
kingdom	**reino** (m)	[ʀ'ɐjnu]
prince	**príncipe** (m)	[pɾ'ĩsipə]
princess	**princesa** (f)	[prĩs'ezɐ]
president	**presidente** (m)	[prəzid'ẽtə]
vice-president	**vice-presidente** (m)	[v'isə prəzid'ẽtə]
senator	**senador** (m)	[sənɐd'oɾ]
monarch	**monarca** (m)	[mun'arkɐ]
ruler (sovereign)	**governante** (m)	[guvərn'ãtə]
dictator	**ditador** (m)	[ditɐd'oɾ]
tyrant	**tirano** (m)	[tiɾ'ɐnu]

magnate	**magnata** (m)	[mɐgn'atɐ]
director	**diretor** (m)	[dirɛt'or]
chief	**chefe** (m)	[ʃ'ɛfə]
manager (director)	**dirigente** (m)	[diriʒ'ẽtə]
boss	**patrão** (m)	[pɐtr'ãu]
owner	**dono** (m)	[d'onu]
head (~ of delegation)	**chefe** (m)	[ʃ'ɛfə]
authorities	**autoridades** (f pl)	[auturid'adəʃ]
superiors	**superiores** (m pl)	[supərj'orəʃ]
governor	**governador** (m)	[guvərnɐd'or]
consul	**cônsul** (m)	[k'õsul]
diplomat	**diplomata** (m)	[diplum'atɐ]
mayor	**prefeito** (m)	[prəf'ɐjtu]
sheriff	**xerife** (m)	[ʃɛr'ifə]
emperor	**imperador** (m)	[ĩpərɐd'or]
tsar, czar	**czar** (m)	[kz'ar]
pharaoh	**faraó** (m)	[fɐrɐ'ɔ]
khan	**cão** (m)	[k'ãu]

160. Breaking the law. Criminals. Part 1

bandit	**bandido** (m)	[bãd'idu]
crime	**crime** (m)	[kr'imə]
criminal (person)	**criminoso** (m)	[krimin'ozu]
thief	**ladrão** (m)	[lɐdr'ãu]
to steal (vi, vt)	**roubar** (vt)	[ʀob'ar]
stealing (larceny)	**roubo** (m)	[ʀ'obu]
theft	**furto** (m)	[f'urtu]
to kidnap (vt)	**raptar** (vt)	[ʀɐpt'ar]
kidnapping	**rapto** (m)	[ʀ'aptu]
kidnapper	**raptor** (m)	[ʀapt'or]
ransom	**resgate** (m)	[ʀəʒg'atə]
to demand ransom	**pedir resgate**	[pəd'ir ʀəʒg'atə]
to rob (vt)	**roubar** (vt)	[ʀob'ar]
robbery	**assalto, roubo** (m)	[ɐs'altu], [ʀ'obu]
robber	**assaltante** (m)	[ɐsalt'ãtə]
to extort (vt)	**extorquir** (vt)	[əʃturk'ir]
extortionist	**extorsionário** (m)	[əʃtursiun'ariu]
extortion	**extorsão** (f)	[əʃturs'ãu]
to murder, to kill	**matar, assassinar** (vt)	[mɐt'ar], [ɐsɐsin'ar]
murder	**homicídio** (m)	[ɔmis'idiu]

murderer	**homicida, assassino** (m)	[ɔmis'idɐ], [ɐsɐs'inu]
gunshot	**tiro** (m)	[t'iru]
to fire a shot	**dar um tiro**	[dar ũ t'iru]
to shoot to death	**matar a tiro**	[mɐt'ar ɐ t'iru]
to shoot (vi)	**atirar, disparar** (vi)	[ɐtir'ar], [diʃpɐr'ar]
shooting	**tiroteio** (m)	[tirut'ɐju]
incident (fight, etc.)	**acontecimento** (m)	[ɐkõtəsim'ẽtu]
fight, brawl	**porrada** (f)	[puʀ'adɐ]
Help!	**Socorro!**	[suk'oʀu]
victim	**vítima** (f)	[v'itimɐ]
to damage (vt)	**danificar** (vt)	[dɐnifik'ar]
damage	**dano** (m)	[d'ɐnu]
dead body	**cadáver** (m)	[kɐd'avɛr]
grave (~ crime)	**grave**	[gr'avə]
to attack (vt)	**atacar** (vt)	[ɐtɐk'ar]
to beat (dog, person)	**bater** (vt)	[bɐt'er]
to beat up	**espancar** (vt)	[əʃpãk'ar]
to take (rob of sth)	**tirar** (vt)	[tir'ar]
to stab to death	**esfaquear** (vt)	[əʃfɐkj'ar]
to maim (vt)	**mutilar** (vt)	[mutil'ar]
to wound (vt)	**ferir** (vt)	[fər'ir]
blackmail	**chantagem** (f)	[ʃãt'aʒẽj]
to blackmail (vt)	**chantagear** (vt)	[ʃãtɐʒj'ar]
blackmailer	**chantagista** (m)	[ʃãtɐʒ'iʃtɐ]
protection racket	**extorsão** (f)	[əʃturs'ãu]
racketeer	**extorsionário** (m)	[əʃtursiun'ariu]
gangster	**gângster** (m)	[g'ãgʃtɛr]
mafia, Mob	**máfia** (f)	[m'afiɐ]
pickpocket	**carteirista** (m)	[kɐrtɐjr'iʃtɐ]
burglar	**assaltante, ladrão** (m)	[ɐsalt'ãtə], [lɐdr'ãu]
smuggling	**contrabando** (m)	[kõtrɐb'ãdu]
smuggler	**contrabandista** (m)	[kõtrɐbãd'iʃtɐ]
forgery	**falsificação** (f)	[falsifikɐs'ãu]
to forge (counterfeit)	**falsificar** (vt)	[falsifik'ar]
fake (forged)	**falsificado**	[falsifik'adu]

161. Breaking the law. Criminals. Part 2

rape	**violação** (f)	[viulɐs'ãu]
to rape (vt)	**violar** (vt)	[viul'ar]
rapist	**violador** (m)	[viulɐd'or]
maniac	**maníaco** (m)	[mɐn'iɐku]
prostitute (fem.)	**prostituta** (f)	[pruʃtit'utɐ]

prostitution	**prostituição** (f)	[pruʃtituis'ãu]
pimp	**chulo** (m)	[ʃ'ulu]
drug addict	**toxicodependente** (m)	[tɔksikɔdəpẽd'ẽtə]
drug dealer	**traficante** (m)	[trɐfik'ãtə]
to blow up (bomb)	**explodir** (vt)	[əʃplud'ir]
explosion	**explosão** (f)	[əʃpluz'ãu]
to set fire	**incendiar** (vt)	[ĩsẽdj'ar]
incendiary (arsonist)	**incendiário** (m)	[ĩsẽdj'ariu]
terrorism	**terrorismo** (m)	[təʀur'iʒmu]
terrorist	**terrorista** (m)	[təʀur'iʃtɐ]
hostage	**refém** (m)	[ʀəf'ẽj]
to swindle (vt)	**enganar** (vt)	[ẽgɐn'ar]
swindle	**engano** (m)	[ẽg'ɐnu]
swindler	**vigarista** (m)	[vigɐr'iʃtɐ]
to bribe (vt)	**subornar** (vt)	[suburn'ar]
bribery	**suborno** (m)	[sub'ornu]
bribe	**suborno** (m)	[sub'ornu]
poison	**veneno** (m)	[vən'enu]
to poison (vt)	**envenenar** (vt)	[ẽvənən'ar]
to poison oneself	**envenenar-se** (vp)	[ẽvənən'arsə]
suicide (act)	**suicídio** (m)	[suis'idiu]
suicide (person)	**suicida** (m)	[suis'idɐ]
to threaten (vt)	**ameaçar** (vt)	[ɐmiɐs'ar]
threat	**ameaça** (f)	[ɐmj'asɐ]
to make an attempt	**atentar contra a vida de ...**	[ɐtẽt'ar k'õtrɐ ɐ v'idɐ də]
attempt (attack)	**atentado** (m)	[ɐtẽt'adu]
to steal (a car)	**roubar** (vt)	[ʀob'ar]
to hijack (a plane)	**desviar** (vt)	[dəʒvj'ar]
revenge	**vingança** (f)	[vĩg'ãsɐ]
to revenge (vt)	**vingar-se** (vp)	[vĩg'arsə]
to torture (vt)	**torturar** (vt)	[turtur'ar]
torture	**tortura** (f)	[turt'urɐ]
to torment (vt)	**atormentar** (vt)	[ɐturmẽt'ar]
pirate	**pirata** (m)	[pir'atɐ]
hooligan	**desordeiro** (m)	[dəzɔrd'ɐjru]
armed (adj)	**armado**	[ɐrm'adu]
violence	**violência** (f)	[viul'ẽsiɐ]
illegal (unlawful)	**ilegal**	[iləg'al]
spying (n)	**espionagem** (f)	[əʃpiun'aʒẽj]
to spy (vi)	**espionar** (vi)	[əʃpiun'ar]

162. Police. Law. Part 1

justice	**justiça** (f)	[ʒuʃt'isɐ]
court (court room)	**tribunal** (m)	[tribun'al]
judge	**juiz** (m)	[ʒu'iʃ]
jurors	**jurados** (m pl)	[ʒur'aduʃ]
jury trial	**tribunal** (m) **do júri**	[tribun'al du ʒ'uri]
to judge (vt)	**julgar** (vt)	[ʒulg'ar]
lawyer, attorney	**advogado** (m)	[ɐdvug'adu]
accused	**réu** (m)	[ʀ'ɛu]
dock	**banco** (m) **dos réus**	[b'ãku duʃ ʀ'ɛuʃ]
charge	**acusação** (f)	[ɐkuzɐs'ãu]
accused	**acusado** (m)	[ɐkuz'adu]
sentence	**sentença** (f)	[sẽt'ẽsɐ]
to sentence (vt)	**sentenciar** (vt)	[sẽtẽsj'ar]
guilty (culprit)	**culpado** (m)	[kulp'adu]
to punish (vt)	**punir** (vt)	[pun'ir]
punishment	**punição** (f)	[punis'ãu]
fine (penalty)	**multa** (f)	[m'ultɐ]
life imprisonment	**prisão** (f) **perpétua**	[priz'ãu pərp'ɛtuɐ]
death penalty	**pena** (f) **de morte**	[p'enɐ də m'ɔrtə]
electric chair	**cadeira** (f) **elétrica**	[kɐd'ɐjrɐ el'ɛtrikɐ]
gallows	**forca** (f)	[f'orkɐ]
to execute (vt)	**executar** (vt)	[ezəkut'ar]
execution	**execução** (f)	[ezəkus'ãu]
prison, jail	**prisão** (f)	[priz'ãu]
cell	**cela** (f) **de prisão**	[s'ɛlɐ də priz'ãu]
escort	**escolta** (f)	[əʃk'ɔltɐ]
prison guard	**guarda** (m) **prisional**	[gu'ardɐ priziun'al]
prisoner	**preso** (m)	[pr'ezu]
handcuffs	**algemas** (f pl)	[alʒ'emɐʃ]
to handcuff (vt)	**algemar** (vt)	[alʒəm'ar]
prison break	**fuga, evasão** (f)	[f'ugɐ], [evɐz'ãu]
to break out (vi)	**fugir** (vi)	[fuʒ'ir]
to disappear (vi)	**desaparecer** (vi)	[dəzɐpɐrəs'er]
to release (from prison)	**soltar, libertar** (vt)	[solt'ar], [libərt'ar]
amnesty	**amnistia** (f)	[ɐmniʃt'iɐ]
police	**polícia** (f)	[pul'isiɐ]
police officer	**polícia** (m)	[pul'isiɐ]

police station	**esquadra** (f) **de polícia**	[ɐʃku'adrɐ də pul'isiɐ]
billy club	**cassetete** (m)	[kasət'etə]
bullhorn	**megafone** (m)	[mɛgɐf'ɔnə]
patrol car	**carro** (m) **de patrulha**	[k'aʀu də pɐtr'uʎɐ]
siren	**sirene** (f)	[sir'ɛnə]
to turn on the siren	**ligar a sirene**	[lig'ar ɐ sir'ɛnə]
siren call	**toque** (m) **da sirene**	[t'ɔkə dɐ sir'ɛnə]
crime scene	**cena** (f) **do crime**	[s'enɐ du kr'imə]
witness	**testemunha** (f)	[təʃtəm'uɲɐ]
freedom	**liberdade** (f)	[libərd'adə]
accomplice	**cúmplice** (m)	[k'ũplisə]
to flee (vi)	**escapar** (vi)	[əʃkɐp'ar]
trace (to leave a ~)	**traço** (m)	[tr'asu]

163. Police. Law. Part 2

search (investigation)	**procura** (f)	[prɔk'urɐ]
to look for ...	**procurar** (vt)	[prɔkur'ar]
suspicion	**suspeita** (f)	[suʃp'ɐjtɐ]
suspicious (suspect)	**suspeito**	[suʃp'ɐjtu]
to stop (cause to halt)	**parar** (vt)	[pɐr'ar]
to detain (keep in custody)	**deter** (vt)	[dət'er]
case (lawsuit)	**caso** (m)	[k'azu]
investigation	**investigação** (f)	[ĩvəʃtigɐs'ãu]
detective	**detetive** (m)	[dətɛt'ivə]
investigator	**investigador** (m)	[ĩvəʃtigɐd'or]
hypothesis	**versão** (f)	[vərs'ãu]
motive	**motivo** (m)	[mut'ivu]
interrogation	**interrogatório** (m)	[ĩtəʀugɐt'ɔriu]
to interrogate (vt)	**interrogar** (vt)	[ĩtəʀug'ar]
to question (vt)	**questionar** (vt)	[kəʃtiun'ar]
check (identity ~)	**verificação** (f)	[vərifikɐs'ãu]
round-up	**rusga** (f)	[ʀ'uʒgɐ]
search (~ warrant)	**busca** (f)	[b'uʃkɐ]
chase (pursuit)	**perseguição** (f)	[pərsəgis'ãu]
to pursue, to chase	**perseguir** (vt)	[pərsəg'ir]
to track (a criminal)	**seguir** (vt)	[səg'ir]
arrest	**prisão** (f)	[priz'ãu]
to arrest (sb)	**prender** (vt)	[prẽd'er]
to catch (thief, etc.)	**pegar, capturar** (vt)	[pəg'ar], [kaptur'ar]
capture	**captura** (f)	[kapt'urɐ]
document	**documento** (m)	[dukum'ẽtu]
proof (evidence)	**prova** (f)	[pr'ɔvɐ]

to prove (vt)	**provar** (vt)	[pruv'aɾ]
footprint	**pegada** (f)	[pəg'adɐ]
fingerprints	**impressões** (f pl) **digitais**	[ĩprəs'oĩʃ diʒit'ajʃ]
piece of evidence	**prova** (f)	[pr'ɔvɐ]
alibi	**álibi** (m)	['alibi]
innocent (not guilty)	**inocente**	[inus'ẽtə]
injustice	**injustiça** (f)	[ĩʒuʃt'isɐ]
unjust, unfair (adj)	**injusto**	[ĩʒ'uʃtu]
criminal (adj)	**criminal**	[krimin'al]
to confiscate (vt)	**confiscar** (vt)	[kõfiʃk'aɾ]
drug (illegal substance)	**droga** (f)	[dr'ɔgɐ]
weapon, gun	**arma** (f)	['aɾmɐ]
to disarm (vt)	**desarmar** (vt)	[dəzɐrm'aɾ]
to order (command)	**ordenar** (vt)	[ɔrdən'aɾ]
to disappear (vi)	**desaparecer** (vi)	[dəzɐpɐrəs'eɾ]
law	**lei** (f)	[lɐj]
legal, lawful (adj)	**legal**	[ləg'al]
illegal, illicit (adj)	**ilegal**	[iləg'al]
responsibility (blame)	**responsabilidade** (f)	[ʀəʃpõsɐbilid'adə]
responsible (adj)	**responsável**	[ʀəʃpõs'avɛl]

NATURE

The Earth. Part 1

164. Outer space

cosmos	**cosmos** (m)	[k'ɔʒmuʃ]
space (as adj)	**cósmico**	[k'ɔʒmiku]
outer space	**espaço** (m) **cósmico**	[əʃp'asu k'ɔʒmiku]
world	**mundo** (m)	[m'ũdu]
universe	**universo** (m)	[univ'ɛrsu]
galaxy	**galáxia** (f)	[gɐl'aksiɐ]
star	**estrela** (f)	[əʃtr'elɐ]
constellation	**constelação** (f)	[kõʃtəlɐs'ãu]
planet	**planeta** (m)	[plɐn'etɐ]
satellite	**satélite** (m)	[sɐt'ɛlitə]
meteorite	**meteorito** (m)	[mətiuɾ'itu]
comet	**cometa** (m)	[kum'etɐ]
asteroid	**asteroide** (m)	[ɐʃtəɾ'ɔjdə]
orbit	**órbita** (f)	['ɔɾbitɐ]
to revolve (~ around the Earth)	**girar** (vi)	[ʒiɾ'aɾ]
atmosphere	**atmosfera** (f)	[ɐtmuʃf'ɛɾɐ]
the Sun	**Sol** (m)	[sɔl]
solar system	**Sistema** (m) **Solar**	[siʃt'emɐ sul'aɾ]
solar eclipse	**eclipse** (m) **solar**	[ekl'ipsə sul'aɾ]
the Earth	**Terra** (f)	[t'ɛʀɐ]
the Moon	**Lua** (f)	[l'uɐ]
Mars	**Marte** (m)	[m'artə]
Venus	**Vénus** (m)	[v'ɛnuʃ]
Jupiter	**Júpiter** (m)	[ʒ'upitɛɾ]
Saturn	**Saturno** (m)	[sɐt'urnu]
Mercury	**Mercúrio** (m)	[məɾk'uɾiu]
Uranus	**Urano** (m)	[uɾ'ɐnu]
Neptune	**Neptuno** (m)	[nɛpt'unu]
Pluto	**Plutão** (m)	[plut'ãu]
Milky Way	**Via Láctea** (f)	[v'iɐ l'atiɐ]
Great Bear	**Ursa Maior** (f)	[urse mɐj'ɔɾ]

North Star	**Estrela Polar** (f)	[əʃtr'elɐ pul'ar]
Martian	**marciano** (m)	[mɐrsj'ɐnu]
extraterrestrial (n)	**extraterrestre** (m)	[əʃtrɐtəʀ'ɛʃtrə]
alien	**alienígena** (m)	[ɐlien'iʒənɐ]
flying saucer	**disco** (m) **voador**	[d'iʃku vuɐd'or]
spaceship	**nave** (f) **espacial**	[n'avə əʃpesj'al]
space station	**estação** (f) **orbital**	[əʃtɐs'ãu ɔrbit'al]
blast-off	**lançamento** (m)	[lãsɐm'ẽtu]
engine	**motor** (m)	[mut'or]
nozzle	**bocal** (m)	[buk'al]
fuel	**combustível** (m)	[kõbuʃt'ivɛl]
cockpit, flight deck	**cabine** (f)	[kɐb'inə]
antenna	**antena** (f)	[ãt'enɐ]
porthole	**vigia** (f)	[viʒ'iɐ]
solar battery	**bateria** (f) **solar**	[bɐtər'iɐ sul'ar]
spacesuit	**traje** (m) **espacial**	[tr'aʒə əʃpesj'al]
weightlessness	**imponderabilidade** (f)	[ĩpõdərɐbilid'adə]
oxygen	**oxigénio** (m)	[ɔksiʒ'ɛniu]
docking (in space)	**acoplagem** (f)	[ɐkupl'aʒẽj]
to dock (vi, vt)	**fazer uma acoplagem**	[fɐz'er 'umɐ ɐkupl'aʒẽj]
observatory	**observatório** (m)	[ɔbsərvɐt'ɔriu]
telescope	**telescópio** (m)	[tələʃk'ɔpiu]
to observe (vt)	**observar** (vt)	[ɔbsərv'ar]
to explore (vt)	**explorar** (vt)	[əʃplur'ar]

165. The Earth

the Earth	**Terra** (f)	[t'ɛʀɐ]
globe (the Earth)	**globo** (m) **terrestre**	[gl'obu təʀ'ɛʃtrə]
planet	**planeta** (m)	[plɐn'etɐ]
atmosphere	**atmosfera** (f)	[ɐtmuʃf'ɛrɐ]
geography	**geografia** (f)	[ʒiugrɐf'iɐ]
nature	**natureza** (f)	[nɐtur'ezɐ]
globe (table ~)	**globo** (m)	[gl'obu]
map	**mapa** (m)	[m'apɐ]
atlas	**atlas** (m)	['atlɐʃ]
Europe	**Europa** (f)	[eur'ɔpɐ]
Asia	**Ásia** (f)	['aziɐ]
Africa	**África** (f)	['afrikɐ]
Australia	**Austrália** (f)	[auʃtr'aliɐ]
America	**América** (f)	[ɐm'ɛrikɐ]

North America	**América** (f) **do Norte**	[ɐm'ɛrikɐ du n'ɔrtə]
South America	**América** (f) **do Sul**	[ɐm'ɛrikɐ du sul]
Antarctica	**Antártida** (f)	[ɐ̃t'artidɐ]
the Arctic	**Ártico** (m)	['artiku]

166. Cardinal directions

north	**norte** (m)	[n'ɔrtə]
to the north	**para norte**	[p'ɐrɐ n'ɔrtə]
in the north	**no norte**	[nu n'ɔrtə]
northern (adj)	**do norte**	[du n'ɔrtə]
south	**sul** (m)	[sul]
to the south	**para sul**	[p'ɐrɐ sul]
in the south	**no sul**	[nu sul]
southern (adj)	**do sul**	[du sul]
west	**oeste, ocidente** (m)	[ɔ'ɛʃtə], [ɔsid'ẽtə]
to the west	**para oeste**	[p'ɐrɐ ɔ'ɛʃtə]
in the west	**no oeste**	[nu ɔ'ɛʃtə]
western (adj)	**ocidental**	[ɔsidẽt'al]
east	**leste, oriente** (m)	[l'ɛʃtə], [ɔrj'ẽtə]
to the east	**para leste**	[p'ɐrɐ l'ɛʃtə]
in the east	**no leste**	[nu l'ɛʃtə]
eastern (adj)	**oriental**	[ɔriẽt'al]

167. Sea. Ocean

sea	**mar** (m)	[mar]
ocean	**oceano** (m)	[ɔsj'ɐnu]
gulf (bay)	**golfo** (m)	[g'olfu]
straits	**estreito** (m)	[əʃtr'ɐjtu]
solid ground	**terra** (f) **firme**	[t'ɛʀɐ f'irmə]
continent (mainland)	**continente** (m)	[kõtin'ẽtə]
island	**ilha** (f)	['iʎɐ]
peninsula	**península** (f)	[pən'ĩsulɐ]
archipelago	**arquipélago** (m)	[ɐrkip'ɛlɐgu]
bay, cove	**baía** (f)	[bɐ'iɐ]
harbor	**porto** (m)	[p'ortu]
lagoon	**lagoa** (f)	[lɐg'oɐ]
cape	**cabo** (m)	[k'abu]
atoll	**atol** (m)	[ɐt'ɔl]
reef	**recife** (m)	[ʀəs'ifə]

coral	**coral** (m)	[kur'al]
coral reef	**recife** (m) **de coral**	[ʀəs'ifə də kur'al]
deep (adj)	**profundo**	[pruf'ũdu]
depth (deep water)	**profundidade** (f)	[prufũdid'adə]
abyss	**abismo** (m)	[ɐb'iʒmu]
trench (e.g., Mariana ~)	**fossa** (f) **oceânica**	[f'ɔsɐ ɔsj'ɐnikɐ]
current, stream	**corrente** (f)	[kuʀ'ẽtə]
to surround (bathe)	**banhar** (vt)	[bɐɲ'ar]
shore	**litoral** (m)	[litur'al]
coast	**costa** (f)	[k'ɔʃtɐ]
high tide	**maré** (f) **alta**	[mɐr'ɛ 'altɐ]
low tide	**maré** (f) **baixa**	[mɐr'ɛ b'ajʃɐ]
sandbank	**restinga** (f)	[ʀəʃt'ĩgɐ]
bottom	**fundo** (m)	[f'ũdu]
wave	**onda** (f)	['õdɐ]
crest (~ of a wave)	**crista** (f) **da onda**	[kr'iʃtɐ dɐ 'õdɐ]
froth (foam)	**espuma** (f)	[əʃp'umɐ]
storm	**tempestade** (f)	[tẽpəʃt'adə]
hurricane	**furacão** (m)	[furɐk'ãu]
tsunami	**tsunami** (m)	[tsun'ɐmi]
calm (dead ~)	**calmaria** (f)	[kalmɐr'iɐ]
quiet, calm (adj)	**calmo**	[k'almu]
pole	**polo** (m)	[p'ɔlu]
polar (adj)	**polar**	[pul'ar]
latitude	**latitude** (f)	[lɐtit'udə]
longitude	**longitude** (f)	[lõʒit'udə]
parallel	**paralela** (f)	[pɐrɐl'ɛlɐ]
equator	**equador** (m)	[ekwɐd'or]
sky	**céu** (m)	[s'ɛu]
horizon	**horizonte** (m)	[ɔriz'õtə]
air	**ar** (m)	[ar]
lighthouse	**farol** (m)	[fɐr'ɔl]
to dive (vi)	**mergulhar** (vi)	[mərguʎ'ar]
to sink (ab. boat)	**afundar-se** (vp)	[ɐfũd'arsə]
treasures	**tesouros** (m pl)	[təz'oruʃ]

168. Mountains

mountain	**montanha** (f)	[mõt'ɐɲɐ]
mountain range	**cordilheira** (f)	[kurdiʎ'ɐjrɐ]

mountain ridge	**serra** (f)	[s'ɛʀɐ]
summit, top	**cume** (m)	[k'umə]
peak	**pico** (m)	[p'iku]
foot (of mountain)	**sopé** (m)	[sup'ɛ]
slope (mountainside)	**declive** (m)	[dəkl'ivə]
volcano	**vulcão** (m)	[vulk'ãu]
active volcano	**vulcão** (m) **ativo**	[vulk'ãu at'ivu]
dormant volcano	**vulcão** (m) **extinto**	[vulk'ãu əʃt'ĩtu]
eruption	**erupção** (f)	[erups'ãu]
crater	**cratera** (f)	[krɐt'ɛrɐ]
magma	**magma** (m)	[m'agmɐ]
lava	**lava** (f)	[l'avɐ]
molten (~ lava)	**fundido**	[fũd'idu]
canyon	**desfiladeiro** (m)	[dəʃfilɐd'ɐjru]
gorge	**garganta** (f)	[gɐrg'ãtɐ]
crevice	**fenda** (f)	[f'ẽdɐ]
abyss (chasm)	**precipício** (m)	[prəsip'isiu]
pass, col	**passo, colo** (m)	[p'asu], [k'ɔlu]
plateau	**planalto** (m)	[plɐn'altu]
cliff	**falésia** (f)	[fɐl'ɛziɐ]
hill	**colina** (f)	[kul'inɐ]
glacier	**glaciar** (m)	[glɐsj'ar]
waterfall	**queda** (f) **d'água**	[k'ɛdɐ d'agwɐ]
geyser	**géiser** (m)	[ʒ'ɛjzɛr]
lake	**lago** (m)	[l'agu]
plain	**planície** (f)	[plɐn'isiə]
landscape	**paisagem** (f)	[pajz'aʒẽj]
echo	**eco** (m)	['ɛku]
alpinist	**alpinista** (m)	[alpin'iʃtɐ]
rock climber	**escalador** (m)	[əʃkɐlɐd'or]
to conquer (in climbing)	**conquistar** (vt)	[kõkiʃt'ar]
climb (an easy ~)	**subida, escalada** (f)	[sub'idɐ], [əʃkɐl'adɐ]

169. Rivers

river	**rio** (m)	[ʀ'iu]
spring (natural source)	**fonte, nascente** (f)	[f'õtə], [nɐʃs'ẽtə]
riverbed	**leito** (m) **do rio**	[l'ɐjtu du ʀ'iu]
basin	**bacia** (f)	[bɐs'iɐ]
to flow into ...	**desaguar no ...**	[dəzɐgu'ar nu]
tributary	**afluente** (m)	[ɐflu'ẽtə]
bank (of river)	**margem** (f)	[m'arʒẽj]

current, stream	**corrente** (f)	[kuʀ'ẽtə]
downstream (adv)	**rio abaixo**	[ʀ'iu ɐb'ajʃu]
upstream (adv)	**rio acima**	[ʀ'iu ɐs'imɐ]
inundation	**inundação** (f)	[inũdɐs'ãu]
flooding	**cheia** (f)	[ʃ'ɐjɐ]
to overflow (vi)	**transbordar** (vi)	[trãʒburd'ar]
to flood (vt)	**inundar** (vt)	[inũd'ar]
shallows (shoal)	**baixio** (m)	[bajʃ'iu]
rapids	**rápidos** (m pl)	[ʀ'apiduʃ]
dam	**barragem** (f)	[bɐʀ'aʒẽj]
canal	**canal** (m)	[kɐn'al]
artificial lake	**reservatório** (m) **de água**	[ʀəzərvɐt'ɔriu də 'aguɐ]
sluice, lock	**esclusa** (f)	[əʃkl'uzɐ]
water body (pond, etc.)	**corpo** (m) **de água**	[k'orpu də 'aguɐ]
swamp, bog	**pântano** (m)	[p'ãtɐnu]
marsh	**tremedal** (m)	[trəməd'al]
whirlpool	**remoinho** (m)	[ʀəmu'iɲu]
stream (brook)	**arroio, regato** (m)	[ɐʀ'oju], [ʀəg'atu]
drinking (ab. water)	**potável**	[put'avɛl]
fresh (~ water)	**doce**	[d'osə]
ice	**gelo** (m)	[ʒ'elu]
to freeze (ab. river, etc.)	**congelar-se** (vp)	[kõʒəl'arsə]

170. Forest

forest	**floresta** (f), **bosque** (m)	[flur'ɛʃtɐ], [b'ɔʃkə]
forest (as adj)	**florestal**	[flurəʃt'al]
thick forest	**mata** (f) **cerrada**	[m'atɐ səʀ'adɐ]
grove	**arvoredo** (m)	[ɐrvur'edu]
forest clearing	**clareira** (f)	[klɐr'ɐjrɐ]
thicket	**matagal** (f)	[mɐtɐg'al]
scrubland	**mato** (m)	[m'atu]
footpath (troddenpath)	**vereda** (f)	[vər'edɐ]
gully	**ravina** (f)	[ʀɐv'inɐ]
tree	**árvore** (f)	['arvurə]
leaf	**folha** (f)	[f'oʎɐ]
leaves	**folhagem** (f)	[fuʎ'aʒẽj]
fall of leaves	**queda** (f) **das folha**	[k'ɛdɐ dɐʃ f'oʎɐ]
to fall (ab. leaves)	**cair** (vi)	[kɐ'ir]

top (of the tree)	**topo** (m)	[t'opu]
branch	**ramo** (m)	[ʀ'ɐmu]
bough	**galho** (m)	[g'aʎu]
bud (on shrub, tree)	**botão, rebento** (m)	[but'ãu], [ʀəb'ẽtu]
needle (of pine tree)	**agulha** (f)	[ɐg'uʎɐ]
pine cone	**pinha** (f)	[p'iɲɐ]
hollow (in a tree)	**buraco** (m) **de árvore**	[bur'aku də 'arvurə]
nest	**ninho** (m)	[n'iɲu]
burrow (animal hole)	**toca** (f)	[t'ɔkɐ]
trunk	**tronco** (m)	[tr'õku]
root	**raiz** (f)	[ʀɐ'iʃ]
bark	**casca** (f) **de árvore**	[k'aʃkɐ də 'arvurə]
moss	**musgo** (m)	[m'uʒgu]
to uproot (vt)	**arrancar pela raiz**	[ɐʀãk'ar p'elɐ ʀɐ'iʃ]
to chop down	**cortar** (vt)	[kurt'ar]
to deforest (vt)	**desflorestar** (vt)	[dəʃflurəʃt'ar]
tree stump	**toco, cepo** (m)	[t'ɔku], [s'epu]
campfire	**fogueira** (f)	[fug'ɐjrɐ]
forest fire	**incêndio** (m) **florestal**	[ĩs'ẽdiu flurəʃt'al]
to extinguish (vt)	**apagar** (vt)	[ɐpɐg'ar]
forest ranger	**guarda-florestal** (m)	[gu'ardɐ flurəʃt'al]
protection	**proteção** (f)	[prutɛs'ãu]
to protect (~ nature)	**proteger** (vt)	[prutəʒ'er]
poacher	**caçador** (m) **furtivo**	[kɐsɐd'or furt'ivu]
trap (e.g., bear ~)	**armadilha** (f)	[ɐrmɐd'iʎɐ]
to gather, to pick (vt)	**colher** (vt)	[kuʎ'ɛr]
to lose one's way	**perder-se** (vp)	[pərd'ersə]

171. Natural resources

natural resources	**recursos** (m pl) **naturais**	[ʀək'ursuʃ nɐtur'ajʃ]
minerals	**minerais** (m pl)	[minər'ajʃ]
deposits	**depósitos** (m pl)	[dəp'ɔzituʃ]
field (e.g., oilfield)	**jazida** (f)	[ʒɐz'idɐ]
to mine (extract)	**extrair** (vt)	[əʃtrɐ'ir]
mining (extraction)	**extração** (f)	[əʃtras'ãu]
ore	**minério** (m)	[min'ɛriu]
mine (e.g., for coal)	**mina** (f)	[m'inɐ]
mine shaft, pit	**poço** (m) **de mina**	[p'osu də m'inɐ]
miner	**mineiro** (m)	[min'ɐjru]
gas	**gás** (m)	[gaʃ]
gas pipeline	**gasoduto** (m)	[gazɔd'utu]

oil (petroleum)	**petróleo** (m)	[pətr'ɔliu]
oil pipeline	**oleoduto** (m)	[ɔliud'utu]
oil well	**poço** (m) **de petróleo**	[p'osu də pətr'ɔliu]
derrick	**torre** (f) **petrolífera**	[t'oʀə pətrul'ifərɐ]
tanker	**petroleiro** (m)	[pətrul'ɐjru]
sand	**areia** (f)	[ɐr'ɐjɐ]
limestone	**calcário** (m)	[kalk'ariu]
gravel	**cascalho** (m)	[kɐʃk'aʎu]
peat	**turfa** (f)	[t'urfɐ]
clay	**argila** (f)	[ɐrʒ'ilɐ]
coal	**carvão** (m)	[kɐrv'ãu]
iron	**ferro** (m)	[f'ɛʀu]
gold	**ouro** (m)	['oru]
silver	**prata** (f)	[pr'atɐ]
nickel	**níquel** (m)	[n'ikɛl]
copper	**cobre** (m)	[k'ɔbrə]
zinc	**zinco** (m)	[z'ĩku]
manganese	**manganês** (m)	[mãgɐn'eʃ]
mercury	**mercúrio** (m)	[mərk'uriu]
lead	**chumbo** (m)	[ʃ'ũbu]
mineral	**mineral** (m)	[minər'al]
crystal	**cristal** (m)	[kriʃt'al]
marble	**mármore** (m)	[m'armurə]
uranium	**urânio** (m)	[ur'ɐniu]

The Earth. Part 2

172. Weather

weather	**tempo** (m)	[t'ẽpu]
weather forecast	**previsão** (f) **do tempo**	[prəviz'ãu du t'ẽpu]
temperature	**temperatura** (f)	[tẽpərɐt'urɐ]
thermometer	**termómetro** (m)	[tərm'ɔmətru]
barometer	**barómetro** (m)	[bɐr'ɔmətru]
humid (adj)	**húmido**	['umidu]
humidity	**humidade** (f)	[umid'adə]
heat (extreme ~)	**calor** (m)	[kɐl'or]
hot (torrid)	**cálido**	[k'alidu]
it's hot	**está muito calor**	[əʃt'a m'ũjtu kɐl'or]
it's warm	**está calor**	[əʃt'a kɐl'or]
warm (moderately hot)	**quente**	[k'ẽtə]
it's cold	**está frio**	[əʃt'a fr'iu]
cold (adj)	**frio**	[fr'iu]
sun	**sol** (m)	[sɔl]
to shine (vi)	**brilhar** (vi)	[briʎ'ar]
sunny (day)	**de sol, ensolarado**	[də sɔl], [ẽsulɐr'adu]
to come up (vi)	**nascer** (vi)	[nɐʃs'er]
to set (vi)	**pôr-se** (vp)	[p'orsə]
cloud	**nuvem** (f)	[n'uvẽj]
cloudy (adj)	**nublado**	[nubl'adu]
rain cloud	**nuvem** (f) **negra**	[n'uvẽj n'egrɐ]
somber (gloomy)	**escuro, cinzento**	[əʃk'uru], [sĩz'ẽtu]
rain	**chuva** (f)	[ʃ'uvɐ]
it's raining	**está a chover**	[əʃt'a ɐ ʃuv'er]
rainy (day)	**chuvoso**	[ʃuv'ozu]
to drizzle (vi)	**chuviscar** (vi)	[ʃuviʃk'ar]
pouring rain	**chuva** (f) **torrencial**	[ʃ'uvɐ tuʀẽsj'al]
downpour	**chuvada** (f)	[ʃuv'adɐ]
heavy (e.g., ~ rain)	**forte**	[f'ɔrtə]
puddle	**poça** (f)	[p'ɔsɐ]
to get wet (in rain)	**molhar-se** (vp)	[muʎ'arsə]
fog (mist)	**nevoeiro** (m)	[nəvu'ɐjru]
foggy	**de nevoeiro**	[də nəvu'ɐjru]

snow	**neve** (f)	[n'ɛvə]
it's snowing	**está a nevar**	[əʃt'a ɐ nɛv'ar]

173. Severe weather. Natural disasters

thunderstorm	**trovoada** (f)	[truvu'adɐ]
lightning (~ strike)	**relâmpago** (m)	[ʀəl'ãpɐgu]
to flash (vi)	**relampejar** (vi)	[ʀəlãpəʒ'ar]
thunder	**trovão** (m)	[truv'ãu]
to thunder (vi)	**trovejar** (vi)	[truvəʒ'ar]
it's thundering	**está a trovejar**	[əʃt'a ɐ truvəʒ'ar]
hail	**granizo** (m)	[grɐn'izu]
it's hailing	**está a cair granizo**	[əʃt'a ɐ kɐ'ir grɐn'izu]
to flood (vt)	**inundar** (vt)	[inũd'ar]
flood, inundation	**inundação** (f)	[inũdɐs'ãu]
earthquake	**terremoto** (m)	[təʀəm'ɔtu]
tremor, quake	**abalo, tremor** (m)	[ɐb'alu], [trəm'or]
epicenter	**epicentro** (m)	[epis'ẽtru]
eruption	**erupção** (f)	[erups'ãu]
lava	**lava** (f)	[l'avɐ]
twister	**turbilhão** (m)	[turbiʎ'ãu]
tornado	**tornado** (m)	[turn'adu]
typhoon	**tufão** (m)	[tuf'ãu]
hurricane	**furacão** (m)	[furɐk'ãu]
storm	**tempestade** (f)	[tẽpəʃt'adə]
tsunami	**tsunami** (m)	[tsun'ɐmi]
cyclone	**ciclone** (m)	[sikl'ɔnə]
bad weather	**mau tempo** (m)	[m'au t'ẽpu]
fire (accident)	**incêndio** (m)	[ĩs'ẽdiu]
disaster	**catástrofe** (f)	[kɐt'aʃtrufə]
meteorite	**meteorito** (m)	[mətiur'itu]
avalanche	**avalanche** (f)	[ɐvɐl'ãʃə]
snowslide	**deslizamento** (f) **de neve**	[dəʒlizɐm'ẽtu də n'ɛvə]
blizzard	**nevasca** (f)	[nəv'aʃkɐ]
snowstorm	**tempestade** (f) **de neve**	[tẽpəʃt'adə də n'ɛvə]

Fauna

174. Mammals. Predators

predator	**predador** (m)	[prəded'or]
tiger	**tigre** (m)	[t'igrə]
lion	**leão** (m)	[lj'ãu]
wolf	**lobo** (m)	[l'obu]
fox	**raposa** (f)	[ʀɐp'ozɐ]
jaguar	**jaguar** (m)	[ʒɐgu'aɾ]
leopard	**leopardo** (m)	[liup'ardu]
cheetah	**chita** (f)	[ʃ'itɐ]
black panther	**pantera** (f)	[pãt'eɾɐ]
puma	**puma** (m)	[p'umɐ]
snow leopard	**leopardo-das-neves** (m)	[liup'ardu dɐʒ n'ɛvəʃ]
lynx	**lince** (m)	[l'ĩsə]
coyote	**coiote** (m)	[koj'ɔtə]
jackal	**chacal** (m)	[ʃɐk'al]
hyena	**hiena** (f)	[j'enɐ]

175. Wild animals

animal	**animal** (m)	[ɐnim'al]
beast (animal)	**besta** (f)	[b'eʃtɐ]
squirrel	**esquilo** (m)	[əʃk'ilu]
hedgehog	**ouriço** (m)	[or'isu]
hare	**lebre** (f)	[l'ɛbrə]
rabbit	**coelho** (m)	[ku'ɐʎu]
badger	**texugo** (m)	[tɛks'ugu]
raccoon	**guaxinim** (m)	[guaksin'ĩ]
hamster	**hamster** (m)	['ɐmstɐɾ]
marmot	**marmota** (f)	[mɐrm'ɔtɐ]
mole	**toupeira** (f)	[top'ɐjɾɐ]
mouse	**rato** (m)	[ʀ'atu]
rat	**ratazana** (f)	[ʀɐtɐz'ɐnɐ]
bat	**morcego** (m)	[muɾs'egu]
ermine	**arminho** (m)	[ɐrm'iɲu]
sable	**zibelina** (f)	[zibəl'inɐ]

marten	**marta** (f)	[m'artɐ]
weasel	**doninha** (f)	[dun'iɲɐ]
mink	**vison** (m)	[viz'õ]
beaver	**castor** (m)	[kɐʃt'or]
otter	**lontra** (f)	[l'õtrɐ]
horse	**cavalo** (m)	[kɐv'alu]
moose	**alce** (m) **americano**	['alsə ɐmərik'ɐnu]
deer	**veado** (m)	[vj'adu]
camel	**camelo** (m)	[kɐm'elu]
bison	**bisão** (m)	[biz'ãu]
aurochs	**auroque** (m)	[aur'ɔkə]
buffalo	**búfalo** (m)	[b'ufɐlu]
zebra	**zebra** (f)	[z'ɛbrɐ]
antelope	**antílope** (m)	[ãt'ilupə]
roe deer	**corça** (f)	[k'orsɐ]
fallow deer	**gamo** (m)	[g'ɐmu]
chamois	**camurça** (f)	[kɐm'ursɐ]
wild boar	**javali** (m)	[ʒɐvɐl'i]
whale	**baleia** (f)	[bɐl'ɐjɐ]
seal	**foca** (f)	[f'ɔkɐ]
walrus	**morsa** (f)	[m'ɔrsɐ]
fur seal	**urso-marinho** (m)	['ursu mɐr'iɲu]
dolphin	**golfinho** (m)	[golf'iɲu]
bear	**urso** (m)	['ursu]
polar bear	**urso** (m) **branco**	['ursu br'ãku]
panda	**panda** (m)	[p'ãdɐ]
monkey	**macaco** (m)	[mɐk'aku]
chimpanzee	**chimpanzé** (m)	[ʃĩpãz'ɛ]
orangutan	**orangotango** (m)	[ɔrãgut'ãgu]
gorilla	**gorila** (m)	[gur'ilɐ]
macaque	**macaco** (m)	[mɐk'aku]
gibbon	**gibão** (m)	[ʒib'ãu]
elephant	**elefante** (m)	[eləf'ãtə]
rhinoceros	**rinoceronte** (m)	[ʀinɔsər'õtə]
giraffe	**girafa** (f)	[ʒir'afɐ]
hippopotamus	**hipopótamo** (m)	[ipɔp'ɔtɐmu]
kangaroo	**canguru** (m)	[kãgur'u]
koala (bear)	**coala** (m)	[ku'alɐ]
mongoose	**mangusto** (m)	[mãg'uʃtu]
chinchilla	**chinchila** (f)	[ʃĩʃ'ilɐ]
skunk	**doninha-fedorenta** (f)	[duniɲɐ fədur'ẽtɐ]
porcupine	**porco-espinho** (m)	[p'orkɔ əʃp'iɲu]

176. Domestic animals

cat	**gata** (f)	[g'atɐ]
tomcat	**gato** (m) **macho**	[g'atu m'aʃu]
dog	**cão** (m)	[k'ãu]
horse	**cavalo** (m)	[kɐv'alu]
stallion	**garanhão** (m)	[gɐrɐɲ'ãu]
mare	**égua** (f)	['ɛguɐ]
cow	**vaca** (f)	[v'akɐ]
bull	**touro** (m)	[t'oru]
ox	**boi** (m)	[boj]
sheep	**ovelha** (f)	[ɔv'ɐʎɐ]
ram	**carneiro** (m)	[kɐrn'ɐjru]
goat	**cabra** (f)	[k'abrɐ]
billy goat, he-goat	**bode** (m)	[b'ɔdə]
donkey	**burro** (m)	[b'uʀu]
mule	**mula** (f)	[m'ulɐ]
pig	**porco** (m)	[p'orku]
piglet	**porquinho** (m)	[purk'iɲu]
rabbit	**coelho** (m)	[ku'ɐʎu]
hen (chicken)	**galinha** (f)	[gɐl'iɲɐ]
rooster	**galo** (m)	[g'alu]
duck	**pato** (m), **pata** (f)	[p'atu], [p'atɐ]
drake	**pato** (m)	[p'atu]
goose	**ganso** (m)	[g'ãsu]
tom turkey	**peru** (m)	[pər'u]
turkey (hen)	**perua** (f)	[pər'uɐ]
domestic animals	**animais** (m pl) **domésticos**	[ɐnim'ajʃ dum'ɛʃtikuʃ]
tame (e.g., ~ hamster)	**domesticado**	[duməʃtik'adu]
to tame (vt)	**domesticar** (vt)	[duməʃtik'ar]
to breed (vt)	**criar** (vt)	[kri'ar]
farm	**quinta** (f)	[k'ĩtɐ]
poultry	**aves** (f pl) **domésticas**	['avəʃ dum'ɛʃtikɐʃ]
cattle	**gado** (m)	[g'adu]
herd (cattle)	**rebanho** (m), **manada** (f)	[ʀəb'ɐɲu], [mɐn'adɐ]
stable	**estábulo** (m)	[əʃt'abulu]
pigsty	**pocilga** (f)	[pus'ilgɐ]
cowshed	**vacaria** (m)	[vɐkɐr'iɐ]
rabbit hutch	**coelheira** (f)	[kuɛʎ'ɐjrɐ]
hen house	**galinheiro** (m)	[gɐliɲ'ɐjru]

177. Dogs. Dog breeds

dog	**cão** (m)	[k'ãu]
sheepdog	**cão pastor** (m)	[k'ãu pɐʃt'or]
German shepherd dog	**pastor-alemão** (m)	[pɐʃt'or ɐləm'ãu]
poodle	**caniche** (m)	[kan'iʃə]
dachshund	**teckel** (m)	[tɛkk'ɛl]
bulldog	**buldogue** (m)	[buld'ɔgə]
boxer	**boxer** (m)	[b'ɔksɐr]
mastiff	**mastim** (m)	[mɐʃt'ĩ]
rottweiler	**rottweiler** (m)	[ʀɔtv'ajlɐr]
Doberman	**dobermann** (m)	[dɔb'ɛrmɐn]
basset	**basset** (m)	[bas'ɛt]
bobtail	**pastor inglês** (m)	[pɐʃt'or ĩgl'eʃ]
Dalmatian	**dálmata** (m)	[d'almɐtɐ]
cocker spaniel	**cocker spaniel** (m)	[k'ɔkɐr spɐnj'ɛl]
Newfoundland	**terra-nova** (m)	[tɛʀɐn'ɔvɐ]
Saint Bernard	**são-bernardo** (m)	[sãubərn'ardu]
husky	**husky** (m)	['ɐski]
Chow Chow	**Chow-chow** (m)	[ʃɔuʃ'ɔu]
spitz	**spitz alemão** (m)	[ʃp'itz ɐləm'ãu]
pug	**carlindogue** (m)	[kɐrlĩd'ɔgə]

178. Sounds made by animals

barking (n)	**latido** (m)	[lɐt'idu]
to bark (vi)	**ladrar, latir** (vi)	[lɐdr'ar], [lɐt'ir]
to meow (vi)	**miar** (vi)	[mj'ar]
to purr (vi)	**ronronar** (vi)	[ʀõʀun'ar]
to moo (vi)	**mugir** (vi)	[muʒ'ir]
to bellow (bull)	**bramir** (vi)	[brɐm'ir]
to growl (vi)	**rosnar** (vi)	[ʀuʒn'ar]
howl (n)	**uivo** (m)	['ujvu]
to howl (vi)	**uivar** (vi)	[ujv'ar]
to whine (vi)	**ganir** (vi)	[gɐn'ir]
to bleat (sheep)	**balir** (vi)	[bɐl'ir]
to oink, to grunt (pig)	**grunhir** (vi)	[gruɲ'ir]
to squeal (vi)	**guinchar** (vi)	[gĩʃ'ar]
to croak (vi)	**coaxar** (vi)	[kuaʃ'ar]
to buzz (insect)	**zumbir** (vi)	[zũb'ir]
to stridulate (vi)	**estridular, ziziar** (vi)	[əʃtridul'ar], [zizj'ar]

179. Birds

bird	**pássaro, ave** (m)	[p'aseru], ['avə]
pigeon	**pombo** (m)	[p'õbu]
sparrow	**pardal** (m)	[perd'al]
tit	**chapim-real** (m)	[ʃep'ĩ ʀi'al]
magpie	**pega-rabuda** (f)	[p'ɛge ʀab'ude]
raven	**corvo** (m)	[k'orvu]
crow	**gralha** (f) **cinzenta**	[gr'aʎe sĩz'ẽte]
jackdaw	**gralha-de-nuca cinzenta** (f)	[gr'aʎe də n'uke sĩz'ẽte]
rook	**gralha-calva** (f)	[gr'aʎe k'alve]
duck	**pato** (m)	[p'atu]
goose	**ganso** (m)	[g'ãsu]
pheasant	**faisão** (m)	[fajz'ãu]
eagle	**águia** (f)	['agie]
hawk	**açor** (m)	[es'or]
falcon	**falcão** (m)	[falk'ãu]
vulture	**abutre** (m)	[eb'utrə]
condor (Andean ~)	**condor** (m)	[kõd'or]
swan	**cisne** (m)	[s'iʒnə]
crane	**grou** (m)	[gro]
stork	**cegonha** (f)	[səg'oɲe]
parrot	**papagaio** (m)	[pepeg'aju]
hummingbird	**beija-flor** (m)	[b'ejʒe fl'or]
peacock	**pavão** (m)	[pev'ãu]
ostrich	**avestruz** (f)	[evəʃtr'uʃ]
heron	**garça** (f)	[g'arse]
flamingo	**flamingo** (m)	[flem'ĩgu]
pelican	**pelicano** (m)	[pəlik'enu]
nightingale	**rouxinol** (m)	[ʀoʃin'ɔl]
swallow	**andorinha** (f)	[ãdur'iɲe]
thrush	**tordo-zornal** (m)	[t'ɔrdu zurn'al]
song thrush	**tordo-músico** (m)	[t'ɔrdu m'uziku]
blackbird	**melro-preto** (m)	[m'ɛlʀu pr'etu]
swift	**andorinhão** (m)	[ãduriɲ'ãu]
lark	**cotovia** (f)	[kutuv'ie]
quail	**codorna** (f)	[kɔd'ɔrne]
woodpecker	**pica-pau** (m)	[p'ike p'au]
cuckoo	**cuco** (m)	[k'uku]
owl	**coruja** (f)	[kur'uʒe]

eagle owl	**corujão, bufo** (m)	[kɔruʒ'ãu], [b'ufu]
wood grouse	**tetraz-grande** (m)	[tɛtr'aʒ gr'ãdə]
black grouse	**tetraz-lira** (m)	[tɛtr'aʒ l'irɐ]
partridge	**perdiz-cinzenta** (f)	[pərdiʃ sĩz'ẽtɐ]
starling	**estorninho** (m)	[əʃturn'iɲu]
canary	**canário** (m)	[kɐn'ariu]
hazel grouse	**galinha-do-mato** (f)	[gɐl'iɲɐ du m'atu]
chaffinch	**tentilhão** (m)	[tẽtiʎ'ãu]
bullfinch	**dom-fafe** (m)	[dõf'afə]
seagull	**gaivota** (f)	[gajv'ɔtɐ]
albatross	**albatroz** (m)	[albɐtr'ɔʃ]
penguin	**pinguim** (m)	[pĩgu'ĩ]

180. Birds. Singing and sounds

to sing (vi)	**cantar** (vi)	[kãt'ar]
to call (animal, bird)	**gritar** (vi)	[grit'ar]
to crow (rooster)	**cantar (o galo)**	[kãt'ar u g'alu]
cock-a-doodle-doo	**cocorocó** (m)	[kɔkuruk'ɔ]
to cluck (hen)	**cacarejar** (vi)	[kɐkɐrəʒ'ar]
to caw (vi)	**crocitar** (vi)	[krɔsit'ar]
to quack (duck)	**grasnar** (vi)	[grɐʒn'ar]
to cheep (vi)	**piar** (vi)	[pj'ar]
to chirp, to twitter	**chilrear, gorjear** (vi)	[ʃilʀe'ar], [gurʒj'ar]

181. Fish. Marine animals

bream	**brema** (f)	[br'emɐ]
carp	**carpa** (f)	[k'arpɐ]
perch	**perca** (f)	[p'ɛrkɐ]
catfish	**siluro** (m)	[sil'uru]
pike	**lúcio** (m)	[l'usiu]
salmon	**salmão** (m)	[salm'ãu]
sturgeon	**esturjão** (m)	[əʃturʒ'ãu]
herring	**arenque** (m)	[ɐr'ẽkə]
Atlantic salmon	**salmão** (m)	[salm'ãu]
mackerel	**cavala** (m), **sarda** (f)	[kɐv'alɐ], [s'ardɐ]
flatfish	**solha** (f)	[s'oʎɐ]
zander, pike perch	**zander** (m)	[zãd'er]
cod	**bacalhau** (m)	[bɐkɐʎ'au]
tuna	**atum** (m)	[ɐt'ũ]
trout	**truta** (f)	[tr'utɐ]

eel	**enguia** (f)	[ẽg'iɐ]
electric ray	**raia elétrica** (f)	[ʀ'ajɐ el'ɛtrikɐ]
moray eel	**moreia** (f)	[mur'ɐjɐ]
piranha	**piranha** (f)	[pir'ɐɲɐ]
shark	**tubarão** (m)	[tubɐr'ãu]
dolphin	**golfinho** (m)	[golf'iɲu]
whale	**baleia** (f)	[bɐl'ɐjɐ]
crab	**caranguejo** (m)	[kɐrãg'ɐʒu]
jellyfish	**medusa, alforreca** (f)	[məd'uzɐ], [alfuʀ'ɛkɐ]
octopus	**polvo** (m)	[p'olvu]
starfish	**estrela-do-mar** (f)	[əʃtr'elɐ du m'ar]
sea urchin	**ouriço-do-mar** (m)	[or'isu du m'ar]
seahorse	**cavalo-marinho** (m)	[kɐv'alu mɐr'iɲu]
oyster	**ostra** (f)	['ɔʃtrɐ]
shrimp	**camarão** (m)	[kɐmɐr'ãu]
lobster	**lavagante** (m)	[lɐvɐg'ãtə]
spiny lobster	**lagosta** (f)	[lɐg'oʃtɐ]

182. Amphibians. Reptiles

snake	**serpente, cobra** (f)	[sərp'ẽtə], [k'ɔbrɐ]
venomous (snake)	**venenoso**	[vənən'ozu]
viper	**víbora** (f)	[v'iburɐ]
cobra	**cobra-capelo, naja** (f)	[kɔbrɐkɐp'ɛlu], [n'aʒɐ]
python	**piton** (m)	[p'itɔn]
boa	**jiboia** (f)	[ʒib'ɔjɐ]
grass snake	**cobra-de-água** (f)	[kɔbrɐdə'aguɐ]
rattle snake	**cascavel** (f)	[kɐʃkɐv'ɛl]
anaconda	**anaconda** (f)	[ɐnɐk'õdɐ]
lizard	**lagarto** (m)	[lɐg'artu]
iguana	**iguana** (f)	[igu'ɐnɐ]
monitor lizard	**varano** (m)	[vɐr'ɐnu]
salamander	**salamandra** (f)	[sɐlɐm'ãdrɐ]
chameleon	**camaleão** (m)	[kɐmɐlj'ãu]
scorpion	**escorpião** (m)	[əʃkurpj'ãu]
turtle	**tartaruga** (f)	[tɐrtɐr'ugɐ]
frog	**rã** (f)	[ʀã]
toad	**sapo** (m)	[s'apu]
crocodile	**crocodilo** (m)	[krukud'ilu]

183. Insects

insect, bug	**inseto** (m)	[ĩs'ɛtu]
butterfly	**borboleta** (f)	[burbul'etɐ]
ant	**formiga** (f)	[furm'igɐ]
fly	**mosca** (f)	[m'oʃkɐ]
mosquito	**mosquito** (m)	[muʃk'itu]
beetle	**escaravelho** (m)	[əʃkɐrɐv'ɛʎu]
wasp	**vespa** (f)	[v'ɛʃpɐ]
bee	**abelha** (f)	[ɐb'ɐʎɐ]
bumblebee	**zangão** (m)	[zɐ̃g'ɐ̃u]
gadfly	**moscardo** (m)	[muʃk'ardu]
spider	**aranha** (f)	[ɐr'ɐɲɐ]
spider's web	**teia** (f) **de aranha**	[t'ɐjɐ də ɐr'ɐɲɐ]
dragonfly	**libélula** (f)	[lib'ɛlulɐ]
grasshopper	**gafanhoto-do-campo** (m)	[gɐfɐɲ'otu du k'ɐ̃pu]
moth (night butterfly)	**traça** (f)	[tr'asɐ]
cockroach	**barata** (f)	[bɐr'atɐ]
tick	**carraça** (f)	[kɐʀ'asɐ]
flea	**pulga** (f)	[p'ulgɐ]
midge	**borrachudo** (m)	[buʀɐʃ'udu]
locust	**gafanhoto** (m)	[gɐfɐɲ'otu]
snail	**caracol** (m)	[kɐrɐk'ɔl]
cricket	**grilo** (m)	[gr'ilu]
lightning bug	**pirilampo** (m)	[piril'ɐ̃pu]
ladybug	**joaninha** (f)	[ʒuɐn'iɲɐ]
cockchafer	**besouro** (m)	[bəz'oru]
leech	**sanguessuga** (f)	[sɐ̃gəs'ugɐ]
caterpillar	**lagarta** (f)	[lɐg'artɐ]
earthworm	**minhoca** (f)	[miɲ'ɔkɐ]
larva	**larva** (f)	[l'arvɐ]

184. Animals. Body parts

beak	**bico** (m)	[b'iku]
wings	**asas** (f pl)	['azɐʃ]
foot (of bird)	**pata** (f)	[p'atɐ]
feathering	**plumagem** (f)	[plum'aʒɐ̃j]
feather	**pena, pluma** (f)	[p'enɐ], [pl'umɐ]
crest	**crista** (f)	[kr'iʃtɐ]
gill	**brânquias, guelras** (f pl)	[br'ɐ̃kiɐʃ], [g'ɛlʀɐʃ]
spawn	**ovas** (f pl)	['ɔvɐʃ]

larva	**larva** (f)	[l'arvɐ]
fin	**barbatana** (f)	[bɐrbɐt'ɐnɐ]
scales (of fish, reptile)	**escama** (f)	[əʃk'ɐmɐ]
fang (canine)	**canino** (m)	[kɐn'inu]
paw (e.g., cat's ~)	**pata** (f)	[p'atɐ]
muzzle (snout)	**focinho** (m)	[fus'iɲu]
mouth (of cat, dog)	**boca** (f)	[b'okɐ]
tail	**cauda** (f), **rabo** (m)	[k'audɐ], [ʀ'abu]
whiskers	**bigodes** (m pl)	[big'ɔdəʃ]
hoof	**casco** (m)	[k'aʃku]
horn	**corno** (m)	[k'ornu]
carapace	**carapaça** (f)	[kɐrɐp'asɐ]
shell (of mollusk)	**concha** (f)	[k'õʃɐ]
eggshell	**casca** (f) **de ovo**	[k'aʃkɐ də 'ovu]
animal's hair (pelage)	**pelo** (m)	[p'elu]
pelt (hide)	**pele** (f), **couro** (m)	[p'ɛlə], [k'oru]

185. Animals. Habitats

habitat	**habitat** (m)	[abit'atə]
migration	**migração** (f)	[migrɐs'ãu]
mountain	**montanha** (f)	[mõt'ɐɲɐ]
reef	**recife** (m)	[ʀəs'ifə]
cliff	**falésia** (f)	[fɐl'ɛziɐ]
forest	**floresta** (f)	[flur'ɛʃtɐ]
jungle	**selva** (f)	[s'ɛlvɐ]
savanna	**savana** (f)	[sɐv'ɐnɐ]
tundra	**tundra** (f)	[t'ũdrɐ]
steppe	**estepe** (f)	[əʃt'ɛpə]
desert	**deserto** (m)	[dəz'ɛrtu]
oasis	**oásis** (m)	[o'aziʃ]
sea	**mar** (m)	[mar]
lake	**lago** (m)	[l'agu]
ocean	**oceano** (m)	[ɔsj'ɐnu]
swamp	**pântano** (m)	[p'ãtɐnu]
freshwater (adj)	**de água doce**	[də 'agwɐ d'osə]
pond	**lagoa** (f)	[lɐg'oɐ]
river	**rio** (m)	[ʀ'iu]
den	**toca** (f) **do urso**	[t'ɔkɐ du 'ursu]
nest	**ninho** (m)	[n'iɲu]

hollow (in a tree)	**buraco** (m) **de árvore**	[bur'aku də 'arvurə]
burrow (animal hole)	**toca** (f)	[t'ɔkɐ]
anthill	**formigueiro** (m)	[furmig'ɐjru]

Flora

186. Trees

tree	**árvore** (f)	['arvurə]
deciduous (adj)	**decídua**	[dəs'iduɐ]
coniferous (adj)	**conífera**	[kun'ifərɐ]
evergreen (adj)	**perene**	[pər'ɛnə]
apple tree	**macieira** (f)	[mɐsj'ɐjrɐ]
pear tree	**pereira** (f)	[pər'ɐjrɐ]
sweet cherry tree	**cerejeira** (f)	[sərəʒ'ɐjrɐ]
sour cherry tree	**ginjeira** (f)	[ʒĩʒ'ɐjrɐ]
plum tree	**ameixeira** (f)	[ɐmɐjʃ'ɐjrɐ]
birch	**bétula** (f)	[b'ɛtulɐ]
oak	**carvalho** (m)	[kɐrv'aʎu]
linden tree	**tília** (f)	[t'iliɐ]
aspen	**choupo-tremedor** (m)	[ʃ'opu trəməd'or]
maple	**bordo** (m)	[b'ɔrdu]
spruce	**espruce-europeu** (m)	[əʃpr'usə eurup'eu]
pine	**pinheiro** (m)	[piɲ'ɐjru]
larch	**alerce, lariço** (m)	[ɐl'ɛrsə], [lɐr'isu]
fir tree	**abeto** (m)	[ɐb'ɛtu]
cedar	**cedro** (m)	[s'ɛdru]
poplar	**choupo, álamo** (m)	[ʃ'opu], ['alɐmu]
rowan	**tramazeira** (f)	[trɐmɐz'ɐjrɐ]
willow	**salgueiro** (m)	[salg'ɐjru]
alder	**amieiro** (m)	[ɐmj'ɐjru]
beech	**faia** (f)	[f'ajɐ]
elm	**ulmeiro** (m)	[ulm'ɐjru]
ash (tree)	**freixo** (m)	[fr'ɐjʃu]
chestnut	**castanheiro** (m)	[kɐʃtɐɲ'ɐjru]
magnolia	**magnólia** (f)	[mɐgn'ɔliɐ]
palm tree	**palmeira** (f)	[palm'ɐjrɐ]
cypress	**cipreste** (m)	[sipr'ɛʃtə]
mangrove	**mangue** (m)	[m'ãgə]
baobab	**embondeiro, baobá** (m)	[ẽbõd'ɐjru], [baub'a]
eucalyptus	**eucalipto** (m)	[eukɐl'iptu]
sequoia	**sequoia** (f)	[səku'ɔjɐ]

187. Shrubs

bush	**arbusto** (m)	[ɐrb'uʃtu]
shrub	**arbusto** (m), **moita** (f)	[ɐrb'uʃtu], [m'ojtɐ]
grapevine	**videira** (f)	[vid'ɐjrɐ]
vineyard	**vinhedo** (m)	[viɲ'edu]
raspberry bush	**framboeseira** (f)	[frãbuez'ɐjrɐ]
blackcurrant bush	**groselheira-preta** (f)	[gruzəʎɐjrɐ pr'etɐ]
redcurrant bush	**groselheira-vermelha** (f)	[gruzəʎ'ɐjrɐ vərm'ɐʎɐ]
gooseberry bush	**groselheira** (f) **espinhosa**	[gruzəʎ'ɐjrɐ əʃpiɲ'ɔzɐ]
acacia	**acácia** (f)	[ɐk'asiɐ]
barberry	**bérberis** (f)	[b'ɛrbəriʃ]
jasmine	**jasmim** (m)	[ʒɐʒm'ĩ]
juniper	**junípero** (m)	[ʒun'ipəru]
rosebush	**roseira** (f)	[ʀuz'ɐjrɐ]
dog rose	**roseira** (f) **brava**	[ʀuz'ɐjrɐ br'avɐ]

188. Mushrooms

mushroom	**cogumelo** (m)	[kugum'ɛlu]
edible mushroom	**cogumelo** (m) **comestível**	[kugum'ɛlu kuməʃt'ivɛl]
toadstool	**cogumelo** (m) **venenoso**	[kugum'ɛlu vənən'ozu]
cap (of mushroom)	**chapéu** (m)	[ʃɐp'ɛu]
stipe (of mushroom)	**pé, caule** (m)	[pɛ], [k'aulə]
cep (Boletus edulis)	**cepe-de-bordéus** (m)	[s'ɛpə də burd'ɛuʃ]
orange-cap boletus	**boleto** (m) **áspero**	[bul'etu 'aʃpəru]
birch bolete	**boleto** (m) **castanho**	[bul'etu kɐʃt'ɐɲu]
chanterelle	**cantarelo** (m)	[kãtɐr'ɛlu]
russula	**rússula** (f)	[ʀ'usulɐ]
morel	**morchela** (f)	[murʃ'ɛlɐ]
fly agaric	**agário-das-moscas** (m)	[ɐg'ariu dɐʒ m'oʃkɐʃ]
death cap	**cicuta** (f) **verde**	[sik'utɐ v'erdə]

189. Fruits. Berries

fruit	**fruta** (f)	[fr'utɐ]
fruits	**frutas** (f pl)	[fr'utɐʃ]
apple	**maçã** (f)	[mɐs'ã]
pear	**pera** (f)	[p'erɐ]
plum	**ameixa** (f)	[ɐm'ɐjʃɐ]
strawberry	**morango** (m)	[mur'ãgu]

sour cherry	**ginja** (f)	[ʒ'ĩʒɐ]
sweet cherry	**cereja** (f)	[sər'ɐʒɐ]
grape	**uva** (f)	['uvɐ]
raspberry	**framboesa** (f)	[frãbu'ezɐ]
blackcurrant	**groselha** (f) **preta**	[gruz'ɐʎɐ pr'etɐ]
redcurrant	**groselha** (f) **vermelha**	[gruz'ɐʎɐ vərm'ɐʎɐ]
gooseberry	**groselha** (f) **espinhosa**	[gruz'ɐʎɐ əʃpiɲ'ɔzɐ]
cranberry	**oxicoco** (m)	[ɔksik'oku]
orange	**laranja** (f)	[lɐr'ãʒɐ]
mandarin	**tangerina** (f)	[tãʒər'inɐ]
pineapple	**ananás** (m)	[ɐnɐn'aʃ]
banana	**banana** (f)	[bɐn'ɐnɐ]
date	**tâmara** (f)	[t'ɐmɐrɐ]
lemon	**limão** (m)	[lim'ãu]
apricot	**damasco** (m)	[dɐm'aʃku]
peach	**pêssego** (m)	[p'esəgu]
kiwi	**kiwi** (m)	[kiv'i]
grapefruit	**toranja** (f)	[tur'ãʒɐ]
berry	**baga** (f)	[b'agɐ]
berries	**bagas** (f pl)	[b'agɐʃ]
cowberry	**arando** (m) **vermelho**	[ɐr'ãdu vərm'ɐʎu]
field strawberry	**morango-silvestre** (m)	[mur'ãgu silv'ɛʃtrə]
bilberry	**mirtilo** (m)	[mirt'ilu]

190. Flowers. Plants

flower	**flor** (f)	[flor]
bouquet (of flowers)	**ramo** (m) **de flores**	[ʀ'ɐmu də fl'orəʃ]
rose (flower)	**rosa** (f)	[ʀ'ɔzɐ]
tulip	**tulipa** (f)	[tul'ipɐ]
carnation	**cravo** (m)	[kr'avu]
gladiolus	**gladíolo** (m)	[glɐd'iulu]
cornflower	**centáurea** (f)	[sẽt'auriɐ]
bluebell	**campânula** (f)	[kãp'ɐnulɐ]
dandelion	**dente-de-leão** (m)	[d'ẽtə də li'ãu]
camomile	**camomila** (f)	[kamum'ilɐ]
aloe	**aloé** (m)	[ɐlu'ɛ]
cactus	**cato** (m)	[k'atu]
rubber plant, ficus	**fícus** (m)	[f'ikuʃ]
lily	**lírio** (m)	[l'iriu]
geranium	**gerânio** (m)	[ʒər'eniu]
hyacinth	**jacinto** (m)	[ʒɐs'ĩtu]

mimosa	**mimosa** (f)	[mim'ɔzɐ]
narcissus	**narciso** (m)	[nars'izu]
nasturtium	**capuchinha** (f)	[kɐpuʃ'iɲɐ]
orchid	**orquídea** (f)	[ɔrk'idiɐ]
peony	**peónia** (f)	[pj'ɔniɐ]
violet	**violeta** (f)	[viul'etɐ]
pansy	**amor-perfeito** (m)	[ɐm'or pərf'ɐjtu]
forget-me-not	**não-me-esqueças** (m)	[n'ãu mə əʃk'esɐʃ]
daisy	**margarida** (f)	[mɐrgɐr'idɐ]
poppy	**papoula** (f)	[pɐp'olɐ]
hemp	**cânhamo** (m)	[k'ɐɲɐmu]
mint	**hortelã** (f)	[ɔrtəl'ã]
lily of the valley	**lírio-do-vale** (m)	[l'iriu du v'alə]
snowdrop	**campânula-branca** (f)	[kãpɐnulɐ br'ãkɐ]
nettle	**urtiga** (f)	[urt'igɐ]
sorrel	**azeda** (f)	[ɐz'edɐ]
water lily	**nenúfar** (m)	[nən'ufar]
fern	**feto** (m), **samambaia** (f)	[f'ɛtu], [sɐmãb'ajɐ]
lichen	**líquen** (m)	[l'ikɛn]
tropical greenhouse	**estufa** (f)	[əʃt'ufɐ]
grass lawn	**relvado** (m)	[ʀɛlv'adu]
flowerbed	**canteiro** (m) **de flores**	[kãt'ɐjru də fl'orəʃ]
plant	**planta** (f)	[pl'ãtɐ]
grass, herb	**erva** (f)	['ɛrvɐ]
blade of grass	**folha** (f) **de erva**	[f'oʎɐ də 'ɛrvɐ]
leaf	**folha** (f)	[f'oʎɐ]
petal	**pétala** (f)	[p'ɛtɐlɐ]
stem	**talo** (m)	[t'alu]
tuber	**tubérculo** (m)	[tub'ɛrkulu]
young plant (shoot)	**broto, rebento** (m)	[br'out], [ʀəb'ẽtu]
thorn	**espinho** (m)	[əʃp'iɲu]
to blossom (vi)	**florescer** (vi)	[flurəʃs'er]
to fade, to wither	**murchar** (vi)	[murʃ'ar]
smell (odor)	**cheiro** (m)	[ʃ'ɐjru]
to cut (flowers)	**cortar** (vt)	[kurt'ar]
to pick (a flower)	**colher** (vt)	[kuʎ'ɛr]

191. Cereals, grains

grain	**grão** (m)	[gr'ãu]
cereal crops	**cereais** (m pl)	[sərj'ajʃ]

ear (of barley, etc.)	**espiga** (f)	[əʃp'igɐ]
wheat	**trigo** (m)	[tr'igu]
rye	**centeio** (m)	[sẽt'ɐju]
oats	**aveia** (f)	[ɐv'ɐjɐ]
millet	**milho-miúdo** (m)	[m'iʎu mi'udu]
barley	**cevada** (f)	[səv'adɐ]
corn	**milho** (m)	[m'iʎu]
rice	**arroz** (m)	[ɐʀ'ɔʒ]
buckwheat	**trigo-sarraceno** (m)	[tr'igu saʀɐs'enu]
pea plant	**ervilha** (f)	[erv'iʎɐ]
kidney bean	**feijão** (m)	[fɐjʒ'ãu]
soy	**soja** (f)	[s'ɔʒɐ]
lentil	**lentilha** (f)	[lẽt'iʎɐ]
beans (pulse crops)	**fava** (f)	[f'avɐ]

REGIONAL GEOGRAPHY

Countries. Nationalities

192. Politics. Government. Part 1

politics	**política** (f)	[pul'itikɐ]
political (adj)	**político**	[pul'itiku]
politician	**político** (m)	[pul'itiku]
state (country)	**estado** (m)	[əʃt'adu]
citizen	**cidadão** (m)	[sidɐd'ãu]
citizenship	**cidadania** (f)	[sidɐdɐn'iɐ]
national emblem	**brasão** (m) **de armas**	[brɐz'ãu də 'armɐʃ]
national anthem	**hino** (m) **nacional**	['inu nɐsjun'al]
government	**governo** (m)	[guv'ernu]
head of state	**Chefe** (m) **de Estado**	[ʃ'ɛfə də əʃt'adu]
parliament	**parlamento** (m)	[pɐrlɐm'ẽtu]
party	**partido** (m)	[pɐrt'idu]
capitalism	**capitalismo** (m)	[kɐpitɐl'iʒmu]
capitalist (adj)	**capitalista**	[kɐpitɐl'iʃtɐ]
socialism	**socialismo** (m)	[susiɐl'iʒmu]
socialist (adj)	**socialista**	[susiɐl'iʃtɐ]
communism	**comunismo** (m)	[kumun'iʒmu]
communist (adj)	**comunista**	[kumun'iʃtɐ]
communist (n)	**comunista** (m)	[kumun'iʃtɐ]
democracy	**democracia** (f)	[dəmukrɐs'iɐ]
democrat	**democrata** (m)	[dəmukr'atɐ]
democratic (adj)	**democrático**	[dəmukr'atiku]
Democratic party	**Partido** (m) **Democrático**	[pɐrt'idu dəmukr'atiku]
liberal (n)	**liberal** (m)	[libər'al]
liberal (adj)	**liberal**	[libər'al]
conservative (n)	**conservador** (m)	[kõsərvɐd'or]
conservative (adj)	**conservador**	[kõsərvɐd'or]
republic (n)	**república** (f)	[ʀɛp'ublikɐ]
republican (n)	**republicano** (m)	[ʀɛpublik'ɐnu]
Republican party	**Partido** (m) **Republicano**	[pɐrt'idu ʀɛpublik'ɐnu]

poll, elections	**eleições** (f pl)	[elɐjs'ojʃ]
to elect (vt)	**eleger** (vt)	[eləʒ'er]
elector, voter	**eleitor** (m)	[elɐjt'or]
election campaign	**campanha** (f) **eleitoral**	[kɐ̃p'ɐɲɐ elɐjtur'al]
voting (n)	**votação** (f)	[vutɐs'ɐ̃u]
to vote (vi)	**votar** (vi)	[vut'ar]
suffrage, right to vote	**direito** (m) **de voto**	[dir'ɐjtu də v'ɔtu]
candidate	**candidato** (m)	[kɐ̃did'atu]
to be a candidate	**candidatar-se** (vi)	[kɐ̃didɐt'arsə]
campaign	**campanha** (f)	[kɐ̃p'ɐɲɐ]
opposition (as adj)	**da oposição**	[dɐ ɔpuzis'ɐ̃u]
opposition (n)	**oposição** (f)	[ɔpuzis'ɐ̃u]
visit	**visita** (f)	[viz'itɐ]
official visit	**visita** (f) **oficial**	[viz'itɐ ɔfisj'al]
international (adj)	**internacional**	[ĩtərnɐsiun'al]
negotiations	**negociações** (f pl)	[nəgusiɐs'ojʃ]
to negotiate (vi)	**negociar** (vi)	[nəgusj'ar]

193. Politics. Government. Part 2

society	**sociedade** (f)	[susiɛd'adə]
constitution	**constituição** (f)	[kõʃtituis'ɐ̃u]
power (political control)	**poder** (m)	[pud'er]
corruption	**corrupção** (f)	[kuʀups'ɐ̃u]
law (justice)	**lei** (f)	[lɐj]
legal (legitimate)	**legal**	[ləg'al]
justice (fairness)	**justiça** (f)	[ʒuʃt'isɐ]
just (fair)	**justo**	[ʒ'uʃtu]
committee	**comité** (m)	[kumit'ɛ]
bill (draft law)	**projeto-lei** (m)	[pruʒ'ɛtu l'ɐj]
budget	**orçamento** (m)	[ɔrsɐm'ẽtu]
policy	**política** (f)	[pul'itikɐ]
reform	**reforma** (f)	[ʀəf'ɔrmɐ]
radical (adj)	**radical**	[ʀɐdik'al]
power (strength, force)	**força** (f)	[f'orsɐ]
powerful (adj)	**poderoso**	[pudər'ozu]
supporter	**partidário** (m)	[pɐrtid'ariu]
influence	**influência** (f)	[ĩflu'ẽsiɐ]
regime (e.g., military ~)	**regime** (m)	[ʀəʒ'imə]
conflict	**conflito** (m)	[kõfl'itu]

conspiracy (plot)	**conspiração** (f)	[kõʃpirɐs'ãu]
provocation	**provocação** (f)	[pruvukɐs'ãu]
to overthrow (regime, etc.)	**derrubar** (vt)	[dəʀub'ar]
overthrow (of government)	**derrube** (m), **queda** (f)	[dəʀ'ubə], [k'ɛdɐ]
revolution	**revolução** (f)	[ʀəvulus'ãu]
coup d'état	**golpe** (m) **de Estado**	[g'ɔlpə də əʃt'adu]
military coup	**golpe** (m) **militar**	[g'ɔlpə milit'ar]
crisis	**crise** (f)	[kr'izə]
economic recession	**recessão** (f) **económica**	[ʀəsəs'ãu ekun'ɔmikɐ]
demonstrator (protester)	**manifestante** (m)	[mɐnifəʃt'ãtə]
demonstration	**manifestação** (f)	[mɐnifəʃtɐs'ãu]
martial law	**lei** (f) **marcial**	[lɐj mɐrsj'al]
military base	**base** (f) **militar**	[b'azə milit'ar]
stability	**estabilidade** (f)	[əʃtɐbilid'adə]
stable (adj)	**estável**	[əʃt'avɛl]
exploitation	**exploração** (f)	[əʃplurɐs'ãu]
to exploit (workers)	**explorar** (vt)	[əʃplur'ar]
racism	**racismo** (m)	[ʀas'iʒmu]
racist	**racista** (m)	[ʀas'iʃtɐ]
fascism	**fascismo** (m)	[fɐʃs'iʒmu]
fascist	**fascista** (m)	[fɐʃs'iʃtɐ]

194. Countries. Miscellaneous

foreigner	**estrangeiro** (m)	[əʃtrãʒ'ɐjru]
foreign (adj)	**estrangeiro**	[əʃtrãʒ'ɐjru]
abroad (adv)	**no estrangeiro**	[nu əʃtrãʒ'ɐjru]
emigrant	**emigrante** (m)	[emigr'ãtə]
emigration	**emigração** (f)	[emigrɐs'ãu]
to emigrate (vi)	**emigrar** (vi)	[emigr'ar]
the West	**Ocidente** (m)	[ɔsid'ẽtə]
the East	**Oriente** (m)	[ɔrj'ẽtə]
the Far East	**Extremo Oriente** (m)	[əʃtr'emu ɔrj'ẽtə]
civilization	**civilização** (f)	[sivilizɐs'ãu]
humanity (mankind)	**humanidade** (f)	[umɐnid'adə]
world (earth)	**mundo** (m)	[m'ũdu]
peace	**paz** (f)	[paʒ]
worldwide (adj)	**mundial**	[mũdj'al]
homeland	**pátria** (f)	[p'atriɐ]
people (population)	**povo** (m)	[p'ovu]

population	**população** (f)	[pupulɐs'ãu]
people (a lot of ~)	**gente** (f)	[ʒ'ẽtə]
nation (people)	**nação** (f)	[nɐs'ãu]
generation	**geração** (f)	[ʒɛrɐs'ãu]
territory (area)	**território** (m)	[təʀit'ɔriu]
region	**região** (f)	[ʀəʒj'ãu]
state (part of a country)	**estado** (m)	[əʃt'adu]
tradition	**tradição** (f)	[trɐdis'ãu]
custom (tradition)	**costume** (m)	[kuʃt'umə]
ecology	**ecologia** (f)	[ɛkuluʒ'iɐ]
Indian (Native American)	**índio** (m)	['ĩdiu]
Gipsy (masc.)	**cigano** (m)	[sig'ɐnu]
Gipsy (fem.)	**cigana** (f)	[sig'ɐnɐ]
Gipsy (adj)	**cigano**	[sig'ɐnu]
empire	**império** (m)	[ĩp'ɛriu]
colony	**colónia** (f)	[kul'ɔniɐ]
slavery	**escravidão** (f)	[əʃkrɐvid'ãu]
invasion	**invasão** (f)	[ĩvaz'ãu]
famine	**fome** (f)	[f'ɔmə]

195. Major religious groups. Confessions

religion	**religião** (f)	[ʀəliʒj'ãu]
religious (adj)	**religioso**	[ʀəliʒj'ozu]
faith, belief	**crença** (f)	[kr'ẽsɐ]
to believe (in God)	**crer** (vt)	[krer]
believer	**crente** (m)	[kr'ẽtə]
atheism	**ateísmo** (m)	[ɐte'iʒmu]
atheist	**ateu** (m)	[ɐt'eu]
Christianity	**cristianismo** (m)	[kriʃtiɐn'iʒmu]
Christian (n)	**cristão** (m)	[kriʃt'ãu]
Christian (adj)	**cristão**	[kriʃt'ãu]
Catholicism	**catolicismo** (m)	[kɐtulis'iʒmu]
Catholic (n)	**católico** (m)	[kɐt'ɔliku]
Catholic (adj)	**católico**	[kɐt'ɔliku]
Protestantism	**protestantismo** (m)	[prutəʃtãt'iʒmu]
Protestant Church	**Igreja** (f) **Protestante**	[igr'ɐʒɐ prutəʃt'ãtə]
Protestant	**protestante** (m)	[prutəʃt'ãtə]
Orthodoxy	**ortodoxia** (f)	[ɔrtɔdɔks'iɐ]
Orthodox Church	**Igreja** (f) **Ortodoxa**	[igr'ɐʒɐ ɔrtɔd'ɔksɐ]

Orthodox	**ortodoxo** (m)	[ɔrtɔd'ɔksu]
Presbyterianism	**presbiterianismo** (m)	[prəʒbitəriɐn'iʒmu]
Presbyterian Church	**Igreja** (f) **Presbiteriana**	[igr'ɐʒɐ prəʒbitərj'ɐnɐ]
Presbyterian (n)	**presbiteriano** (m)	[prəʒbitərj'ɐnu]
Lutheranism	**Igreja** (f) **Luterana**	[igr'ɐʒɐ lutər'ɐnɐ]
Lutheran (n)	**luterano** (m)	[lutər'ɐnu]
Baptist Church	**Igreja** (f) **Batista**	[igr'ɐʒɐ bat'iʃtɐ]
Baptist (n)	**batista** (m)	[bat'iʃtɐ]
Anglican Church	**Igreja** (f) **Anglicana**	[igr'ɐʒɐ ãglik'ɐnɐ]
Anglican (n)	**anglicano** (m)	[ãglik'ɐnu]
Mormonism	**mormonismo** (m)	[murmun'iʒmu]
Mormon (n)	**mórmon** (m)	[m'ɔrmɔn]
Judaism	**Judaísmo** (m)	[ʒudɐ'iʒmu]
Jew (n)	**judeu** (m)	[ʒud'eu]
Buddhism	**budismo** (m)	[bud'iʒmu]
Buddhist (n)	**budista** (m)	[bud'iʃtɐ]
Hinduism	**hinduísmo** (m)	[ĩdu'iʒmu]
Hindu (n)	**hindu** (m)	[ĩd'u]
Islam	**Islão** (m)	[iʒl'ãu]
Muslim (n)	**muçulmano** (m)	[musulm'ɐnu]
Muslim (adj)	**muçulmano**	[musulm'ɐnu]
Shiah Islam	**Xiismo** (m)	[ʃi'iʒmu]
Shiite (n)	**xiita** (m)	[ʃi'itɐ]
Sunni Islam	**sunismo** (m)	[sun'iʒmu]
Sunnite (n)	**sunita** (m)	[sun'itɐ]

196. Religions. Priests

priest	**padre** (m)	[p'adrə]
the Pope	**Papa** (m)	[p'apɐ]
monk, friar	**monge** (m)	[m'õʒə]
nun	**freira** (f)	[fr'ɐjrɐ]
pastor	**pastor** (m)	[pɐʃt'or]
abbot	**abade** (m)	[ɐb'adə]
vicar (parish priest)	**vigário** (m)	[vig'ariu]
bishop	**bispo** (m)	[b'iʃpu]
cardinal	**cardeal** (m)	[kɐrdj'al]
preacher	**pregador** (m)	[prəgɐd'or]
preaching	**sermão** (m)	[sərm'ãu]

parishioners	**paroquianos** (pl)	[pɐrukj'ɐnuʃ]
believer	**crente** (m)	[kr'ẽtə]
atheist	**ateu** (m)	[ɐt'eu]

197. Faith. Christianity. Islam

Adam	**Adão**	[ɐd'ãu]
Eve	**Eva**	['ɛvɐ]
God	**Deus** (m)	[d'euʃ]
the Lord	**Senhor** (m)	[səɲ'oɾ]
the Almighty	**Todo Poderoso** (m)	[t'odu pudəɾ'ozu]
sin	**pecado** (m)	[pək'adu]
to sin (vi)	**pecar** (vi)	[pək'aɾ]
sinner (masc.)	**pecador** (m)	[pəkɐd'oɾ]
sinner (fem.)	**pecadora** (f)	[pəkɐd'oɾɐ]
hell	**inferno** (m)	[ĩf'ɛrnu]
paradise	**paraíso** (m)	[pɐɾɐ'izu]
Jesus	**Jesus**	[ʒəz'uʃ]
Jesus Christ	**Jesus Cristo**	[ʒəz'uʃ kɾ'iʃtu]
the Holy Spirit	**Espírito** (m) **Santo**	[əʃp'iɾitu s'ãtu]
the Savior	**Salvador** (m)	[salvɐd'oɾ]
the Virgin Mary	**Virgem Maria** (f)	[v'iɾʒẽj mɐɾ'iɐ]
the Devil	**Diabo** (m)	[dj'abu]
devil's (adj)	**diabólico**	[diɐb'ɔliku]
Satan	**Satanás** (m)	[sɐtɐn'aʃ]
satanic (adj)	**satânico**	[sɐt'ɐniku]
angel	**anjo** (m)	['ãʒu]
guardian angel	**anjo** (m) **da guarda**	['ãʒu dɐ gu'aɾdɐ]
angelic (adj)	**angélico**	[ãʒ'ɛliku]
apostle	**apóstolo** (m)	[ɐp'ɔʃtulu]
archangel	**arcanjo** (m)	[ɐrk'ãʒu]
the Antichrist	**anticristo** (m)	[ãtikɾ'iʃtu]
Church	**Igreja** (f)	[igɾ'ɐʒɐ]
Bible	**Bíblia** (f)	[b'ibliɐ]
biblical (adj)	**bíblico**	[b'ibliku]
Old Testament	**Velho Testamento** (m)	[v'ɛʎu təʃtɐm'ẽtu]
New Testament	**Novo Testamento** (m)	[n'ovu təʃtɐm'ẽtu]
Gospel	**Evangelho** (m)	[evãʒ'ɛʎu]
Holy Scripture	**Sagradas Escrituras** (f pl)	[sɐgɾ'adɐʃ əʃkɾit'uɾɐʃ]
heaven	**Céu** (m)	[s'ɛu]

Commandment	**mandamento** (m)	[mãdem'ẽtu]
prophet	**profeta** (m)	[pruf'ɛtɐ]
prophecy	**profecia** (f)	[prufəs'iɐ]
Allah	**Alá**	[al'a]
Mohammed	**Maomé**	[maum'ɛ]
the Koran	**Corão, Alcorão** (m)	[kur'ãu], [alkur'ãu]
mosque	**mesquita** (f)	[məʃk'itɐ]
mullah	**mulá** (m)	[mul'a]
prayer	**oração** (f)	[ɔrɐs'ãu]
to pray (vi, vt)	**rezar, orar** (vi)	[ʀəz'ar], [ɔr'ar]
pilgrimage	**peregrinação** (f)	[pərəgrinɐs'ãu]
pilgrim	**peregrino** (m)	[pərəgr'inu]
Mecca	**Meca** (f)	[m'ɛkɐ]
church	**igreja** (f)	[igr'ɐʒɐ]
temple	**templo** (m)	[t'ẽplu]
cathedral	**catedral** (f)	[kɐtədr'al]
Gothic (adj)	**gótico**	[g'ɔtiku]
synagogue	**sinagoga** (f)	[sinɐg'ɔgɐ]
mosque	**mesquita** (f)	[məʃk'itɐ]
chapel	**capela** (f)	[kɐp'ɛlɐ]
abbey	**abadia** (f)	[ɐbɐd'iɐ]
convent	**convento** (m)	[kõv'ẽtu]
monastery	**mosteiro** (m)	[muʃt'ɐjru]
bell (in church)	**sino** (m)	[s'inu]
bell tower	**campanário** (m)	[kãpɐn'ariu]
to ring (ab. bells)	**repicar** (vi)	[ʀəpik'ar]
cross	**cruz** (f)	[kruʃ]
cupola (roof)	**cúpula** (f)	[k'upulɐ]
icon	**ícone** (m)	['ikɔnə]
soul	**alma** (f)	['almɐ]
fate (destiny)	**destino** (m)	[dəʃt'inu]
evil (n)	**mal** (m)	[mal]
good (n)	**bem** (m)	[bẽj]
vampire	**vampiro** (m)	[vãp'iru]
witch (sorceress)	**bruxa** (f)	[br'uʃɐ]
demon	**demónio** (m)	[dəm'ɔniu]
devil	**diabo** (m)	[dj'abu]
spirit	**espírito** (m)	[əʃp'iritu]
redemption (giving us ~)	**redenção** (f)	[ʀədẽs'ãu]
to redeem (vt)	**redimir** (vt)	[ʀədim'ir]
church service, mass	**missa** (f)	[m'isɐ]
to say mass	**celebrar a missa**	[sələbr'ar ɐ m'isɐ]

confession	**confissão** (f)	[kõfis'ãu]
to confess (vi)	**confessar-se** (vp)	[kõfəs'arsə]
saint (n)	**santo** (m)	[s'ãtu]
sacred (holy)	**sagrado**	[sɐgr'adu]
holy water	**água** (f) **benta**	['agwɐ b'ẽtɐ]
ritual (n)	**ritual** (m)	[ʀitu'al]
ritual (adj)	**ritual**	[ʀitu'al]
sacrifice	**sacrifício** (m)	[sɐkrif'isiu]
superstition	**superstição** (f)	[supərʃtis'ãu]
superstitious (adj)	**supersticioso**	[supərʃtisj'ozu]
afterlife	**vida** (f) **depois da morte**	[v'idɐ dəp'ojʃ dɐ m'ɔrtə]
eternal life	**vida** (f) **eterna**	[v'idɐ et'ɛrnɐ]

MISCELLANEOUS

198. Various useful words

background (green ~)	**fundo** (m)	[f'ũdu]
balance (of situation)	**equilíbrio** (m)	[ekil'ibriu]
barrier (obstacle)	**barreira** (f)	[bɐʀ'ɐjrɐ]
base (basis)	**base** (f)	[b'azə]
beginning	**começo** (m)	[kum'esu]
category	**categoria** (f)	[kɐtəgur'iɐ]
cause (reason)	**causa** (f)	[k'auzɐ]
choice	**variedade** (f)	[vɐriɛd'adə]
coincidence	**coincidência** (f)	[kuĩsid'ẽsiɐ]
comfortable (~ chair)	**cómodo**	[k'ɔmudu]
comparison	**comparação** (f)	[kõpɐrɐs'ãu]
compensation	**compensação** (f)	[kõpẽsɐs'ãu]
degree (extent, amount)	**grau** (m)	[gr'au]
development	**desenvolvimento** (m)	[dəzẽvɔlvim'ẽtu]
difference	**diferença** (f)	[difər'ẽsɐ]
effect (e.g., of drugs)	**efeito** (m)	[ef'ɐjtu]
effort (exertion)	**esforço** (m)	[əʃf'orsu]
element	**elemento** (m)	[eləm'ẽtu]
end (finish)	**fim** (m)	[fĩ]
example (illustration)	**exemplo** (m)	[ez'ẽplu]
fact	**facto** (m)	[f'aktu]
frequent (adj)	**frequente**	[frəku'ẽtə]
growth (development)	**crescimento** (m)	[krəʃsim'ẽtu]
help	**ajuda** (f)	[ɐʒ'udɐ]
ideal	**ideal**	[idj'al]
kind (sort, type)	**tipo** (m)	[t'ipu]
labyrinth	**labirinto** (m)	[lɐbir'ĩtu]
mistake, error	**erro** (m)	['eʀu]
moment	**momento** (m)	[mum'ẽtu]
object (thing)	**objeto** (m)	[ɔbʒ'ɛtu]
obstacle	**obstáculo** (m)	[ɔbʃt'akulu]
original (original copy)	**original** (m)	[ɔriʒin'al]
part (~ of sth)	**parte** (f)	[p'artə]
particle, small part	**partícula** (f)	[pɐrt'ikulɐ]
pause (break)	**pausa** (f)	[p'auzɐ]

position | **posição** (f) | [puzis'ãu]
principle | **princípio** (m) | [prĩs'ipiu]
problem | **problema** (m) | [prubl'emɐ]

process | **processo** (m) | [prus'ɛsu]
progress | **progresso** (m) | [prugr'ɛsu]
property (quality) | **propriedade** (f) | [prupriɛd'adə]
reaction | **reação** (f) | [ʀias'ãu]
risk | **risco** (m) | [ʀ'iʃku]

secret | **mistério** (m) | [miʃt'ɛriu]
section (sector) | **secção** (f) | [sɛks'ãu]
series | **série** (f) | [s'ɛriə]
shape (outer form) | **forma** (f) | [f'ɔrmɐ]
situation | **situação** (f) | [situɐs'ãu]

solution | **solução** (f) | [sulus'ãu]
standard (adj) | **padrão** | [pɐdr'ãu]
standard (level of quality) | **padrão** (m) | [pɐdr'ãu]
stop (pause) | **paragem** (f) | [pɐr'aʒẽj]
style | **estilo** (m) | [əʃt'ilu]
system | **sistema** (m) | [siʃt'emɐ]

table (chart) | **tabela** (f) | [tɐb'ɛlɐ]
tempo, rate | **ritmo** (m) | [ʀ'itmu]
term (word, expression) | **termo** (m) | [t'ermu]
thing (object, item) | **coisa** (f) | [k'ojzɐ]
truth | **verdade** (f) | [vərd'adə]
turn (please wait your ~) | **vez** (f) | [veʒ]
type (sort, kind) | **tipo** (m) | [t'ipu]

urgent (adj) | **urgente** | [urʒ'ẽtə]
urgently (adv) | **urgentemente** | [urʒẽtəm'ẽtə]
utility (usefulness) | **utilidade** (f) | [utilid'adə]

variant (alternative) | **variante** (f) | [vɐrj'ãtə]
way (means, method) | **modo** (m) | [m'ɔdu]
zone | **zona** (f) | [z'onɐ]

CPSIA information can be obtained
at www.ICGtesting.com
Printed in the USA
BVHW01s0158200118
505801BV00009B/32/P